STATE TAXATION OF BUSINESS

Issues and Policy Options

Edited by THOMAS F. POGUE

Foreword by FREDERICK D. STOCKER

Published in cooperation with the National Tax Association

PRAEGER

Westport, Connecticut
London

Library of Congress Cataloging-in-Publication Data

State taxation of business : issues and policy options / edited by
   Thomas F. Pogue.
      p.   cm.
     "Published in cooperation with the National Tax Association."
     Includes bibliographical references and index.
     ISBN 0-275-94125-6
     1. Corporations—Taxation—United States—States. 2. Business
enterprises—Taxation—United States—States.   I. Pogue, Thomas F.
II. National Tax Association.
    HD2753.U6S78   1992
    336.24'3'0973—dc20   92-15767

British Library Cataloguing in Publication Data is available.

Library of Congress Catalog Card Number: 92-15767
ISBN: 0-275-94125-6

First published in 1992

Praeger Publishers, 88 Post Road West, Westport, CT 06881
An imprint of Greenwood Publishing Group, Inc.

Printed in the United States of America

The paper used in this book complies with the
Permanent Paper Standard issued by the National
Information Standards Organization (Z39.48-1984).

10 9 8 7 6 5 4 3 2 1

Contents

Tables and Figures

TABLES

FIGURES

Foreword

The oldest principle of tax policy is that the best tax is one that somebody else pays. This principle helps explain the appeal of business taxes, which place no direct and obvious burden on the average citizen. Business taxpayers may raise loud complaints, but they represent relatively few votes. Moreover, in many peoples' eyes, they seem readily able to pay.

It takes but a moment's reflection to realize that all business taxes, in the final analysis, rest on living and breathing people. But often it is difficult to ascertain just who these people are—owners (or stockholders) in the business, or customers, or workers, or perhaps owners of land in the taxing jurisdiction. Some business taxes are shifted out of state, but nobody knows just how much. These uncertainties may trouble analysts of tax policy but do little to diminish the political appeal of business taxes.

The fact that all business taxes eventually are paid by individuals does not necessarily mean that such taxes should be repealed. For one thing, business activities use government services (police and fire protection, the courts) and taxes represent a (perhaps crude) way of charging business for these government inputs.

The search continues for a plausible rationale for state taxation of business, and for guidelines for translating that rationale into tax policies and laws.

Today, these long standing and fundamental questions of why and how states should tax business are complicated by economic and technological changes that render existing business tax structures increasingly obsolete. Financial services and telecommunications, for example, no longer are taxed appropriately under traditional state laws. New business tax instruments also are under consideration for controlling industrial and hazardous waste. More broadly, the growth of national and international markets has focused attention on the ways business taxes may affect states' competitive positions, and that of the Nation.

On March 7-8, 1991, the National Tax Association sponsored a seminar in San Antonio at which many of the nation's leading authorities on taxation debated a variety of issues related to state taxation of business. In attendance were academic students of taxation, corporate tax executives, private tax attorneys, and government officials responsible for making state tax policy and for tax administration. This volume grows out of that seminar.

These collected papers do not pretend to offer a program for state business tax reform. As is clear, the issues are complicated and controversial. Solutions involve difficult trade-offs, for example between tax neutrality and administrative feasibility, between tax equity and simplicity of tax compliance. Today more than ever revenue needs constrain the states in implementing otherwise desirable reforms. Understanding the problems and the policy options is just the first step toward reform.

For eighty-five years the National Tax Association has worked to advance understanding of the theory and practice of taxation at all levels of government. The Association is nonpartisan and nonpolitical and represents no special interest or viewpoint. With a membership comprised of taxpayer representatives, government administrators, tax practitioners, and academic scholars, NTA fosters objective analysis and vigorous debate among contrasting viewpoints.

The seminar papers are presented here in that spirit. It is to be hoped that by advancing understanding they will hasten policy improvements in this critical area of taxation.

The seminar was a project of the NTA Committee on State Income and Business Taxation, chaired by James F. Buresh, of Sears Roebuck and Company. The program was planned by a committee headed by Prof. Thomas F. Pogue, of the University of Iowa, who also serves as editor of this volume. Others on the program committee were Dan Bucks, of the Multistate Tax Commission; Harley T. Duncan, of the Federation of Tax Administrators; Robert D. Ebel, of KPMG Peat Marwick; Fred Ferguson, of Price Waterhouse; Steven D. Gold, of the Center for the Study of the States, Rockefeller Institute; Harold A. Hovey, of State Policy Research, Inc.; James A. Papke, of Purdue University; John L. Mikesell, of Indiana University; and James H. Peters, McDermott, Will & Emery, Chicago. The Association expresses appreciation to each.

Frederick D. Stocker
Executive Director
The National Tax Association

Introduction

Taxes on business comprise about 30 percent of the total tax revenue of state and local governments. Although no single definition of "business tax" is widely accepted, most definitions include only taxes collected from business entities rather than from individuals, and most definitions encompass taxes on a business's income, ownership of assets, purchases of inputs, and sales of products and services.

Regardless of how business taxes are defined, there can be little doubt that businesses today must comply with an increasingly complex set of taxes. Virtually all businesses are subject to multiple forms of taxation, and most operate within the jurisdiction of several, if not many, local and state governments. The current system of state and local business taxes, created by more than a century of legislation and court decisions, is not the result of systematic application of well thought out rationales for business taxation; instead, it is the product of many marginal responses to changes in the nature and location of economic activity.

Increasingly, business taxpayers and their accountants and tax specialists are joined by tax administrators, legislators, and other public officials in questioning the desirability of the current system. The principal questions raised, broadly stated, are "How should businesses be taxed?" and "How does present practice compare with and depart from this prescription?" These questions were addressed from a variety of perspectives in papers presented at a seminar sponsored by the National Tax Association in March 1991, and they are now published in this volume. The individual papers have not been edited so as to place them within a single, consistent framework—that of the academic economist. The wide range of viewpoints and the manner in which issues are articulated and analyzed have been retained, thus offering readers a cross-section of current thinking about states' business tax policies. The result, I think, is a valuable reference for anyone concerned with business tax issues in the coming decade.

The book consists of seven main parts, the first of which provides a conceptual framework for defining business taxes, measuring their levels and consequences, comparing interstate differences in business tax practices, and evaluating alternative business tax policies. Data is presented showing current levels, trends, and interstate differences in business taxation. The political and economic rationales for taxing business and the implications of those rationales for tax policy are also examined. The remaining parts employ the perspectives and concepts developed in the first part to analyze business tax policy in areas that are important today and will become increasingly so.

Although recognizing that businesses may in fact be taxed for many reasons, the authors in Part I identify only three distinct *economic* rationales for taxing business: (1) to "charge" for the services supplied by government to business; (2) to confront businesses with the "external" costs of their activities; and (3) to tax individuals indirectly. Examples of services provided by government to businesses are police and fire protection and the civil court system. Examples of external costs are environmental damages (air, water, soil pollution) caused by activities of business.

Any economic rationale for taxing businesses should recognize that taxes on businesses are borne ultimately by individuals. A business has no tax-paying capability independent of the individuals who transact with it—its workers, customers, suppliers, and owners. This fact does not, however, imply that a government might just as well tax individuals directly rather than indirectly via business taxes. Taxes on individuals usually are ineffective means of charging businesses for services supplied by government and correcting for external costs of their activities. The desirability of taxing businesses for the costs that their activities generate is not eliminated or reduced by the fact that taxes on businesses are ultimately borne by individuals.

Whatever the rationale for imposing taxes on business, to do so it is necessary to establish *nexus* (i.e., that the businesses to be taxed have a presence in the state) and to define a tax base and a schedule of tax rates to be applied to the base to determine tax liability. Commonly employed business tax bases are corporate income, sales and gross receipts, and business property. If the objective is to tax businesses for the services that they receive from government, then the base should be proportional to the value (or cost) of those services. There is no reason to believe that close correlation with value of services received was an important factor in the choice of the bases presently in use. Corporate net income is clearly not closely correlated with value of services received. Other business tax bases (e.g., gross receipts and value of real property) may be roughly correlated with value of services, but as Oakland explains in Chapter 2, it is difficult to argue that these bases are the best available proxies for value of services.

The tax bases of multistate businesses, however defined, must be *apportioned* among the states within which they operate. For example, to tax the net income of corporations, states must have rules that determine how much of the income of a corporation is "earned" and subject to taxation in each of the states in which it operates. For corporate income and other tax bases as well, this apportionment problem has become increasingly difficult to solve nonarbitrarily, as economic enterprises and the products and services that they produce have become increasingly complex. The statutes and court and administrative rulings that govern business taxation reflect, in their complexity and continuous change, the complexity and dynamics of the U.S. and world economies.

Part II deals with the apportionment problems that arise in connection with states' taxation of corporate income. A central issue in this part, and in Parts IV and V as well, is whether multistate companies can be taxed fairly and without seriously distorting the efficiency of the economy. Ideally, the apportionment rules used by the various states should be consistent in the sense that all of the income of each corporation is apportioned either to a state or to foreign sources. With such apportionment, a corporation would never be subject to state-level taxation of more than 100 percent of its income.

Over the years, the Multistate Tax Compact and the Uniform Division of Income for Tax Purposes Act (UDITPA) have been important tools for promoting uniform apportionment rules that would achieve this ideal. However, as the authors of Part II make clear, current practice remains far from ideal, primarily because states seek to apply apportionment rules that they believe are to their individual advantage. States tend to apply rules that (they believe) will either maximize their corporate income tax base or give their state an advantage as a location for corporate operation. States continue to follow independent and largely uncoordinated tax policies. The resulting nonuniformity and complexity of statutes and administrative rules adds greatly to administration and compliance costs, a point emphasized repeatedly throughout Parts II through VI.

Tax exporting occurs when taxes levied by a government are borne in full or in part by individuals who reside outside the government's jurisdiction. It has long been recognized as an important consequence of decentralized taxation. As Oakland explains in Chapter 2, tax exporting is an objective of and rationale for particular forms of business taxation. He also explains that market adjustments limit state and local governments' ability to export taxes.

The treatment of tax exporting in Part III is concerned mainly with the exporting of state corporation income taxes that occurs when the sales factor is given more weight than the payroll and property factors in apportioning corporate income. States that apportion in this manner are attempting to place relatively light income tax burdens on corporations that produce for export; they are taxing favorably those corporations that have a relatively low fraction of sales and a relatively high fraction of payroll and property within the state. The door was opened to this practice by U.S. Supreme Court's 1978 decision in *Moorman Manufacturing Company v. Bair.*

Parts IV through VI examine the especially difficult issues of apportionment and nexus that have arisen in the taxation of telecommunication, financial, and insurance companies because of changes in technology, government regulation, and business organization. These changes have created as yet unresolved problems of tax administration and compliance that are altering the manner in which, and even the extent to which, states can tax businesses.

Part VII considers how business taxes might be and are used to control and to apportion the environmental costs of business activities, which are an increasingly important concern of government and business as well as the public in general. The outlook is that environmentally motivated taxation will be increasingly important form of business taxation.

I
State Business Taxation: Description and Rationales

This part provides background data on state business taxation and evaluates various rationales that have been, or might be, offered for such taxation. Although Galginaitis (Chapter 1) and Oakland (Chapter 2) define business taxes somewhat differently, both estimate that these taxes account for 25-30 percent of total state and local tax revenues. Oakland considers a number of possible rationales for taxing business. The strongest *economic* justification is for taxes that serve either as charges for services provided by government to business or as charges for *unpriced* inputs and outputs (i.e., the "external" costs of business activity). Both Galginaitis and Aten (Chapter 3) agree with this conclusion. Galginaitis also sees a role for business taxes as a means of taxing individuals. Other rationales are capture of locational rents (Oakland) and administrative convenience (Galginaitis). Aten explains that *tax competition* need not limit local governments' ability to tax business for services provided, while emphasizing that *local* taxes on business are unsuitable as means of financing social welfare programs. Oakland argues that the bases of traditional business taxes—corporate income, sales and gross receipts, and franchise—are not correlated with the value of public services provided to business; neither are they correlated closely with external costs. These taxes therefore distort the relative prices of private goods and the location of business activity. Consequently, he prefers value-added as a base for taxing business.

1
What Taxes Do States Impose on Business?
STEVEN GALGINAITIS

The history of state business taxation is as old as the United States itself. By 1776, tariffs, excise taxes, and real estate taxes were being levied on businesses throughout the thirteen original states. Yet, despite over 200 years of practical experience, economists and policymakers still struggle with the question: What taxes do states impose on business?

One would think that the answer would be simply an empirical exercise. If you want to know what taxes states impose on business, just read the tax law and examine the sources of state tax revenue. However, the question, like most in public finance economics, probes into microeconomic theory; and so it is not simple to answer partly because it is ambiguous. The term "impose" can imply two different economic concepts: impact and incidence. What taxes impact, or are initially imposed on business, can to a large degree be answered by examining the tax laws and the general revenue sources of the various states. However, which taxes are ultimately borne by business is a more complex question requiring analysis of the incidence of taxes.

This chapter provides a basic description of state business taxation. It is divided into three main sections. The first section examines why a state should tax business at all. The second section provides a brief discussion of the concept of tax incidence and its implications for state business tax burden. The third section discusses initial tax impact, with greater detail on three types of state taxes that can impact directly on business: the corporate income tax, the sales tax, and the property tax.

WHY TAX BUSINESS?

The party on whom a tax is levied bears the legal responsibility of paying the tax. Taxes can be levied directly on people (for example, the individual income tax) or business (for example, the corporate income tax). Ultimately, however, only people pay taxes. The economic burden of a tax can be shifted from business to people through higher prices, lower returns to factors of production, and/or lower returns on owner equity. The distribution of the ultimate economic burden of a tax is referred to as the "incidence" or "ultimate impact" of the tax. This economic fact raises a question. Why, if taxes are ultimately paid by people anyway, should a state bother to tax businesses?

There are at least three reasons. The first is one of administrative simplicity. It is often administratively easier to tax income at the source of that income rather than at its point of receipt.

Second, even though businesses are legal, nonpersonal entities, they do benefit from public services, such as fire and police protection, judicial services, and the maintenance of the transportation infrastructure. The public services received by a business are also indirectly received by the people who work for it, the customers who buy its products, and its owners. Therefore, in order to collect for the public services to a business that indirectly benefit people, it makes sense to levy a tax on the business. This tax can then be shifted by the business to the beneficiaries of the public services.

The third reason states should tax business has to do with the inherent openness of a state's economy. Because a state has no authority to restrict the free flow of goods and services or the factors of production across its borders (the national government can through tariffs and quotas), the only way to tax nonresident consumers and owners of a business is to tax the income at its source (e.g., as corporate profits) before the product or the profits leaves the state.

TAX INCIDENCE

Determining who ultimately bears the burden of a tax is an extremely complex undertaking. The economic literature provides guidance, but it does not yield unambiguous results. The degree to which a tax can be shifted, so that its impact differs from its incidence, depends largely on price elasticities of demand and supply, and, therefore, on the economic factors that determine those elasticities. The more price-inelastic is the demand for a commodity and/or the more elastic is its supply, the more likely the tax burden is to fall on the consumer.

Tax shifting and incidence depend on the extent of market concentration, that is, the extent to which firms see their pricing and output decisions as having an important influence on market prices. Firms that operate in national markets may be less able to raise prices, and therefore less likely to shift the tax burden to the consumer, than firms that only operate in local or regional markets.[1] Also, the degree to which the government regulates market prices is a determinant of tax incidence.

Three other key problems arise in estimating tax incidence. First, people can act simultaneously as different economic agents. For example, a consumer can also be a supplier of labor and a stockholder in a corporation. The degree to which this person bears the burden of a particular tax is the sum of the three incidences.

Second, real-world taxes are hybrid taxes. That is, they are not pure income taxes or pure sales taxes but are composed of discrete elements. For example, some states include a tax on capital as part of the income tax base. This hybridization complicates incidence calculations.

Finally, the degree of mobility of factors of production also complicates tax burden analysis. If the cost of doing business in one jurisdiction is too high (i.e., the rate of return is too low) because of a tax, then capital can move to another jurisdiction. This action can alter the return to capital and labor in the taxing jurisdiction and thus convert what is by design a tax on capital into a tax on labor.

In short, all taxes are ultimately paid by people in their roles as consumers, suppliers of the factors of production, or as owners of equity. Therefore, when the question—What taxes do states impose on business?—is asked, one perfectly correct answer is none! This, however, trivializes the importance of understanding and examining the initial impact of a tax.

TAX IMPACT

Tax impact matters. At least five points can be made in support of this statement. First, although numerous studies have concluded that state tax costs are a relatively small share of total business costs, state tax costs must be considered in making managerial decisions. In particular, taxes may reduce rates of return, influence business location, and, more generally, alter economic incentives and thereby prevent markets from allocating resources efficiently.

Second, policymakers are often concerned with the "tax climate" and "tax image" of a state. Policy discussions of this nature often center on the business tax structure and industry burdens and costs. These are impact issues.

Third, the debate over horizontal equity of business taxation among industries, inputs, and site locations centers on impact, not incidence. This can be particularly true if the state's major industries produce for out-of-state markets.

Fourth, because of the open nature of state economies, using business as a tax-collecting intermediary may be the only procedure available for assessing individuals, wherever they may reside, for the benefits of state services that initially accrue to the business.

Finally, impact is important because even if state tax incidence could be quantified, the impact determination would be prerequisite to any further discussions about tax incidence.

Many taxes obviously impact directly on business. Corporate income taxes, which use as a tax base some measure of net income, impact directly on business. Taxes based on business equity or capital and surplus, as well as modified value-added taxes such as Michigan's Single Business Tax, impact directly on business. Because of this direct relationship, one can measure the degree of impact by looking at the state revenue generated by these taxes. There are many other taxes, however, that have a less distinct impact.

Business shares the impact of some taxes with individuals. Income generated by sole proprietorships, partnerships, and subchapter S corporations are taxed as personal income in most states; therefore, business pays a share of the individual income tax. Property, sales, and excise taxes are levied on business as well as individuals. The business share of these taxes is not clear, however, because revenue from these taxes is generally not tracked by type of taxpayer.

The remainder of this section examines state corporate income taxes and sales taxes, and state plus local property taxes. Based on prior research, business' share of the initial impact of these taxes is roughly calculated. This calculation is provided not only as an approximation of the impact of state taxes on business but also as an illustration of the difficulties in quantifying business' tax burden.

Corporate Income Tax

In 1911, Wisconsin became the first state to tax corporate income. Since then, forty-four other states have enacted corporate income taxes.[2]

In 1976, Michigan repealed its corporate income tax and enacted a modified value-added tax (the Single Business Tax). Table 1.1 shows the primary corporate tax bases by state. Forty-five states use net income as the tax base, three use gross receipts, and twenty-four use capital stock or net worth. Some states use two or more of these bases. For the states that have a corporate income tax, the rates range from 1 percent in both Alaska and Arkansas to 13.8 percent (including the 20 percent surcharge) in Connecticut. Five states have no corporate income tax (Nevada, South Dakota, Texas, Washington, and Wyoming).

By looking at historical data, one can determine the general trends in the absolute amount (as measured by tax receipts) and the relative burden (as measured by the ratio of tax revenue to corporate profits) of corporate income taxation. Table 1.2 shows the state and federal revenue from corporate income tax from 1948 through 1989. It also shows total U.S. corporate profits for the same time period. The last two columns of Table 1.2 show the ratio of state and federal corporate income tax revenue to corporate profits.[3] These "tax rates" are not true effective tax rates because no adjustment is made for differences between economic income and corporate profits as defined for national income accounting (e.g., economic depreciation versus national income accounting capital consumption adjustment). But the calculated tax rates do illustrate the general trend in corporate income taxation.

The tax rate series are presented in Figure 1.1, which shows that the general trend in the state corporate income tax rate has been increasing. The rate remained around 2 percent from 1948 through the mid-1960s. Since then, it has increased to over 6 percent, with a peak of over 9 percent in 1982. This spike during the 1980-1982 period is probably due to reduced corporate profits during the recession, rather than to legislated increases in tax liability.

Figure 1.1 shows that the federal calculated rate increased to a peak of 54 percent in 1951 and then decreased fairly steadily until the late-1960s. The 1970s were marked by a series of ups and downs. The 1980s began with a sharp decrease until 1986, when the rate increased again. The 1980 spike can again be attributed to depressed corporate profits during the recession, and the increases in 1986 through 1988 are a result of the federal Tax Reform Act of 1986, which was designed to increase corporate income tax liabilities relative to individual income tax liabilities.

Some general conclusions can be drawn from these tax rates. From the late 1940s through the late 1970s, the state corporate income tax rate was rising while the federal corporate income tax rate was falling. Both rates spiked during the recession of the early 1980s because of the fall

TABLE 1.1
Corporate Tax Bases by State

State	Gross Receipts[1]	Net Income[2]	Capital Stock or Net Worth
Alabama		X	X
Alaska		X	
Arizona		X	
Arkansas		X	X
California		X	
Colorado		X	
Connecticut		X	
Delaware		X	[3]
Dist. of Columbia		X	
Florida		X	
Georgia		X	X
Hawaii	X	X	
Idaho		X	
Illinois		X	X
Indiana	X	X	
Iowa		X	[4]
Kansas		X	X
Kentucky		X	X
Louisiana		X	X
Maine		X	
Maryland		X	
Massachusetts		X[5]	X
Michigan[6]			
Minnesota		X	
Mississippi		X	X
Missouri		X	X
Montana		X	
Nebraska		X	X
Nevada			
New Hampshire		X	
New Jersey		X	
New Mexico		X	
New York		X	X
North Carolina		X	X
North Dakota		X	

TABLE 1.1 (continued)

State	Gross Receipts[1]	Net Income[2]	Capital Stock or Net Worth
Ohio		X	X
Oklahoma		X	X
Oregon		X	
Pennsylvania		X	X
Rhode Island		X	X
South Carolina		X[7]	X
South Dakota			
Tennessee		X	X
Texas			X
Utah		X	
Vermont		X	
Virginia		X	
Washington	X		
West Virginia		X	X
Wisconsin		X	
Wyoming			X
Totals	3	45	24

Sources: U.S. Advisory Commission on Intergovernmental Relations, *Significant Features of Fiscal Federalism*, 1991, Washington, D.C.; Policy Economics Group, KPMG Peat Marwick, *A Report on the Connecticut Business Tax Structure*, 1990, Washington, D.C.; Commerce Clearing House, *All States Tax Guide*, Vol. 1.

[1]Column includes only general business taxes based on business gross receipts. Does not include various special business taxes which may be based on gross receipts, such as insurance gross premiums or utility taxes.

[2]Some corporate income tax bases, such as Connecticut's, have a capital stock component.

[3]Delaware has two separate corporate taxes: income and franchise, which is based on capital stock outstanding. The corporate franchise tax is for the privilege of being incorporated in the state.

[4]Iowa annual filing fee with the secretary of state is no longer based on value of capital stock; $30 fee for all corporations.

[5]Massachusetts also has a nonincome measure of the tax based on tangible personal property or net worth allocable to the state.

[6]Michigan levies a single business tax, which is a modified value-added tax.

[7]South Dakota employs a limited income tax on certain banks and financial institutions.

TABLE 1.2
State and Federal Corporate Income Tax Revenue

Year	Corp. Income Tax Revenue ($billion)		Corp. Profits ($billion)	Calculated Tax Rate	
	State	Federal		St. (%)	Fed. (%)
1948	.6	11.7	30.3	1.9	38.6
1949	.6	9.6	28.0	2.3	34.3
1950	.6	17.1	34.9	1.7	49.0
1951	.7	21.7	39.9	1.7	54.4
1952	.8	18.6	37.5	2.2	49.6
1953	.8	19.5	37.7	2.1	51.7
1954	.7	16.8	36.6	2.1	45.9
1955	.7	21.0	47.1	1.6	44.6
1956	.9	21.0	45.7	1.9	46.0
1957	1.0	20.4	45.3	2.2	45.0
1958	1.0	18.0	40.3	2.5	44.7
1959	1.0	22.4	51.4	1.9	43.6
1960	1.2	21.5	49.5	2.4	43.4
1961	1.3	21.5	50.3	2.5	42.7
1962	1.3	22.5	58.3	2.2	38.6
1963	1.5	24.5	63.6	2.4	38.5
1964	1.7	26.2	70.7	2.4	37.1
1965	1.9	28.9	81.3	2.4	35.5
1966	2.0	31.5	86.6	2.4	36.4
1967	2.2	30.1	84.1	2.6	35.8
1968	2.5	36.1	90.7	2.8	39.8
1969	3.2	36.1	87.4	3.6	41.3
1970	3.7	30.7	74.7	5.0	41.1
1971	3.4	33.4	87.1	3.9	38.3
1972	4.4	36.6	100.7	4.4	36.3
1973	5.4	43.3	113.3	4.8	38.2
1974	6.0	45.1	101.7	5.9	44.3
1975	6.6	43.6	117.6	5.6	37.1
1976	7.3	54.6	145.2	5.0	37.6
1977	9.2	61.6	174.8	5.2	35.2
1978	10.7	71.4	197.2	5.4	36.2
1979	12.1	74.4	200.1	6.1	37.2
1980	13.3	70.3	177.2	7.5	39.7
1981	14.1	65.7	188.0	7.5	34.9

TABLE 1.2 (continued)

Year	Corp. Income Tax Revenue ($billion)		Corp. Profits ($billion)	Calculated Tax Rate	
	State	Federal		St. (%)	Fed. (%)
1982	14.0	49.1	150.0	9.3	32.7
1983	13.2	61.3	213.7	6.2	28.7
1984	15.5	75.2	266.9	5.8	28.2
1985	17.6	76.2	282.3	6.2	27.0
1986	18.4	83.8	282.1	6.5	29.7
1987	20.7	103.2	308.3	6.7	33.5
1988	21.7	110.5	337.6	6.4	32.7
1989	23.9	110.4	311.6	7.7	35.4

Sources: State revenues from U.S. Advisory Commission on Intergovernmental Relations, *Significant Features of Fiscal Federalism*, Vol. 2, 1990, Washington, D.C. Federal revenues and profits from *Economic Report of the President*, 1991, U.S. Government Printing Office, Washington, D.C.

in corporate profits. Since the mid-1980s, both rates have been increasing, at least partly due to the federal Tax Reform Act of 1986.

Sales Tax

Table 1.3 presents general revenue by source for 1989. General sales taxes accounted for over 28 percent of states' total general revenue and over 48 percent of total tax revenue. However, how the initial impact of the sales tax splits between individuals and businesses is unclear from the numbers.

Recent empirical studies have calculated the importance of the business share of state sales taxes. Pollock (1991) calculated the business share of sales tax in Connecticut. His calculations centered on three main components: business intermediate purchases, business capital purchases, and consumer purchases. The sales tax paid on each type of purchase was calculated by multiplying each flow of purchase, classified by industry and commodity, by the effective tax rate for that purchase. The flow of each type of purchase was calculated using data from a variety of sources, including: U.S. input-output tables, the U.S. Department of Commerce's *Annual Survey of Manufactures* and *County Business*

Patterns, Standard and Poor's Compustat, and data supplied by the State of Connecticut. The study concluded that 45 percent of Connecticut's sales tax is imposed on business. Pollock also pointed out that business-to-business purchases are an important part of almost all state sales tax

FIGURE 1.1
Ratio of Corporate Income Tax Revenue to Corporate Profits

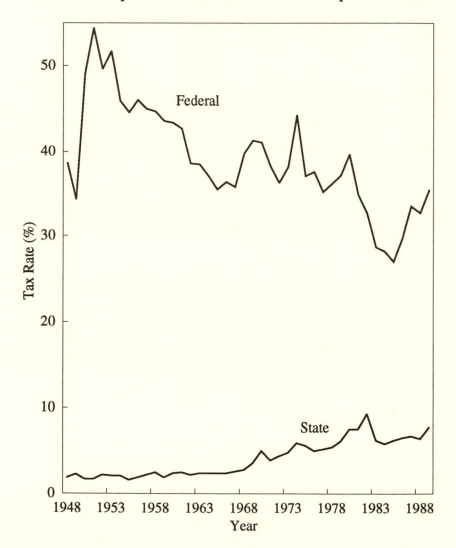

bases, despite ostensible efforts to levy the tax only on final sales.

Ring (1989) conducted an empirical study that estimated the individual and corporate shares of state sales tax. He estimated that the share of general sales tax paid by producers ranges from 18 percent in Massachusetts to 65 percent in Louisiana, with a weighted average of 41 percent.

Applying Ring's percentages against states 1989 sales tax revenue yields a business share of state general sales tax of $57,464 million, or about 41 percent of total general sales taxes. Ring's study is based on 1979 data, and the current calculation does not account for any changes in tax rates, definitions of tax base, or other economic conditions

TABLE 1.3
State General Revenue, FY 1989
(millions of current dollars)

Revenue Source	All State Governments	All State and Local Governments
Total General Revenue	482,477	785,844
Total Taxes	284,169	468,647
Property	5,417	142,525
General Sales	138,249	166,016
Individual Income[1]	88,819	123,729
Corporation Income	23,861	N.A.
All Other Taxes	27,822	36,378
Intergovernmental Revenue	108,235	125,824
Current Charges	38,553	104,578
All Other Revenue	51,520	86,795

Sources: Data supplied by the U.S. Department of Commerce, Bureau of the Census. Published sources: U.S. Bureau of Census, *Government Finances in 1988-89* and *State Government Finances in 1989*.

[1]State and local total includes both individual and corporate income tax revenue.

Table 1.4
State and Local Property Tax Revenue, 1989
(millions of dollars)

State	Revenue	State	Revenue
Alabama	609.4	Montana	547.4
Alaska	662.4	Nebraska	1,124.1
Arizona	2,133.9	Nevada	429.1
Arkansas	506.5	New Hampshire	1,170.7
California	15,789.1	New Jersey	8,168.1
Colorado	2,106.8	New Mexico	274.3
Connecticut	3,249.0	New York	16,684.4
Delaware	186.0	North Carolina	2,112.6
Florida	6,954.2	North Dakota	290.9
Georgia	2,855.2	Ohio	5,193.3
Hawaii	372.6	Oklahoma	862.3
Idaho	391.1	Oregon	2,240.7
Illinois	7,663.4	Pennsylvania	5,628.3
Indiana	2,686.3	Rhode Island	735.1
Iowa	1,772.5	South Carolina	1,239.6
Kansas	1,550.1	South Dakota	388.9
Kentucky	850.4	Tennessee	1,464.3
Louisiana	1,058.1	Texas	10,410.6
Maine	813.9	Utah	716.4
Maryland	2,564.6	Vermont	413.6
Massachusetts	4,395.3	Virginia	3,299.8
Michigan	7,086.1	Washington	2,581.3
Minnesota	2,868.0	West Virginia	440.6
Mississippi	763.9	Wisconsin	3,455.2
Missouri	1,640.1	Wyoming	413.4

Source: U.S. Advisory Commission on Intergovernmental Relations, *Significant Features of Fiscal Federalism*, 1991, Washington, D.C.

between 1979 and 1989. The figures do serve, however, as a rough approximation of the initial impact of state general sales taxes on business.

Property Tax

Table 1.3 shows that state property tax accounts for only about 1 percent of total state general revenue and about 2 percent of total state tax revenue. This is because most property taxes are levied by local governments. This is true despite the fact that some states tax commercial and industrial property at higher rates than residential.

Much anecdotal evidence circulating in recent years attributes the greatest business tax burden to state and local property taxes. Referring back to Table 1.3, over 29 percent of total local general revenue and over 74 percent of total local tax revenue are from property taxes. Over 18 percent of total state and local general revenue and over 30 percent of state and local tax revenue are from property taxes. For these reasons, the following analysis includes both state and local property taxes.

The business share of property tax is even more difficult to determine than the sales tax. Estimates of the business property tax base have been published,[4] but the wide range of rates and exemptions at both the state and local levels makes the determination of the business share quite difficult.

One study that estimated the business share of state and local property taxes was conducted by Reschovsky et al. (1983). Reschovsky updated an unpublished 1977 U.S. Advisory Commission on Intergovernmental Relations (ACIR) study using 1980 data. He assumed the same proportion of total state and local property taxes comes from business as ACIR estimated for 1977. Using this same methodology for the 1989 data shown in Table 1.4 (which shows 1989 state and local property tax revenue by state) yields a business share of state and local property tax of $49,670 million, or about 35 percent of total property taxes. As with the sales tax numbers above, this calculation does not take into account tax rate, tax base, or other changes that occurred between 1980 and 1989. The number serves as a rough approximation of the initial impact of state and local property taxes on business.

CONCLUSION

Using rough calculations based on previous studies, the total impact of the "big three" taxes (corporate income, sales, and property) on business in 1989 was $130,995 million. This is the sum of state corporate income taxes ($23,861 million), state general sales taxes ($57,464 million), and state and local property taxes ($49,670 million). The total is approximately 43 percent of the total for those three taxes.

This chapter is not intended to definitively (or even rigorously attempt to) quantify the state taxes with an initial impact on business. It is intended only to be a brief summary of the issues that one must consider when evaluating the impact of state taxes on business. It is also intended to provide some fundamental data on the historic and current revenue sources of the states.

Today's economic environment makes state business taxation policy more important than ever. Budget crises and interstate competition for business location have made business taxes a major concern of state policymakers. Many states are considering far-reaching changes in their business taxes, not only to raise revenues but also to provide for healthier economic conditions. To understand what needs to be done, one needs to understand present conditions. This chapter is designed to provide some insight into what taxes states currently impose on business.

NOTES

I wish to thank Robert Ebel for his helpful comments, Clay Dursthoff for his expertise with ACIR data, and Shelley LeMessurier for her skilled editing. Any remaining errors are my own.

1. For a more detailed discussion, see Pollock (1991).

2. U.S. Advisory Commission on Intergovernmental Relations, *Significant Features of Fiscal Federalism*, Vol. 1 (1991), p. 32.

3. It would be interesting to do this calculation using state corporate profits data. The U.S. Bureau of Economic Analysis has done some estimation of corporate profits by state as a part of its gross state product study, *Survey of Current Business* (December 1991).

4. For example, see *State Fiscal Capacity and Effort*, published annually by the U.S. Advisory Commission on Intergovernmental Relations, Washington, D.C.

2
How Should Businesses
Be Taxed?

WILLIAM H. OAKLAND

The theme of this volume is state taxation of business. In this chapter, I examine both the economic rationale(s) for such taxation and the forms it should take.

When first presented with the assignment, I thought my task would mainly involve surveying the literature on this important question and then reporting the consensus of economists' opinion. It would be an understatement to say I was shocked to find little in the recent literature that explicitly addresses the question of how business should be taxed. Indeed, I was able to find a cryptic reference by Jim Papke to a pre-World War II paper by Mable Walker written for the Tax Policy League in 1937.[1] Otherwise, I had to go back to my doctoral dissertation to find a reference to a paper by Studenski (1940) on the subject "Toward a Theory of Business Taxation."

This is not meant to imply that the literature is devoid of papers dealing with business taxation. The reality is just the opposite. However, the preponderance of the literature deals with the consequences of taxes levied on businesses. There is little discussion of why such taxes are imposed in the first place. The exception that makes the rule involves the U.S. Corporation Income Tax, where the tax has been defended in terms of improving the performance of the U.S. Personal Income Tax.[2] Because it involves taxing a portion of profits at several levels, and because of other nonneutralities, the federal profits tax has come under heavy attack with many critics calling for outright repeal. But this discussion is largely beside the point for state taxation of business, where considerations arising from taxpayer mobility are of paramount importance.

Much of the following discussion, therefore, has been developed through introspection as well as from more than two decades of wrestling with matters of state and local tax policy in four states.

NATURE AND EXTENT OF BUSINESS TAXATION

Direct taxation of business has proven to be a very profitable activity for state and local governments. Although it cannot be measured precisely, such taxation likely accounts for nearly one-third of all taxes collected by state and local governmental units. This may come as a surprise to some observers because the tax most readily identified as a business tax, the corporation income tax, scarcely accounts for 20 percent of the total. The bulk of business tax collections come from levies that are not levied on business per se, such as the property tax and the general sales tax. Perhaps as much as one-third of the former and one-fourth of the latter are collected from business enterprises.[3] A rough estimate is provided in Table 2.1.

The figures in Table 2.1 for property tax and general sales tax are based on business shares of one-third and one-fourth, respectively. Also, the figures exclude specific excise taxes, such as gasoline charges. Therefore, I believe that the 27 percent share is conservative.

DEFINITION OF A BUSINESS TAX

Because there is the possibility and, indeed, even the likelihood, of tax shifting, there is no fully satisfactory definition of a business tax. For the purposes of the present discussion, a business tax will be defined as any tax on a business's purchase of inputs, its ownership of assets, its earnings, or its right to do business. Included in this definition are payroll taxes for which the business is the statutory taxpayer, property taxes on business property, general and partial sales taxes on business purchase of equipment or materials, corporate profits taxes, severance taxes, and business license taxes.

Common to all of these examples is that the tax liability is tied to the purchase or use of inputs into the production process. In some cases, such as payroll taxes, the tax is based on the flow of input services purchased. In other cases, such as the property tax, the tax is based on ownership of capital inputs. In still others, such as profits taxes or severance taxes, the tax is based on the flow of services provided by inputs owned by the firm.[4]

TABLE 2.1
State and Local Business Taxes, 1987
($billions)

Type of Tax	Revenue Collected
Property Taxes	30.4
General Sales Taxes	24.2
Unemployment Tax	23.7
Corporate Income Tax	22.7
Business License Taxes	5.8
Insurance Premiums	6.4
Severance Tax	4.0
Total Business Taxes	117.2
Total Taxes	428.8
Business Share	27.3%

Source: U.S. Department of Commerce, Bureau of Census, *Census of Governments, 1987*.

The arbitrary nature of this definition is highlighted by the treatment of payroll taxes, whereby those levied on the worker are excluded, whereas those levied on the firm are included. Because the long-run incidence of the two levies should be identical, in theory, the distinction is meaningless. Fortunately, however, at the state and local levels, there are few instances of payroll taxes assessed on the worker.

Note that we have excluded any tax levied on the sales of goods and services by a business, whether or not it is the statutory taxpayer. It is assumed that the government intends for such taxes to be paid by the buyer. Such an assumption may be warranted for general sales or gross receipts taxes, for partial excises on goods sold by public utilities, or for which the demand is inelastic, such as tobacco or alcohol. On the other hand, it may be a bad assumption for partial excises on goods for which close substitutes are available, such as taxes upon hotel rooms or theater tickets. Alternative potential sites for consumption may render the demand for such services highly elastic to price increases arising from localized taxation. Once again, our procedure may be defended on the basis that such taxes, to the extent they exist, constitute but an insignificant fraction of state and local revenues. Nevertheless, they highlight the difficulties in achieving a fully satisfactory definition.

Finally, our definition does not allow for tax liabilities that arise from the personal income tax. Profits of partnerships and proprietorships are subject to this tax. Symmetry with corporate profits taxes would seem to dictate that such tax payments be included as business levies. A moment's reflection, however, suggests otherwise. The personal income tax applies to all earnings of capital, whether they take the form of dividends, capital gains, or profits of unincorporated enterprise. Hence, it is not a tax on the employment of capital in the unincorporated sector per se. To the extent that proprietors or partners could have redirected their investments to stocks, bonds, or land, a similar personal income tax liability would be due.[5]

MOTIVES FOR BUSINESS TAXATION

Businesses are taxed for a number of reasons. Unfortunately, not all can be justified by traditional principles (e.g., equity and efficiency) of taxation. Sometimes business taxes exist because of political expediency. On other occasions, they may be adopted because of incorrect perceptions as to who bears the burden of the tax. Even when some form of business taxation can be justified, however, there may be preferable alternatives.

The Political Motive

Business taxation is sometimes popular among elected officials because it masks the true cost of government programs. Business taxes often have low visibility among taxpayers. Because they do not have to pay the taxes directly, taxpayers may be unaware of burdens they bear from higher prices or lower wages. Public officials can thus claim credit for the benefit of public programs without having to bear their political cost.

If true, this would be a powerful reason to avoid business taxation. Decisions about whether to expand public services should be made in light of the opportunity costs of such action. This takes on added force if one has a jaundiced view of the motives of government officials. Even if one believes that taxpayers are often uninformed about the benefits of government programs as well as the taxes that finance them, this cannot serve as a justification for business taxes. Equal ignorance should not be the basis for public policy. Instead, the thrust should be to increase the information flow to the citizen-worker.

Ability to Pay

Some might defend business taxation on the grounds of ability to pay. Because business firms often have vast resources under their control, they may be posited to have "deep pockets" for tax purposes. The same reasoning that is applied to apportion personal taxes among individuals is thus extended to include the business sector. The flaw with this reasoning is that businesses are not ultimate economic entities.

Only people can bear the burden of taxes. Therefore, business tax payments must come at the expense of those who deal with the firm: customers, suppliers, workers, lenders, landlords, or owners. There can be no presumption that the division of the tax burden among these groups will obey principles of ability to pay. This is true for the largest of business firms as well as for the smallest. Indeed, it may be particularly true for large firms because of the heterogeneity of the individuals that interact with it. Even in the event that the owners of the firm bear the burden of business taxes—and there is strong reason to believe otherwise—there is no guarantee that the burden will be distributed progressively. Ownership of business firms is widespread, including retirement and pension plans of workers who cannot be presumed to be included among the affluent. Ironically, this is more likely to be the case for "rich" firms like IBM or GE than for closely held small firms.

If a state or local government wishes to distribute taxes according to ability to pay, it should do so through a tax that takes into account the personal circumstances of individual taxpayers, such as the personal income tax, or through sales taxes on goods for which the income elasticity of demand is greater than unity. The use of business taxes for this purpose is simply too unwieldy and indiscriminate to achieve this goal.

Soak the Rich

A related argument, popular among those with populist convictions, is that business taxes can be justified because the owners of businesses (the "capitalists") tend to be rich and thus deserve to pay something additional for the cost of government. We have already pointed out that the ownership of most large firms spans all income classes. However, it still is the case that, *on average*, those who own businesses tend to be in the upper reaches of the income scale. Hence, to the extent that business taxes fall on owners, the rich will pay a disproportionate share of these taxes.

In the short run, when capital investment is fixed in place, there may be some element of validity to such reasoning. Owners of capital will simply be forced to accept lower returns on existing investments. Attempts to increase product prices will often be obviated because of competition from businesses located in other jurisdictions. Moreover, because capital costs are fixed in the short run, most firms will not find it profitable to change price and output strategy.[6]

In the long run, however, matters are much different. Because capital investment is highly mobile, firms can shift business taxes to others. Unless offset by public service benefits, such taxes will cause an outflight of capital from the jurisdiction. In response, prices of goods will rise or other costs will have to go down to offset the tax cost. Depending on the mix of these reactions, customers, suppliers, or workers will more or less suffer the burden of the tax. And there is no reason to expect such individuals to reside in the upper economic strata.[7]

One might object to this criticism on the grounds that long-run shifting of business taxes would not occur if all communities levied similar tax burdens on business, for in this event there would be no motive for capital outflow because relocation would offer no tax relief. To the extent that a community restrains its business taxes to some national norm, therefore, it might be argued that business would be unable to shift its tax burden to others. Such reasoning overlooks the fact, however, that even if every community imposes the *same* tax burden on business, any *one* community can, by eliminating its business taxes, attract additional capital investment. This will in turn increase the prices that can be paid to local owners of factors of production or lower the prices that firms can charge their local customers. The choice to tax business is in fact the choice to forego these advantages. Even in such an idealized environment, therefore, business taxes are in effect shifted to other groups. Soaking the rich through business taxes is simply not a strategy open to state and local governments in the long run.

Nevertheless, in practice, many communities may attempt to enjoy the short-run benefits of business taxation. Politicians often have limited time horizons. They may be tempted by the short-run advantages of targeting the rich for special taxation, leaving the longer-term economic development consequences for their successors. This proclivity will not go unnoticed by the business community. Communities with strong populist traditions will be approached with circumspection by the business investor. The end result may not be much different than the long-run scenario painted above. In this event, even the short-term benefits of business taxation are not achieved.

Export the Tax Burden

A popular rationale for business taxation is that it extends the reach of the taxing jurisdiction to residents of other jurisdictions. This is alleged to occur when businesses sell part or all of their product to out-of-jurisdiction individuals or firms. The belief is that businesses will raise their prices to recapture the tax payment assessed them. In effect, the tax burden is "exported" to nonresidents. Tax exporting can also occur even if taxes are absorbed by profits or shifted backward to other factors of production. As long as some owners of business or of other factors reside out of state, the tax burden will be shared with nonresidents. Absentee ownership of businesses and often of land and natural resources inputs is not uncommon. Indeed, it is typical for large publicly held corporations.

Although the policy of tax exporting may be questioned on moral or ethical grounds, it clearly has tremendous political appeal. If carried out successfully, citizens of the jurisdictions are able to enjoy public services at a reduced cost. Any political leader who eschews such opportunities would soon be seeking a new career. Moreover, exporting can be rationalized in defensive terms as being necessary to offset those taxes imported into the jurisdiction.

Although the case for exporting taxes, if possible, is compelling, it is often quite beside the point. In fact, there are very few genuine opportunities for tax exporting. Clearly, if the business firm is engaged in competition with firms outside its jurisdiction, it will not be able to recapture the tax in higher prices. To attempt to do so would simply result in lost sales. At the same time, if the domestic firm were to absorb the tax through lower profits, its owners would have the incentive to relocate to another jurisdiction, as discussed above.

The only way a firm engaged in interstate or international competition can continue to compete in the face of higher business taxes is if workers agree to take lower wages and/or landlords agree to accept lower rents so as to offset the tax burden. The reduction in wages surely does not result in tax exportation. To the extent that landowners reside outside the jurisdiction, some exportation may occur. But even this possibility may vanish if the tax is anticipated and local residents own the land at the time the tax is imposed.[8]

If, on the other hand, the products produced by business enterprise are consumed totally by residents of the jurisdiction, prices might be raised in response to business taxes. But then there wouldn't be any exporting because the consumers reside within the jurisdiction.

Thus, the opportunities for exportation are extremely limited. They arise principally from some unique resource that enables businesses within the jurisdiction to enjoy a competitive advantage over "foreign" businesses. It must also be the case that ownership of this unique resource must rest at least in part with nonresidents and that the taxes not be foreseen at the time the nonresidents acquired the resource.

This is a formidable list of requirements, characterizing only a small portion of the businesses within most jurisdictions. And even in these cases, a broad-based business tax may be a relatively clumsy instrument to achieve exportation. It would make far more sense to tax the unique resource directly, as in the case of severance taxation, or to tax the products using the unique resource, as in the case of tourist taxes or land taxes. We will deal with these options in greater detail below.

Before leaving the question of tax exporting, we need to dispose of another mechanism through which it is often alleged that a jurisdiction can export its tax burden. This process is through the federal income tax system. Because a tax on business is a cost that is deductible in calculating federal income tax liability, the imposition of $1 in tax will initially reduce profits by only $(1 - t)$, where t is the marginal federal tax rate. It would seem, therefore, that the federal government pays part of the firm's tax liability. Because this loss of federal revenue is shared by the nation as a whole, it would not be far from the truth for the jurisdiction to attribute this loss to nonresidents.

As far as it goes, this argument is correct. However, it does not go far enough. If it is true as we have argued, that the net return to investment in a community cannot be reduced by local taxation, then, in fact, there will be no reduction in federal income tax receipts caused by a local business tax. To maintain its net return, each business in the taxing community must raise output prices or lower input prices to fully offset the local tax. If it does so, its pretax profits will be unchanged, and it will pay the same federal income tax as before, with its customers and input suppliers absorbing the full amount of the local tax. No additional exporting will result through the federal income tax. Only if input and/or output prices do not rise enough to restore after-tax business profits will federal tax liabilities shrink. But in this case, the gainers are the nonresident capitalists, and the losers are the residents of the nation as a whole. Local taxpayers are affected only in their role as citizens of the country as a whole—and this effect is negative, as opposed to the positive effect one associates with tax exporting.

Close Loopholes in the Personal Income Tax System

A major business tax, the U.S. Corporation Income Tax, is frequently defended on the grounds that it is necessary to plug an important loophole in the U.S. Personal Income Tax arising from the ability to defer the personal tax via retaining earnings in corporate enterprises. At the very least, this allows individuals the opportunity to postpone the tax liability on retained corporation profits, and, because of the absence of constructive realization at death, may lead to the avoidance of the tax altogether.

Because most states also impose personal income taxes, can it be that their taxation of corporation income can also be justified in similar terms?

The answer is a resounding no. Only if local corporations are owned entirely by local residents, can the analogy be drawn with the federal corporation income tax. However, foreign (nonlocal) ownership is the rule rather than the exception. This means that the earnings of local citizens from holdings of corporation shares are derived mainly from business activity outside of the jurisdiction. Therefore, the local corporate income tax can do little to offset the retained earnings loophole in the state's personal income tax attributed to nonresidents. Indeed, in the presence of a domestic corporation income tax, resident individuals will have the incentive to shift their holdings to out-of-state corporations, so the loophole will be closed only for those cases where such shifts are impractical. Partial closure might be construed as horizontally inequitable and worse than no closure at all.

Payment for Services Rendered

Perhaps the most compelling motive for the taxation of business enterprise is to recapture the costs of services rendered by government to the business sector. The benefit principle has long served as one of the two major pillars of tax equity. Although conceived as a criterion for the taxation of individuals, it is easily extended to the finance of services to business. In the private sector, benefit charges in the form of input prices provides the basis for defraying the costs of private inputs to production. Unless a similar method is used to pay for public inputs, market prices will no longer accurately signal the relative scarcity of different goods. Therefore, more than equity is at issue here; efficiency seems to require benefit finance so that market prices can play their intended role.[9]

Despite this impeccable logic, the present system of business taxation seems only loosely tied to benefits of government services. In part, this reflects the difficulty in assigning benefits. More important, however, may be the attempt to achieve some of the less noble motives already discussed. We shall return below to the problems of implementing the benefit principle.

Payment for Environmental Damage

Closely associated with the benefit principle is the taxation of business to compensate for environmental damage. Instead of charging for governmental inputs, the focus is on charging for otherwise unpriced environmental inputs or outputs. Not only are such charges necessary to achieve correct relative private goods prices, they may be necessary if business enterprise is to locate at the most efficient site for the conduct of operations. Unless host communities are appropriately compensated they may take steps to exclude the offending enterprise.[10]

Taxation for Locational Rents

Business taxation might be justified as a means for capturing locational rents which arise from some resource that is relatively scarce or specific to the jurisdiction. Examples include mineral deposits, natural harbors, proximity to political centers, and favorable climate. Each of these attributes would lead, in the first instance, to higher operating margins for certain businesses located within the jurisdiction. It is to be expected that the community will want to capture or at least share in the benefits of these natural advantages. Selective business taxation may indeed be one means of so doing. Hence, in order to accomplish this end, states impose severance taxes on mineral extraction and special sales taxes on restaurants and hotels.

Because the pecuniary returns to natural resources often accrue to the owner of the land in the jurisdiction, it will often be that individual, not the business, that will bear the incidence of the tax. In effect, the higher profits get transformed into higher land values as business firms compete for scarce sites within the community. This suggests an alternative method for the community to share in its natural resource wealth—taxation of site rents or land values. Although interest in land taxes has received considerable attention by intellectuals, it has had much less success among practitioners. Taxation of land remains tied to the taxation of structures, equipment, and housing under local property taxes. And the level of property tax rates is only partially related to capturing resource rents.

The taxation of business to capture resource rents requires, in most instances, a targeted approach. That is to say, business taxes should be targeted to those industries that potentially profit from the natural resource. Rarely, if ever, will general taxation of business be appropriate. Only a handful of the business now on the books can possibly be justified by this motive.

IMPLEMENTATION OF BUSINESS TAXES

We now turn to the question of how business taxes should be implemented to achieve the purposes set out in the preceding sections. Three legitimate justifications were given for business taxation: (1) to enable the jurisdiction to spread the benefits of unique resources among its citizens as a whole; (2) to compensate the jurisdiction for environmental damage associated with business activity; and (3) to compensate the community for the costs of public services rendered to business firms.

We have already indicated that for rent capture, specific rather than general business taxes are appropriate. The same would be true for most types of environmental costs. Differences in environmental impact among firms with respect to environmental impact are much more important to public policy than environmental damage caused by businesses in general. The only example of environmental damage common to all firms is traffic congestion, and even here there are enormous differences depending on location. Therefore, charges for environment should be targeted to specific polluters and the extent of the charge tailored to the degree of damage.

Benefit Principle

Firm-, Industry-, or Location-Specific Services. If a service is rendered to a particular business firm, say extending sewer and water facilities, implementation of the benefit principle would call for a user charge or special assessment. To the extent that a service is rendered to all firms within a particular commercial sector, the services could be financed by a charge on the output of the industry—such as a selective excise tax. Finally, if the service is rendered to all firms within a specific geographic area, a benefit tax would require some sort of spatially restricted fee. The basis for such a fee might be lot or building size, lot or building value, number of employees, payroll, or some other measure of business activity. If the government service to the firm is proportional to one of these indices, the choice is clear. However, should there be no clear connection or should the connection be different for different firms, a choice among lesser evils needs to be made. Because this issue also arises with respect to services benefitting the business sector in general, its discussion is deferred until later.

General Services. Implementation of taxes to support general business services is far more problematic. First, benefits of some government services are very difficult to quantify. For example, benefits from the legal system, police protection, public health, and so forth are impossible to measure; therefore, allocation of benefits to specific firms becomes quite a chancy business. The best that can be expected under such circumstances is a rough application of the benefit principle. A second problem concerns the identification of services that should be considered beneficial to business. For example, it is widely accepted that education leads to a more productive work force. It is tempting to conclude, therefore, that the business community should share in the costs of public education. However, under the market system, individuals are compensated according to their productivity. To tax the business community for educational costs is to make them pay twice. This example suggests that business benefit taxation be confined to those services that are provided to it directly, rather than to labor or other resources that it uses in its operations.

After the appropriate services to be financed by general taxes on business are identified, there is the question of how to divide their costs among individual firms. Sometimes the choice is easy, for example, fuel consumption to pay for business highway services. Even here, however, special levies may be necessary, such as taxes based on weight. In general, if the service is linked to the employment of some particular input, a tax on that input is most appropriate. Thus, fire protection services could be financed by taxes that are proportional to the value of plant, equipment, and inventories. Here a property tax is a suitable business levy.

For many services, however, there is no obvious link between benefits and the employment of any particular input, nor any other facet of business operations. In such cases, any allocation method can be shown to be deficient. Some methods, however, may be more deficient than others. If the tax allocation method causes firms to alter their choice of production process, organization mode, or location, it creates economic waste or what public finance scholars call *deadweight loss*. All other things being equal, we want to minimize such losses.

At the same time, the allocation method should be perceived as being fair. It should not unduly punish some firms or reward others because of some irrelevant characteristic of the firm's operations. Some analysts might interpret this as also calling for taking into account a firm's ability to bear taxes. As we shall see below, this argument is far from compelling.

CHOICE OF TAX BASE TO FINANCE GENERAL BUSINESS SERVICES

When the benefits of government services are closely associated with some objective indicator, the assignment of tax share should be assigned accordingly. In the absence of such a correlation, we need to devise an allocator that is economically neutral and equitable.

Allocation According to the Use of Specific Input(s)

Taxes could be assigned according to the relative use of some productive input. For example, taxes could be collected in accordance with a firm's payroll, its purchases of electricity, or its ownership of real property.

Electricity purchases would seem to be an unsuitable allocator. Firms differ widely in electricity consumption and in a matter that would seem unrelated to their benefits of general public services. Not only would such a tax be arbitrary, but it would also induce firms to reduce their use of purchased electricity, either by generating their own power, or by using alternative energy sources. Each of these responses would raise the private and social costs of doing business.

The electricity example is used not to suggest it as a serious candidate for an allocator but to highlight the problems that arise when some specific input is used as a tax base. The use of payroll or business property raises similar problems, though not as dramatic. Industries differ sharply in the relative use of capital and labor. To use either as the allocator would clearly burden some activities relative to others. Moreover, firms would have the incentive to conserve on the chosen input item in order to soften the blow of the tax.

Allocation According to Output

If a firm's tax is based on output rather than input, it will not have an incentive to alter its method of production. Two measures of output suggest themselves: gross receipts and value-added. Gross receipts are not a good index because firms differ sharply in their use of goods purchased for fabrication and for direct resale. Firms engaging in wholesale or retail trade would be severely impacted by such a tax, as would manufacturers that fabricate semifinished products. Also, gross receipts taxes would tend to be pyramided. In effect, the same good gets taxed at each stage of the production process. Because goods and services differ in the number of stages required for their completion, there would be major differences in the tax burden imbedded in the price of different goods.

The value-added measure of output is devoid of such disadvantages. By excluding purchased inputs from the tax base, pyramiding is avoided and the trade sectors are not disproportionately burdened. It is therefore preferred to gross receipts. Some may question whether a value-added tax could be easily implemented, because it is a concept used only by economists, at least in the United States. Present business taxes require, however, all of the information necessary for a value-added tax return. This is because value-added can be measured from either the income or expense side of the firm's income statement. A firm's value-added consists of its wages, profits, interest rates, and depreciation expense.[11] Each of these items is currently reported in connection with personal and/or corporation income tax returns.

Allocation According to Profit

The final candidate for an allocator to be considered is some measure of firm profitability. This approach has similarities to the ability-to-pay criterion for individual taxes. Only those firms showing a profit would contribute to the cost of public services, and those that do would be taxed in proportion to their earnings.

Such an approach clearly conflicts with the benefit principle, and thus is associated with a basic lack of neutrality arising from the failure to require all firms to pay the costs of all of their inputs, both private and governmental. Thus, goods provided by marginally profitable firms would tend to be artificially cheaper. In effect, the profit tax places a price umbrella over such marginal firms. As Dan Troop Smith (1964) put it, profits taxes subsidize inefficient firms at the expense of efficient ones.

A second major defect with the profits approach is that as currently applied it is not a true profits tax. Included in the measure of profits is the return to equity capital, and, for many small businesses, the implicit wages of management. As a consequence, it suffers from the same nonneutralities as specific factor taxation. Capital-intensive activities and small business enterprises would be singled out for disproportionate taxes. Although the latter could be avoided by excluding small businesses, other nonneutralities would be introduced, favoring some industries at the expense of others.

A third nonneutrality arises from the fact that most if not all profits taxes in place are restricted to corporate business. Because some industries are more suitable for the corporate form of business than others, profits taxes will impact relative prices. Moreover, the most rapidly growing sector of the economy, the service sector, involves significant noncorporate business. Over time, therefore, profits taxes restricted to corporations will fail to keep pace with the growth of the government services provided to business.

Whatever their other merits, and we have been unable to find many, profits taxes are inherently unsuitable as a means of financing government services to business. The main advantage of such taxes is that they don't have to be paid unless profits are earned, which is highly popular in business circles. However appealing this may be, it should be noted that wages are not eliminated, nor are materials costs eliminated for nonprofitable business. Why then should the costs of government inputs not be paid when rendered? If the government wants to subsidize particular businesses, it should do so explicitly. Or if it wishes to defer taxes until more prosperous times, it could do so directly. But it should not eliminate the tax liability entirely for firms that do not make a profit.

Origin vs. Destination Principle

Any discussion of an appropriate business tax base would be incomplete without some consideration of whether business taxes should be based on point of consumption of a firm's product (destination principle) or the point of production of the product (origin principle). This distinction is of utmost importance for open economies where products are often consumed in tax jurisdictions other than where they are produced. If the object is to tax where production takes place, then the origin principle is appropriate. If the object is to tax goods where they are consumed, then the destination principle is relevant.

For the purpose of business taxation the intent is to assess producing firms the costs of government services rendered to them. Because a measure of output is used to allocate these costs, the location of production, that is, the origin principle, is the correct measure. At first glance, this might appear to put domestic firms that sell to out-of-jurisdiction customers at a competitive disadvantage with foreign firms because the latter are not subject to tax. It might also seem to encourage the importation of materials rather than to use domestically produced materials, because the foreign materials do not bear any domestic tax burden. Both of these observations are erroneous, however. If a domestic firm's tax liability accurately reflects its use of government services, then there is no net disadvantage to domestic firms relative to foreign firms, who do not get benefits of the government services. Similarly, to the extent that foreign-produced materials have benefitted from government services and they are taxed accordingly, their prices will include a charge for public services. It is only if benefit taxes are not levied elsewhere that a disadvantage will face local producers. But that would be true of any subsidy given to their rivals. Economic principles have long advocated free and open trade, without artificial subsidies. Therefore, origin principles should guide business taxation.

CONCLUSION

The objective of this chapter is to examine the rational economic basis for the taxation of business enterprises by state and local governments. Several logical bases have been explored. With the exception of capturing resource rents for the community at large, business taxes can be justified on the basis of the benefit principle, charging business firms for their use of government services or otherwise unpriced environmental inputs. With a few notable exceptions, such as gasoline taxes and property taxes to pay for fire protection services, most business taxes now in place serve this purpose poorly. Major existing forms of general business taxation distort business firms' choices of productive inputs and location, and unfairly concentrate the tax burden on certain industries and categories of business organization. In general, too much emphasis is given to a firm's use of capital inputs and its total sales in determining its tax allocation. Moreover, the current business tax system places excessive emphasis on the corporate form of business organization.

It seems fair to say that these deficiencies are more serious at the state than at the local level, principally because provision and financing at the local level guarantees some degree of benefit taxation. Only firms within the providing jurisdiction are called on to pay for local business services. Moreover, the bias against the corporate form is usually absent from local business tax structures. The major problems from local business taxation arise from inappropriate *levels* of taxation and heavy reliance on the property tax.

The most obvious reform, particularly at the state level, would be to move away from general sales taxes and corporate income and franchise taxes toward value-added taxes. By widening the base to include all forms of business organization, tax rates could be reduced and tax burdens could be shared more equitably. This would also relieve the existing bias against capital and material modes of production. Moreover, by adopting an origin principle valued-added tax, business location decisions would be less distorted.

Although the proposed reform is straightforward, its adoption seems remote. Only Michigan has adopted a value-added tax, and even there the tax is frequently based on destination rather than origin. While a state value-added tax has frequently been advocated by state tax studies, such proposals have usually been ignored or opposed by legislatures. In part, this reflects the difficulty of achieving any significant reform. In part, however, it reflects the lack of familiarity with the value-added tax concept. To many legislators and businesses, the value-added tax is a European construct that has fostered high levels of government taxation and spending. This type of opposition would soften if the U.S. government were to adopt a value-added tax. Until then, the principal option is for fiscal experts to keep raising the value-added tax as an option.

NOTES

1. See Walker (1937).

2. See, e.g., Goode (1951).

3. Precise figures are scarce in the literature. See, however, Wheaton (1983) and, more recently, Ring (1989). The latter estimated the business share of the sales tax to be 40 percent. In my home state of Louisiana, I have estimated (1988) the share of sales tax to be 35 percent and the property tax share to be 40 percent.

4. License taxes may appear to be an exception to the general rule because they may be viewed as a price to be in business in the first place. While this may be true in principle, most license taxes are based on the amount of input employed or output generated. For example, franchise taxes are typically based on some measure of capital investment or profits earned. Occupational license taxes are typically tied to total sales, a measure of total output, or, equivalently, to the use of inputs in general.

5. To the extent that the profits of unincorporated enterprise reflect opportunity wages to owners, a similar argument can also be made. The personal income tax does not single out compensation in the unincorporated sector, but applies to wages in all market activities.

6. However, the business community may anticipate such taxes and therefore build such costs into their initial investment decision. This is addressed explicitly in the discussion following.

7. If some capital outflight does nevertheless occur, it will depress returns in other regions as well. Some have argued that the reduction may be as large as the direct tax liability itself. However, this does not lessen the burden on customers, suppliers, and workers mentioned above. Therefore, the "soak the rich" strategy is achieved only at the expense of potentially regressive side effects.

8. That is, the bids for local lands would reflect anticipated future tax burdens. Assuming local residents owned land rights initially, they would thus bear the burden of expected future taxes.

9. If the government services have the properties of a pure public good, the benefit charge would not be necessary or desirable.

10. Fischel (1976) has explored the consequences of unpriced environmental costs for local land use policy. Fox (1978) has investigated their relevance to local tax policy.

11. It is also possible to identify value-added through the subtraction method, that is, sales minus purchased materials. In a closed economy, the two measures would give the same result. However, in an open economy, the adding-up method described in the text is appropriate for the so-called origin principle of taxation. The subtraction method is more compatible with the destination principle. This issue is explored at greater length in the discussion following.

3
Local Business Taxation and the Tiebout Model
ROBERT H. ATEN

This chapter is intended to be provocative. It addresses the murky theory of local business taxation, which involves the interaction of several of the more complex topics of public finance—including the economic theory of federalism and the general theory of business taxation.

This chapter does not address the complex problem of tax incidence beyond noting that businesses are not considered a repository of taxes in incidence theory. All taxes are ultimately paid by people, not businesses. Thus, any taxes paid by business firms must either be shifted to customers or employees of businesses, or, if not shifted, be borne by owners of businesses.

The economic theory of federalism establishes the standards against which local taxation of business should be both measured and judged. The theory addresses the equity and efficiency considerations encompassing which levels of government should carry out which activities—in other words, who should raise taxes and other revenues, and who should spend the resulting monies. In the division of governmental budgets among allocation, stabilization, and distribution activities, local governments are assigned many responsibilities for allocating funds among functions whose geographic scope is limited (Musgrave, 1959). Higher levels of government carry out most stabilization and distribution responsibilities. It has more recently been recognized that local governments also carry out stabilization and distribution activities, and this is probably desirable (Oates, 1990). Local taxation of business fits comfortably within that tradition as one revenue source to help finance the largely allocative responsibilities of local governments.

THE TIEBOUT MODEL

According to the Tiebout model, efficient provision of local government services requires benefit taxation. Consumer-taxpayers achieve efficiency by matching their tastes for the delivery of local public services with actual local government performance by "voting with their feet." That is, voters move to the jurisdiction in which public service levels best suit their preferences, given the "tax price" paid for the services. After 35 years, theorists are still uncomfortable with Tiebout's elegant creation. One principal problem is that the assumptions of the model do not appear to be in accord with many stylized facts of local government finance in the United States. For example, many local taxes are not benefit taxes; not everyone lives exclusively on capital income; and the *ex ante* distribution of income is not equal.[1] Nonetheless, there is much to be said for the principal insight of the Tiebout model which derives the conditions for efficient local government behavior from the relationships among such factors as congestion, the geographic availability of certain public goods, and the mobility of households. The Tiebout model certainly creates a presumption that, at the margin, local delivery of goods and services by governments should be financed by local benefit taxes.

THE TIEBOUT MODEL AND THE PRISONERS' DILEMMA

The debate over the correctness of the Tiebout model is central to the determination of the appropriate role for local business taxation. If correct, the model suggests that local businesses should only be taxed to finance benefits they receive from local governments. For those who favor broad local taxation of business to finance local social programs, reliance on the Tiebout model is anathema. Thus, the implications of the model are extremely controversial.

Apart from its relatively unrealistic assumptions, there is one other principal objection to the Tiebout model, namely, that local government taxation is inherently a matter in which jurisdictions compete with each other in a process that systematically reduces taxes on business and individuals. This process of competitive tax reductions without limit may be likened to a form of the game-theoretic "prisoners' dilemma" that is said to be applicable to local governments as they deal with businesses seeking special tax exemptions or favors. The concern is that, as a result of this process, fiscal resources are likely to be insufficient to support adequate local public services.

In the two-person prisoners' dilemma, the prisoners are safe from prosecution if both prisoners do not confess. However, they are questioned separately. The first prisoner to confess will receive a light sentence in exchange for cooperation. The one who does not confess will be heavily punished. Thus, the incentive is to confess, even though that makes the confessing prisoner worse off than if neither confesses.

By analogy, a business is said to be able to obtain separate commitments from each of several local governments for tax subsidies and other benefits in exchange for, say, its commitment to locate a new factory within the government's jurisdiction. The business, in this view, will site the factory in the jurisdiction that provides the best package of tax subsidies and other benefits. Individual governments do not know what benefits each of the others is offering and therefore often offer too many concessions out of their fear of losing the factory.

In the tax competition literature, therefore, the standard conclusion is that as long as prisoners (local governments) stick together, there will be no confessions (competitive tax reductions to business). However, because, like prisoners, local governments cannot hold out in the face of the strong threats against them, too many tax reductions will be provided to business. Therefore, it is often argued that the Tiebout model and its implications are incorrect because of competitive tax reductions by local governments.[2]

The problem with this line of reasoning is that local governments differ from prisoners in that they *can* communicate with each other about tax matters. A recent example occurred in 1990 in the U.S. Northeast. After a sustained period of economic growth lasting the better part of a decade, governments there had adapted to having available an annual bonus of additional revenues. By 1990, however, a regional recession was underway, a precursor of the 1990-1991 national recession. As a result, northeastern governments faced the necessity of increasing tax rates to maintain their balanced budgets without major service-level reductions.[3] Because of the recession, and because corporate profits slacken (or decline) during recessions more than most other taxes, state tax receipts from business corporate profits were particularly hard hit. Nearly all states in the region wanted to raise business tax rates to compensate for their revenue losses.[4]

In several public forums, Governor Mario Cuomo of New York State led the way out of the prisoners' dilemma by strongly exhorting his fellow governors to join him in raising business taxes to provide needed revenues.[5] He called on his fellow governors not to be intimidated by threats by businesses to leave the northeastern United States if their taxes were raised. In effect, he said that if all northeastern states were to simultaneously increase their business taxes, there would be no retaliation in the form of a business exodus from the region. Although businesses could leave any one state, Governor Cuomo implicitly argued, they could not profit by leaving the region. He was successful in the short run in that public officials in several states in the region immediately surrounding New York developed sufficient courage to raise business taxes in 1990. Any adverse long-run consequences of the increased taxes for the economy of the region remain to be seen.

The lesson from this informal but successful concerted effort by states to raise taxes on businesses during a recession is that the tax competition argument against the Tiebout model is overstated. State and local governments *do* have the capacity and willingness jointly to protect themselves against competitive reductions in business taxes in difficult economic times.

A skeptic of the Tiebout model might still argue that governmental behavior in difficult economic times is not the issue. Such a skeptic might note that the real issue for those who believe in the importance of tax competition is the behavior of business in ordinary times. The skeptic could argue that in ordinary times business firms have the capacity to undermine the tax base of local governments by successfully seeking special tax reductions that reduce the efficiency and fairness of business taxation. In extraordinary times, so the argument might go, everyone would recognize the emergency nature of the situation. In ordinary times, the prisoners' dilemma might still prevent local governments from raising business taxes when that is appropriate and encourage them to make competitive tax reductions. There is some merit to this concern, but I suggest its implications are not what they might seem.

EXCESS BURDEN AND RAMSEY PRICING

Tax reductions favoring business are often efficient in the sense that they reduce the excess burden from taxation. Although a detailed discussion of excess burden is beyond the scope of this chapter, the significance of an appropriate theoretical foundation for local business taxation is such that mention should be made.

In the simplest and most well-known case, the standard equation for the calculation of excess burden for commodity taxation is[6]

$$W = \frac{1}{2} pqt^2E \tag{1}$$

where W is the welfare loss (excess burden) due to a tax change, p and q are the pretax price and quantity, respectively, of the commodity being taxed, t is the tax rate, and E is the price elasticity of demand.

The fact that the tax rate term is squared in the expression provides a significant portion of the intellectual justification for the efforts made during the 1980s to keep tax rates low. After all, W increases by the square of the tax rate, t, which enormously increases the impact of that term in the calculation of excess burden.

Although the ongoing debate on tax policy has clearly recognized that excess burden depends on the level of tax rates, it has not considered the implications of the link between excess burden and price elasticity. If the commodities sold by businesses have different price elasticities of demand, equal tax rates across commodities will obviously not minimize the total excess burden arising from the sum of the excess burdens from each separate commodity taxed. Baumol and Bradford (1970) explain the analysis of Frank Ramsey (1927), which shows that the tax rate on each commodity that minimizes excess burden in such circumstances is the square root of the reciprocal of the price elasticity term. One implication of Ramsey's analysis is that a separate tax rate is required for each separate commodity taxed to achieve economic efficiency.

Although this conclusion is theoretically sound, tax policymakers and even theorists have reasonably shrunk from its main implications. No one wants to establish such a complex system of business taxation. Moreover, to equalize excess burden, commodities with low price elasticities of demand should have high tax rates, and vice versa. Elasticities of demand for necessities are generally low, whereas those for luxuries are generally high. Thus, minimizing excess burden would require high tax rates on necessities and low rates on luxuries. This conclusion is so repellant to most theorists that the implications for tax policy of the price elasticity term in equation (1) are conveniently ignored.

I share the general reluctance to advocate the sort of tax system suggested by that interpretation of equation (1). However, this is not the only possible interpretation. Another view addresses the tax competition argument previously discussed. In local business taxation, Ramsey pricing suggests that governments should not, on efficiency grounds, abstain from offering separate lower tax rates to business firms. This could happen when firms suggest lower rates as a requirement for locating or remaining in a particular jurisdiction. Thus, what are called competitive price reductions in the anti-Tiebout model literature could be seen as a step toward economic efficiency, because their adoption would reduce excess burden.

This does not mean governments should automatically agree to proposals for tax reductions to business. Business firms will naturally seek the lowest level of taxation they can obtain, whether or not they face debilitating competition. If tax reductions are not required to help compensate for a large price elasticity of demand faced by the firm (or elasticities of both supply and demand in the more realistic case), then such reductions would not yield improvements in economic efficiency, and governments should not grant them.

Governments have a difficult time determining when they should be responsive to the importuning of firms and selectively decrease business taxes. There is no easy answer to this problem, and history offers many examples of failure by governments to make appropriate judgments.[7] Nevertheless, governments have *some* capacity to demand sufficient information to help them determine whether businesses are facing such significant competition that efficient tax reductions would be required to keep them in business in that locality.[8] Governments will certainly make errors while attempting to make and carry out decisions in this framework. That should not prevent them from taking actions that they see as in their interest and that theory suggests would also improve economic efficiency.[9]

UNEQUAL FISCAL CAPACITIES

A final problem facing those who would rely on local business taxation to help finance local governments is the unequal distribution of business activity among jurisdictions. Such differences are startling[10] and contribute to the larger problem of unequal fiscal capacity among U.S. jurisdictions. The conceptual answer to this problem is reasonably clear from the economic theory of federalism. In addition to open-ended categorical matching grants to compensate for benefit spillovers among jurisdictions, the central government should also provide closed-ended general-purpose grants to help ensure that local governments have fiscal capacities reasonably commensurate with their responsibilities.[11] Local governments should be permitted, subject to appropriate standards established by the central government, to make their own determinations about which commodities to tax and how much. Governments could decide to compete in various ways: (1) as low-tax low-service jurisdictions (New Hampshire has chosen this course); (2) as high-tax, high-service jurisdictions (New York State and City are clear examples); or (3) specializing in providing particular types of governmental services (Florida, e.g., has specialized its tax structure to appeal to the retired elderly who also enjoy its favorable climate).

CONCLUSION

Administrative convenience and a partially legitimate fear of falling into the prisoners' dilemma do help justify the standard approach of local governments to business taxation. However, limitations on local taxation of business generally can reasonably be defended through an analogue with the Tiebout model. Arguments against such limitations are both substantially overstated and do not properly take into consideration the consequences for local business taxation of reasonable strategies to reduce excess burden and the resultant efficiency losses. Although I reject going all the way to minimize excess burden by providing separate tax rates for each commodity facing business taxation, theory does justify local government aid to particular firms through selective business tax reductions.[12] These subsidies should not, of course, substitute for efforts by those firms to meet competition through investment in new plant and equipment or other efforts to seek improvements in productive efficiency.

The implications of Tiebout's analysis are reasonably clear. Local governments should rely principally on benefit taxation. Although there are intellectual arguments against such a reliance, there is also a powerful case favoring it. By analogy, firms should pay local business taxes to the extent that they benefit from local government services.[13]

By and large, any inequities resulting from this framework of taxation are, the business of the national government. Although this chapter probably suggests the correct general framework for efficient taxation of businesses at the local level, not too much should be made of modest deviations from this general approach. The reason is that the Tiebout model should be seen as a partially flawed representation of reality.

It is perhaps too bad that the theory of local business taxation cannot yield determinate results providing easy guidance to practitioners. However, I believe the views of the tax policy community should reflect the sort of ambiguity discussed in this chapter, rather than erroneous simplifications. Given the real limitations of the theoretical case favoring the use of a benefit taxation model at the local level, probably not too much more should be expected or said.

NOTES

The author is grateful to Steven D. Gold, Director of the Center for the Study of the States, State University of New York, and to the participants in the seminar on Local Business Taxation in Ferrara, Italy, for helpful comments. This chapter draws heavily on a previous paper by the author, "Local Business Taxation: The Case of Infrastructure Finance in the United States," which was given at the Italian seminar.

1. These counterfactual assumptions are a serious methodological problem, according to one school of thought (advanced initially by Milton Friedman), only if the predictions of the model do not bear fruit.

2. A more sophisticated offshoot of this argument has poor citizens chasing the rich from one jurisdiction to another to seek higher levels of public services financed by the rich. This is less an argument against the Tiebout model than a reasonable complaint about the operation of the current system of grants and subsidies in the U.S. federal system.

3. Whether the appropriate step might not have been to reduce services is not the question here.

4. Personal tax increases were also under consideration, but that is a different topic.

5. By 1991, the national recession had begun to cause significant service-level reductions in New York, suggesting that Governor Cuomo may have misread the economic signals in 1990. In 1991, New York relied much more heavily on expenditure reductions to close its budget gap.

6. This assumes constant long-run costs to eliminate the supply elasticity term. In the case in which the supply elasticity is included, the expression becomes more complex but remains similar. For a factor of production such as corporate capital the analysis of effects of a tax on commodity sales would become still more complex.

7. There are differing opinions about the reasons for this failure. See, for example, Pomp (1986) and Ledebur and Hamilton (1986).

8. Expressed another way, that the price elasticities of demand or supply for their products are so large.

9. This too has been considered in the literature on optimal taxation. See Baumol and Bradford (1970).

10. Large diversified states and localities collect taxes from business sources that are simply not available to most small or rural jurisdictions.

11. Designing a framework that would distribute general-purpose grant funds in ways that would significantly equalize fiscal capacity is very difficult. This is true because of both theoretical issues and data problems.

12. Hovey (1986) makes the case that economic development pressures may cause states to neglect social welfare concerns. Both the large (7 percent per year) increase in federal governmental transfer payments and the many federal mandates imposed on states for social welfare programs during the 1980s suggest Hovey's concern is

somewhat overblown—the failure of public and private efforts to eliminate poverty and other social problems in the United States notwithstanding.

13. Although it could be construed that way, in my view, this may not be too narrow a framework. Businesses may see themselves as benefiting from sound police, fire, and garbage collection services, from good schools in which the children of their employees are educated, and from reasonable social services to the poor. All these may ensure that the local community enjoys a reputation as having a suitable business climate. Businesses may be willing to pay taxes to help finance such activities, even though the reach of some of these taxes may not be as narrow as the traditional view of benefit taxes would suggest.

II
State Taxation
of Corporate Income

States currently tax corporate income according to complex rules that vary significantly from state to state. As a result, state corporate income taxes are costly to administer and to comply with. And because they alter relative costs and prices, they distort private sector resource allocation.

The authors of this part suggest and evaluate several approaches to reducing the adverse economic effects of the present state-level system of taxing corporate income. Chapters 4 and 6 consider in detail how the rules that govern states' taxation of corporate income can be made more uniform and less complex. In Chapter 4, Carlson et al. examine various approaches to reforming UDITPA. The need for this reform arises from changes in the nature of goods and services and the manner in which they are produced, particularly the increased importance of the service sector and the implicit increase in intangible services and assets.

Strauss, in Chapter 6, analyses the pros and cons of having the federal government collect state corporate income taxes as it collects the federal tax. The state taxes would be levied on the federal corporate income tax base; in other words, they would be "piggybacked" on the federal tax. A three-factor formula would be applied uniformly to apportion income among states. Each state would set the schedule of rates to be applied to the corporate income apportioned to it.

Francis and McGavin, in Chapter 5, are also concerned that states have manipulated apportionment formulas to their individual advantage. They suggest that states pursue economic development and other objectives by means other than formula manipulation. They join Carlson et al. and Strauss in calling for a uniform three-factor formula. But they would "double-weight" the sales factor, giving sales a weight of 50 percent and payroll and property each a weight of 25 percent.

In Mattson's view (Chapter 7) states' taxation of corporate income, as currently practiced, discourages foreign investment by U.S.-owned global corporations and thereby inhibits their ability to compete internationally. States' methods of apportioning the foreign source income of such corporations are "uncoordinated and inconsistent." Also, revenues from state taxes on corporate income have, over the past two decades, increased relative to federal revenues. Mattson calls for eliminating discriminatory taxation of the dividends that U.S.-owned corporations receive from their foreign operations, as well as for lower tax rates.

4
Perspectives on the Reform of UDITPA

GEORGE N. CARLSON, GERALD M. GODSHAW,
and JEFFREY L. HYDE

In the summer of 1957, the National Conference of Commissioners on Uniform State Laws and the House of Delegates of the American Bar Association each met separately and gave their collective approval to the Uniform Division of Income for Tax Purposes Act (hereinafter referred to as UDITPA or Act). The basic purposes of UDITPA were to bring simplification and equity to the area of state income taxation. UDITPA did not, however, intend to address all areas of state taxation that were not uniform at the time. The Act avoided discussing the issue of jurisdictional nexus necessary to impose a tax. Also, the Act did not address the various rules employed by the states to determine the tax base. Furthermore, the adoption of UDITPA was purely voluntary among the states.

BACKGROUND OF REFORM ISSUES

As a model uniform act, UDITPA had some acceptance, but not overly so. It received a boost when in 1966 a group of state tax administrators led by the Special Committee of the Council of State Governments developed and approved the Multistate Tax Compact (Compact). As with UDITPA, acceptance of the Compact was voluntary; by July 1967, twelve states had joined. Membership in the Compact has fluctuated, allowing states to be full or associate members with no restrictions on the option of membership chosen at any time. The Compact established the Multistate Tax Commission (MTC) to be the ruling body and arbiter of the provisions of the Compact. The purpose of the Compact, much like UDITPA, was to provide solutions and additional facilities for dealing with state tax issues of multistate businesses. Also, the Compact meant to provide a continuing forum for resolution of issues affecting the various states in an attempt to achieve uniform state taxation.

To facilitate uniform taxation, the Compact adopted and incorporated UDITPA as Article IV of the Compact. This still did not mandate acceptance of UDITPA. The Compact recommended UDITPA and required only that it be an option to existing allocation and apportionment procedures. In this manner, the Compact attempted to achieve the goals of UDITPA of equity and simplification. The Compact still left acceptance of the form and principles of UDITPA to voluntary compliance. One note of caution at this point: UDITPA, as a separate uniform act, is only one provision of the Compact, which has 12 articles. Through its regulation-promulgating procedures, the MTC has taken the lead in developing and interpreting the goals and provisions of UDITPA.

From the outset, however, various commentators took issue with the Act, questioning its purpose and means to introduce uniformity into an otherwise disorganized area of taxation (Wilkie, 1959; Edelmann, 1958). As the name suggests, UDITPA was meant to address the division of income—in other words, allocation and apportionment issues. One of the drafters of the Act, William J. Pierce, wrote that the Act was intended to institute a fair and equitable measurement procedure for states that had enacted net income taxes or taxes measured by net income (Pierce, 1957, p. 748). It was therefore the stated goals of UDITPA to codify only the issue of dividing income among the several states. In fact, UDITPA is based on two significant assumptions which highlight this limited purpose. First, UDITPA assumes there is no issue with the state's jurisdiction to impose a net income tax. Second, UDITPA is not meant to define the tax base, but it does attempt to define which types of income are allocable as opposed to apportionable (Pierce, 1957, p. 747).

Accordingly, to the drafters, the issues concerning acceptance were limited to practical business issues. It was expected that each state would review the Act with regard to the revenue impact on that state. It was not anticipated that the constitutional constraints of due process and commerce clause scrutiny would be of concern. Up until the time of the drafting of UDITPA, there had been a host of court challenges to state taxes in general. These challenges had been based on the principles of due process and commerce clause as the state taxes were applied to the respective taxpayers.[1] Furthermore, the drafters recognized that the tax base would not be completely uniform; political considerations would almost always prohibit such uniformity. Therefore, UDITPA was careful not to address the component parts of the tax base but merely to provide an equitable means of dividing income among the states.[2]

It is very important to note, in the context of any discussion of UDITPA, that it was a methodology intended for use in the taxation of manufacturing and mercantile operations. Section 2 of UDITPA exempts individuals, financial organizations, and public utilities. In 1957, it was believed that through legislation, the states that taxed these classifications had already adequately addressed the means to divide income among jurisdictions. Therefore, the method to allocate income contemplated by UDITPA was inappropriate in those circumstances. Accordingly, UDITPA was to be the method designed specifically for manufacturing and merchandise businesses.

To accept the purpose of UDITPA, the draftsmen of the Act had to acknowledge the problems in state income taxation previously addressed by others. The first issue was the inefficiency in compliance costs due to the variety of methods used to apportion the state tax bases. Taxpayers were forced to accumulate and to maintain several different accounting records. More disconcerting to taxpayers, the sum of the methods seldom resulted in an accurate assessment of income subject to tax. It was just as likely that more than 100 percent of the income was taxed as it was that significantly less than 100 percent was taxed. It was the intent, therefore, to construct a system whereby all of the income was taxed (no more and no less). Any new system had to simplify the compliance and enforcement functions (Pierce, 1957, p. 748).

Although UDITPA was to invoke a new realm of fairness and equitable taxation through uniformity, Sections 4-8 of the Act accepted state taxation schemes currently used in 1957. These sections specifically allocated rents, capital gains, interest and dividends, and patent and copyright royalties. The drafters acknowledged that the legislatures of the day had established existing methods to tax such activity, and UDITPA incorporated those methods directly. This acceptance of prevailing rules would seem to be a recognition that UDITPA was meant to be incorporated into state taxing schemes without creating wholesale changes that might disrupt state revenues.[3]

Sections 9-17 of the Act are the heart of UDITPA and establish the standard three-factor apportionment scheme. In these sections, the drafters tried to stress to foreseen critics that the purpose of UDITPA was the measurement of a preexisting tax base (Pierce, 1957, p. 750). The factors, as developed, included items that either were not part of the tax base or were thought to be distortional of operations.[4] The purpose, however, was to develop a system to measure business activity without altering the tax base. UDITPA was offered not as a panacea of state income taxation, but more as a means to lessen the issues and problems existing in state taxation in the 1950s. Its purpose was uniformity in one aspect of state taxation—division of income. Its goal in another aspect was fairness and equity. One question that begs the fairness issue is whether nonuniform tax bases can be divided uniformly. This nonuniformity issue remains a critical concern of both state policymakers and the business community, and may lay at the heart of the controversy surrounding UDITPA.

The provisions of UDITPA reflect the primary business activities of the United States in 1957. States have modified UDITPA,[5] but for the most part the provisions of UDITPA continue to emphasize the division of income based on three factors—property, payroll, and gross receipts (or "sales" as used in this chapter). Whereas UDITPA is heavily focused on a manufacturing and mercantile business society, the United States of the 1990s and foreseeably the next century is drifting away from that base. Is UDITPA elastic enough to evolve with the businesses of the future? The purpose of the UDITPA is fair and equitable division of income. Is it accomplishing that goal?

PERSPECTIVES ON REFORM

The issues surrounding the potential reform of UDITPA generally revolve around how income is defined, allocated, and apportioned to the individual states. The issues of nexus, or what constitutes a presence in a state, is not addressed in this section as that is beyond the immediate scope of this chapter. The need for reforming some aspects of UDITPA stems not so much from the intended vagueness of the 1957 guidelines but from the changing world environment. That is, the increased importance of the nonmanufacturing and nonmercantile sectors (in contrast to the manufacturing and mercantile sectors specifically targeted by UDITPA) in today's economy warrants a reopening of the UDITPA guidelines, as do the changing sources of income to corporations. Three areas needing clarification in UDITPA are identified below.

Allocation of Intangible Income

The growing importance of technical know-how, trademarks, trade names, and other intangible assets merits an examination of when the return from intangible assets is included or excluded from the income tax base. The tendency to allocate the income attributable to an intangible asset to the place of domicile may overlook the importance of where the income resulting from the intangible asset is generated. That is, some intangibles may have market value beyond the places where they are developed. Placing the income from an intangible in the tax base of the state in which it is developed and then including it in the apportionable base can create a double taxation scenario, just as excluding the income from the tax base and only partially including it in the tax base of the state of domicile can result in undertaxation.

Currently, the definition, under UDITPA, of business intangible income can be interpreted in ambiguous ways. Business income, under UDITPA, is defined as "income arising from transactions and activity in the regular course of the taxpayer's trade or business."[6] This definition of business income is designed to include income from intangible property when such property is an integral part of the firm's regular business operations. Nonbusiness income is allocated to the individual state of domicile or location of asset producing the income. Nonbusiness income includes any income not related to the principle trade or business activity, such as dividends, interest, rents, or royalties.[7] Clearly, these definitions lead to some ambiguity as to whether or not license fees, rents, and royalties are business or nonbusiness income.

Analysis. The arguments relevant to the taxation of income from intangibles stem from a perception of where the value of an intangible lies. For example, a well-recognized name in consumer products has some values in terms of garnering a larger market share or fetching a higher price. However, the manufacturer of that product contends that its primary business is not the creation of trade names and that the value of the trade name reflects a buildup of a reputation, developed in the place of domicile and not integral to the business. This argument essentially restates the business proposition that the tax base in a particular jurisdiction ought to reflect the income directly sourced to that jurisdiction and the source of the trade name intangible rests with the place of domicile.

States may contend that such a trade name is integral to the success of the business, and, therefore, any income from the intangible ought to be included in the apportionable base and not allocated to the state of domicile. Such an apportionment reflects the notion that the trade name in and of itself may have little value without the perception of the consumer located in the taxing jurisdictions.

Although some states may mandate that a royalty paid to related entities (as might be the case in the above example) be included in the apportionable income base, such an inclusion is controversial and may not accurately represent an allocation of the income to its source. To some extent, UDITPA is designed to avoid determining the ultimate source of the income—unlike the current international standard—by permitting the use of formulary apportionment.

More significant problems stem from the lack of uniformity among states. If some states insist that many intangible assets are not integral to the business and the business is domiciled in their state at the same time other states maintain the intangible is an integral part of the business, the income from the intangible could confront excessive taxation.

Alternatives. Although there is no clear answer as to whether the income from certain intangibles should be regarded as business or nonbusiness income, a clearer set of UDITPA guidelines would avoid much confusion. Absent clarifying changes in UDITPA guidelines, individual states would have to determine under the facts and circumstances which intangibles contribute to business income. This "do nothing" option may appeal to those who wish to give wide discretion to states or those who feel the current guidelines do not pose significant problems. However, the current ambiguity only creates uncertainty in the business community.

An alternative to no change would be to clearly define intangibles associated with business and nonbusiness income. This option would allow for a uniform policy across states concerning which earnings from intangibles would be allocable to specific states and which would not. The difficulty with this approach rests in clearly identifying the facts and circumstances in which the income from intangibles is business income and apportionable. Some state statutes might serve as guides for the determination. For example, when royalties or other payments to related parties for intangibles are instituted, the income from the intangibles could be apportionable. This alternative still does not address the concerns of businesses that feel that income should be allocated back to its origins.

Another alternative would be to create a list of intangibles which are and are not allocable. Despite its apparent administrative neatness, this alternative can create a variety of difficulties. First, defining the income from an intangible requires analytically determining what portion of profits is related to intangible assets and what portion is a result of other factors such as manufacturing or marketing. Second, a concrete list would not allow the flexibility of fitting the facts and circumstances to individual taxpayers. For example, a patent in one firm's case could be integral in locking the competition out of a product line, implying the return on the patent should be apportionable, whereas other patents may have a value in terms of licensing them to unrelated parties when they are not used by the patent owner. Finally, such a list would itself be politically contentious.

Treatment of Foreign Source Income

One of the areas that merits consideration as part of UDITPA reform deals with the taxation of income earned outside the United States by U.S.-backed multinational corporations. The need to address this area of taxation has become far more pronounced since UDITPA was promulgated in 1957. In the last thirty-five years, the world, or global, economy has become a reality. In response U.S. businesses have recognized the necessity to go abroad in pursuit of lower-cost sources of supply and to exploit new markets. Faced with strong competition from businesses located in other countries, U.S. businesses have demonstrated that they realize they must expand internationally merely to survive. It is in light of this new international economy that consideration should be given to modifying UDITPA to provide states and businesses with guidelines for the tax treatment of income earned outside the United States by U.S.-based multinationals.

At the present time, the methods used by the states for taxing income earned outside the United States, by the non-U.S. subsidiary of a U.S.-based corporation, can be placed into two broad categories: allocation or formula apportionment. In many states, foreign source income, such as dividends, royalties, and interest becomes part of the state tax base. In some states, these items of income are allocated specifically to the state of legal or commercial domicile. In other states, foreign source income is treated as business income and is subject to apportionment by whatever formula is used by the state. That formula, however, typically reflects just U.S. business activity, often measured by payroll, property, and sales. Thus, even though foreign income may become part of the state tax base, the foreign business factors associated with that income (such as payroll, property, and sales) are not part of the apportionment formula. The inevitable result of this treatment is that foreign income becomes subject to state taxation. Justice Stewart criticized this inconsistent (in his view) treatment of foreign income and business activities in his dissent in *Mobil Oil Corp. v. State Commissioner of Taxes of Vermont* (1980). A few states have specific exemptions for certain items of foreign source income.

The second method, used most notably by the state of California, is worldwide combined reporting. Under this method, all income earned by the affiliated members of a unitary business is calculated on a global or worldwide basis, thus including corporations organized or chartered outside the United States. Then, that income is apportioned according to the formula used by the state, but the formula, unlike the treatment described above, includes the foreign (and domestic) business activities of the combined group.

Although the question of whether the states should tax foreign source income remains an unsettled issue, it is clear, under either of these methods, that the state income tax liability of a business is indeed affected by its international operations. That is, if a U.S. corporation is subject to state tax on dividends and royalty income received from a foreign subsidiary, or if a foreign subsidiary becomes part of the combined worldwide group, the state tax liability of the domestically based corporation is likely to be different than if it had no such affiliates with international operations, or if foreign income and activities were ignored for state tax purposes. Thus, it is appropriate that UDITPA be modified to provide guidelines on this issue.

Analysis. Before identifying the available alternatives, it is constructive to review the arguments pertaining to state taxation of foreign source income. Business tends to view state corporate income tax systems as source based. According to this view, the state corporate tax system should apply to income earned or sourced within the state, but it should not apply to income earned outside the state, and certainly not to income earned outside the United States. Assuming that the factors of payroll, property, and sales in the UDITPA-mandated formula are reasonably related to where income is generated, the three-factor formula endorsed by UDITPA may come reasonably close to achieving the objective of taxing income earned within a particular geographic location. Business, however, often objects to state tax systems that include foreign source dividends, royalties, and interest in the income tax base as constituting extraterritorial taxation. The essence of this argument is that these items are sure to be subject to state taxation if they become part of the business income base to be apportioned by the traditional three-factor formula. Even more clearly, dividends, interest, and royalties received from abroad are a part of the state tax base when specifically allocated to the state of legal or commercial domicile. In either case, business objects to this treatment as being at odds with the notion of a source-based tax.

Business has been even more vocal in its opposition to worldwide combined reporting. That system is criticized as being inconsistent with the internationally accepted arms-length method, and for creating the likelihood (and perhaps the reality) of double or extraterritorial taxation. Business, for example, observes that an important premise of formula apportionment is that the rate of return on the factors in the formula, such as payroll, is uniform among all jurisdictions in which the business operates. This assumption may be reasonable within the confines of the United States, the argument goes, but it is a questionable assumption in an international context with widely divergent wage rates. If wages are lower abroad, worldwide combination may increase that state tax liability of a domestic corporation by "importing" income earned abroad into the state tax base. Business also criticizes the worldwide combined reporting system as being administratively burdensome. Tax authorities from countries outside the United States also object to worldwide combined reportings for being a violation of international standards.

Not surprisingly, state tax officials see the situation quite differently. Their view is motivated primarily by two concerns: fairness and revenue. With respect to fairness, state officials believe that equity demands that foreign source dividends, royalties, and interest be part of the state tax base. The plea for equity is different from the argument traditionally advanced at the federal level for justifying taxation on a worldwide basis. In the federal context, worldwide taxation is defended on the grounds that the federal government provides benefits and services to U.S. taxpayers wherever they reside or wherever they do business. Thus, according to this view, it is appropriate to tax income on this basis as well. State tax officials, however, contend that it would be unfair to exempt or treat preferentially foreign source dividends, interest, or royalties while taxing those income items in full when generated domestically. As in most tax disputes, there also is a revenue issue. State officials obviously want to protect their revenue base and feel that they need this tool to do so. The adherents of worldwide combined reporting, for example, note that it is essential to address the shifting of profits to lower tax jurisdictions. They also object to the federal rules that label, perhaps artificially, certain items of income as being from a foreign source and thus (potentially) outside the reach of state taxation.

Alternatives. Although the answers to these questions are neither easy nor clear, UDITPA should attempt to address them. Given the growth of the global economy and the divergent interests and views of business and state tax policy officials, it is clear that significant problems exist. Failing to act would be unfortunate; it would recognize the jurisdiction of states to tax foreign source income and permit states to continue to design their own system of taxation, unfettered by any guidelines for taxing international income. This option is attractive to those who argue that there is no compelling reason for state tax systems to treat foreign source income differently than out-of-state income. The option fails to address the concerns of the business community, at a time when the global economy has become a reality.

One alternative would be to prohibit residence states from taxing foreign source income. Under this option, a state that was taxing corporate income solely on the basis of tax (as opposed to commercial or legal) residence would no longer be permitted to tax foreign source income, as defined by federal law, or perhaps by UDITPA. However, a state that taxes corporate income on the basis of commercial or legal domicile could include foreign source income in its tax base. This approach would preclude residence states from subjecting foreign source income to state taxation, either deliberately or inadvertently, through the operation of a particular apportionment formula. Under this approach, nonbusiness corporate foreign income could still be taxed by domiciliary states; to this extent, double taxation could still exist between individual states and foreign countries. Whether or not business-type corporate income was taxed would depend on the mechanics of state apportionment formulas.

Another alternative would be to prohibit the application of the unitary system to foreign corporations. This option was considered at the federal level on a number of occasions in the late 1970s and 1980s. It was also considered by the Reagan administration's Worldwide Unitary Taxation Working Group, but was not adopted. States would be prohibited from including the activities of a non-U.S. subsidiary corporation in a combined report. This option would meet the objections that the worldwide application of the unitary system results in a taxation of foreign source income. State tax administrators would object that this alternative would require them to rely on separate accounting and force them to verify the transfer prices at which intercompany transactions are recorded. Given the difficulty that the Internal Revenue Service has with this problem, state tax administrators argue that they would be faced with an insuperable task.

A third alternative would be to exempt foreign source income. This option, which also has received legislative consideration in the past, would exclude income from sources outside the United States, as defined by the Internal Revenue Code, from the tax base of the states. This limitation would apply to both resident and domiciliary states. It would prohibit a state from including in its tax base foreign source branch earnings, dividends, interest, royalties, rents, capital gains, or any other type of foreign source income paid to a U.S. corporation. Both specific allocation and apportionment of foreign source income would be prohibited. Under this approach, the corporate taxpayer would pay the higher of the foreign or federal tax liability on its foreign source income (due to foreign tax credit rules). This would have the effect of enabling some taxpayers to pay less total tax on their foreign income than on domestic source income, which is taxed at both the federal and state levels. State tax administrators might object to the option if the federal source rules were used to identify foreign source income. They argue that these rules ignore economic realities and could lead to tax avoidance practices. Presumably, state tax administrators would have to rely on the Internal Revenue Service to make most reallocations between domestic and foreign source income.

Apportionment and the Service Sector

When UDITPA was put forth in 1957, the nongovernment service sector represented 12.7 percent of all nonagricultural employment in the United States, whereas today it represents 25.6 percent.[8] The UDITPA guidelines focused on the traditional manufacturing and mercantile sectors of the economy predominant in that time period. Because the service economy has grown and firms now provide services to customers in many states, the definition of the factors used in apportionment has become more critical. Although service industries may have little in the way of property, the sales and employment factors remain relevant.

The focus of much confusion centers on whether sales should be recorded in the jurisdiction where the purchase occurs or whether they should be recorded in the jurisdiction performing the service. The UDITPA guidelines state that sales other than tangible personal property be recognized in the jurisdiction where the cost of performance occurs, or the place from which the services are rendered. Many states contend that the sales ought to be recognized in the jurisdiction benefiting (or making the purchase) from the service provided. This situation can create circumstances leading to either double taxation or undertaxation. If a state adopting the UDITPA guidelines is the domicile for a firm providing services to customers in other states and the recipient of the services is located in a state that apportions the sales to that state, the firm would then be taxed on the same income twice. Conversely, if the firm providing the services were domiciled in the apportionment state and the recipient of the services was located in the state adopting the cost of performance rules, the income from the sale of services to the out-of-state customer might confront reduced overall taxation.

Analysis. The arguments concerning which jurisdiction recognizes the sales of a service company are diverse, depending on the particular state and business. Many states whose residents purchase a variety of services from firms in other states view the present UDITPA guidelines as inherently unfair. These states contend that the service company revenue stems from activity within their state, and just as a manufacturer, under UDITPA, adopts a destination principle for computing the sales factor, so, too, should service companies. Opponents to changing UDITPA counter that, like the pure solicitation function of manufacturing firms under UDITPA, which do not imply nexus, the activities of service providers outside their place of performance represent pure solicitation and do not give rise to nexus.

The potential for over- and undertaxation is magnified when states attach a higher weight to the sales factor. Although attaching increased importance to the sales factor for one state and not others itself creates the potential for over- and undertaxation, the potential disparity is particularly high for service industries. The following extreme case is illustrative. Firm A provides services from state 1 to customers in state 2. All of firm A's customers are located in state 2, which double-weights the sales factor and has adopted a destination principle for services. If state 1 has adopted the UDITPA guidelines and the source of service rules, all of the income of the firm would be subject to taxation in state 1, and 50 percent of the firm's income would be subject to taxation in state 2. In this case, the state income tax base would equal 150 percent of the firm's income.

As the interstate trade in services continues to expand, the problem will only grow as states whose residents purchase services feel their tax base ought to include the income-producing activities generated by their residents. On the other hand, the actual income associated with providing those services rests primarily at the location of the service provider. That is, the provider most likely employs people not located in the state of the customer and provides capital to perform these services outside the sate of the customer.

Alternatives. The appropriate rules for the treatment of sales of services are neither obvious nor easily administrable; however, if UDITPA is to continue as a viable guide to state business taxation in the 1990s, the treatment of interstate sales of services must be addressed. If UDITPA remains unchanged, many states would be free to ignore UDITPA in setting state and local income tax policy. This does not appear to be an attractive option from anyone's perspective. The uncertainty confronting service providers on the potential tax liability outside their place of domicile could clearly impede sound business development. At the same time, certain states may feel compelled not to adopt UDITPA provisions relating to the definition of sales, giving rise to potential double taxation or under-taxation.

Preferable to inaction would be adoption of a destination principle for the service sector. This option would essentially mirror the treatment under UDITPA of manufacturing sales. The key element here would center on the applicability of the destination principle in terms of when the sales effort goes beyond the solicitation function. Although some states have adopted various rules regarding warranty or repair service as constituting more than solicitation in the manufacturing context, a different set of still unclear rules would be needed for service companies. This alternative may also be unattractive when the services provided benefit a multistate corporation and all the benefits (as calculated from the sales factor) are apportioned to the state of domicile of the firm purchasing the service.

A second approach to change would be adoption of an arm's-length standard. Under an arm's-length standard, the value of the marketing and solicitation function would be allocated to the state of residence of the customer. However, developing arm's-length transfer pricing rules on an interstate basis would be overly complex and beyond the scope of any state enforcement policies.

A third approach would be to adopt other formulas for allocating sales. This alternative would set forth guidelines based on efforts of performance by the service provider within the state. For example, the effort might be measured by the time spent by the provider at the customer's location. The difficulty with such formulas is their arbitrariness and that they are likely to differ from state to state, once again implying a potential for double taxation or undertaxation.

Another formulary approach would entail an arbitrary split of the interstate sales of service firms. For example, 50 percent of the sales might be apportioned to the state of domicile of the service provider and 50 percent to the state of the recipient. Although such a sales split methodology might be inconsistent with the facts and circumstances of each case, the uniform adoption of a split would avoid the double and undertaxation problems associated with other options.

CONCLUSION

Although UDITPA was created to address the issue of over- and undertaxation of corporate income at the state level, many of the guidelines contained in UDITPA remain unclear, especially as they relate to today's economic environment. The original Act set forth a framework from which state governments can create their own multistate firm unique to the states in which the firm operates. Although the Act presumes a clear definition of income and nexus, many of the issues raised through implementation of the Act clearly leave the income definition and nexus issues open to debate. Certainly, the changing world economy has meant that some portions of UDITPA are not as relevant as they once were and need clarification.

This chapter identifies three areas in which UDITPA needs reform if it is to remain a standard used by states in allocation and apportioning income of multistate corporations in the 1990s. First, the determination of whether or not the income from certain intangibles is included in the apportionable (as opposed to being allocated to specific states) tax base needs clarification to avoid possible double or undertaxation. Second, the treatment of foreign source income remains a major issue with some states, especially those not adopting the water's-edge principle. The importance of the foreign source income issue will grow as businesses continue to expand internationally. Finally, the treatment of the income accruing to companies providing services in more than one state leads to questions regarding the viability of using the sales factor in apportioning income. The continued growth in the service sector of the economy suggests this issue will remain contentious as states try to expand their tax base.

NOTES

1. In recent years taxpayers have also used due process and the commerce clause as bases to attack a state's measurement methodologies. See *Container Corp. of America v. Franchise Tax Board*, 463 U.S. 159 (1983).

2. This can be seen especially in the comments made in Section 18 of the Act which allows for equitable apportionment provisions in specific situations where the standard provisions are inapplicable. The Act recognizes broad use by several states of separate accounting or other means to accomplish an equitable division of income.

3. The drafters noted that state tax revenues were manipulated by the allocation and apportionment methodologies. It was thought, however, that uniform rules would be better for the business community. If revenue adjustments were needed, it was reasoned that tax rates could be adjusted more easily than apportionment measures. However, this reasoning ignored the political ramifications of adjusting rates and may be a flaw in the ability of UDITPA to reach uniformity.

4. A big concern to some was the inclusion of rents in the property factor and the use of cost versus depreciable value for other property (Wilkie, 1959, p. 71).

5. Primarily, states have weighted the factors differently. Some states double-weight the sales or disregard the other factors. Some states limit the issue of allocable income, treating all income as part of the apportionable tax base.

6. Commerce Clearing House, Inc. (1985, paragraph 8459 1[a]).

7. Commerce Clearing House, Inc. (1985, Paragraph 8459 1[e]).

8. Shares derived from data provided in National Income and Product Accounts.

5
Market Versus Production States: An Economic Analysis of Apportionment Principles

JAMES FRANCIS and BRIAN H. McGAVIN

The apportionment of income among states and other taxing jurisdictions is an issue that continues to confront tax administrators and others working in the area of taxation. At one time the issue was believed to be all but put to rest by the UDITPA compact, but economic and political forces have altered the landscape sufficiently that today many states have or will revisit formulary apportionment. This chapter offers a somewhat nonstandard interpretation of formulary apportionment which we hope will help inform the efforts of those jurisdictions that must revisit the apportionment issue.

We view the apportionment problem as being fundamentally a problem of valuation. If multi-jurisdictional corporate entities are to be liable for tax in a single jurisdiction to the extent that a portion of the value of what they produce arises from activities attributable to that jurisdiction, then the problem is clearly one of apportioning value across jurisdictions. Viewed in this light, we see apportionment as merely another aspect of the general problem of valuation which has vexed economists from the discipline's inception.

APPORTIONMENT AND OBJECTIVE VALUE THEORY

According to the standard three-factor apportionment formula, as enunciated in the UDITPA model of 1956, relative value is proxied by proportionate shares of payroll, property, and sales—each equally weighted. However, in early discussions of apportionment one does see mention of formulae which include only the first two of these—payroll and property. These relate specifically to what might be called the "supply side" of the firm's activities. In standard microeconomic theory, the firm's supply side is depicted using a two-factor production function. This production function is generally written in the form

$$Y = F(K, L)$$

with Y representing physical output, K representing capital input, and L representing labor input.

It seems natural to regard the payroll and property factors of the apportionment formula as attempts to proxy the broad theoretical input categories, labor and capital. Attempting to infer value from factor usage has a venerable history in economics. The first recorded attempt was in *The Wealth of Nations* (Smith, 1963 [1776]), wherein Adam Smith proposed a primitive labor theory of value. Smith's theme was expanded on by David Ricardo, and also by Karl Marx, who used it as the basis for his theory of capitalist exploitation. An apportionment formula that focused exclusively on input usage would therefore seem to amount to applying a "labor theory of value" to the apportionment problem. This perception was corroborated by Beaman (1963) who wrote with respect to a property payroll formula "The argument for this formula is that the sales factor is redundant, capricious, and unnecessary. The advocates of this formula take the economic view that all income, including that from selling, arises from a combination of capital with labor."

APPORTIONMENT AND MAINSTREAM VALUE THEORY

By the late nineteenth century, "objective" value theories had fallen into disrepute with most influential economists, owing to the introduction of the concept of "utility." It was intuitive to most economists that the pleasure or enjoyment associated with the consumption or use of a good must be intrinsically related to its value.[1] Incorporating a sales factor may be viewed as an attempt to include the demand side of the firm's activities in value determination. Therefore, we see that the three-factor formula is actually an amalgam of objectivist and subjectivist value theories. This is eminently appropriate because the dominant theory of value in modern economics also melds these two perspectives. We owe the classic statement of modern value theory to Alfred Marshall (1938) when he addressed the question of whether "cost" or "utility" (i.e., supply or demand) govern value: "We might as reasonably dispute whether it is the upper or the under blade of a pair of scissors that cuts a piece of paper, as whether value is governed by utility or cost of production."

The Marshallian paradigm, of course, dominates the teaching of microeconomics today. From a value-theoretic standpoint, it appears to be essential to include both the supply side and the demand side in apportionment formulae. Further, it appears to be fruitless to conjecture whether supply or demand is relatively more important.

OBJECTIVES OF APPORTIONMENT

Having established that conventional three-factor formulary apportionment is firmly based in standard economic theory, we must now turn to practicalities. In practice, apportionment formulae are constructed with various objectives in mind. The traditional objective of apportionment has been to achieve a fair distribution of corporate income. The concept of fairness recognized by the courts has been most sensitive to protecting taxpayers from double taxation by multiple jurisdictions. Hellerstein (1988b) discusses this under the rubric "internal consistency" and describes judicial attitudes as follows: "A formula ceases to be intrinsically fair when, if applied across all taxing states, it subjects a multistate enterprise to taxation of more than 100 percent of its tax base."

States are quick to assert a second absence of fairness when a formula distributes less than 100 percent of a firm's tax base—the "nowhere" income situation. A strict interpretation of these notions of fairness would necessitate that the apportionment factors sum to one across states for each multistate corporation. Given that the sum of all numerators equals the denominator for each factor, a sufficient condition for this to obtain is that all states use the same weights in their apportionment formulae. Analytically, it does not matter what values are assigned to individual weights. If the weights sum to one and are uniform across states, then the sum of apportionment factors across states for a given company must be one.[2] On the other hand, when states use different weights in their formulae, the sum of a given firm's apportionment factors across states will be one only by chance. The sum will generally be either less than or greater than one depending on a host of considerations.

Recently, several states have made adjustments to their apportionment factors. Often, these adjustments have taken the form of increases in the sales factor relative to the other two factors. An informal survey of states (Table 5.1) that have recently changed from

TABLE 5.1
Revisions in Sales Weights

State	Old (%)	New (%)	Start
Florida	N.A.	50	1971
Wisconsin	33	50	1973
New York	33	50	1978
Connecticut	33	50	1983
Kentucky	33	50	1985
Illinois	33	50	1987
Minnesota	33	50	1987
West Virginia	33	50	1987
Nebraska	33	100	1992
North Carolina	33	50	1989

equal-weighted three-factor apportionment to 50 percent or greater sales-weighted apportionment, indicates that several intend to confer benefits so as to attract new business to the state.

However, a revision of the apportionment formula affects not only new business but also existing business in a state. A few of the surveyed states did acknowledge that "giving a break to business" was a consideration in revising their apportionment formulae.

Formula revision is only one way of conferring benefits on business. As a practical matter it seems to represent something of a meat-axe approach. It is invariably accomplished by large changes in the factor weights that materially affect the entire tax base. The proclivity to formula manipulation may stem from the fact that it is more obscure than other methods of business subsidization; that is to say, the connection between benefactor and beneficiaries is harder to identify than it would be with more direct methods of subsidy.

This political advantage is not without cost, however. The equity of the corporate tax is blemished by every movement away from parity. The efficiency consequences of differential weights and the implications for behavior in the face of uncertain future weights cannot be known with certainty, but they do not seem likely to be salutary. The effect of degraded equity will ultimately be decided in the courts. The effects of degraded efficiency impact the performance of our economy every day.

A REVENUE-NEUTRAL TAX EXEMPTION

As a simple example of the substitutability of formula manipulation and conventional subsidization, consider a tax exemption that is revenue-neutral vis-à-vis a unitary sales weight apportionment formula. Under a unitary sales weight, tax revenue will equal

$$T_u = f_s A$$

where T_u is tax revenue, f_s is the share of sales in a state, and A is federal taxable income. Under an equal-weights formula,

$$T_e = w(f_p + f_n + f_s)A$$

where T_e is tax revenue, f_n is the share of payroll in a state, and f_p is the share of property in a state. Revenue-neutrality requires that

$$T_u = T_e$$

But if the purpose of unitary weighting is a lower tax burden, then for some firms it will be the case that $T_u < T_e$. Therefore, we define

$$T_x = T_e - X$$

where X is an exemption or subtraction from apportioned income computed using a standard apportionment formula. Imposing the requirement that $T_u = T_x$ gives

$$f_s A = w(f_p + f_n + f_s)A - X$$

or

$$X = [w(f_p + f_n + f_s) - f_s]A$$

$$= [(w - 1)f_s + w(f_p + f_n)]A$$

Note that the exemption is a decreasing function of the sales share (f_s). A sufficiently large sales share would imply a negative exemption, which simply means that a firm would be hurt by a unitary sales weight.

The point is that it would be possible to compute an exemption for each firm which would equate both the effects that firm would incur under unitary sales apportionment and equal-weighted apportionment cum exemption. It would be possible to perform a similar exercise for any alternative weighting scheme. The exemption method would obviously not be subject to the same objection raised above against formula manipulation. The effects on individual taxpayers would be clearly observable.

From the standpoint of equity and efficiency, however, the exemption method seems to be less an improvement. Taxpayers would still be treated differentially, and effects similar to overt double taxation or "nowhere" income would not be precluded. There could, however, be some efficiency gains if apportionment weights were stabilized. One complication of the exemption scheme would be the possibility of negative exemptions. Symmetry requires that negative exemptions be imposed, but this might be difficult politically. If negative exemptions are disallowed, the revenue and resource allocation implications of the two regimes will differ.

APPLICATIONS

Given our economic framework for the apportionment problem, other weaknesses of UDITPA become evident. With respect to services, UDITPA defines the sales numerator to include sales when the service is performed either within the state or primarily within the state as measured by cost of performance. This effectively gives 100 percent supply-side weight to services because the jurisdiction of performance is inherently the jurisdiction where capital and labor reside. Sales of services must be reflected in the numerator of the jurisdiction in which the utility or benefit of the consumption of the service is enjoyed in order to properly reflect the effect of demand on the value of the service.

The throwback rule shares a similar flaw. Throwback is designed to deal with the problem of "nowhere" income by attributing to the state of origin a sale that would otherwise be "assigned" to a state where the taxpayer is not jurisdictionally present. Although it does prevent sales factor numerators from summing to less than the sales factor denominator (i.e., it prevents "nowhere" income), it effectively distorts the apportionment of income and diminishes the influence of the sales factor as a proxy for demand by biasing sales toward the state of production.

An alternative to the throwback rule which does not include this flaw is the throwout rule. By deleting from the sales denominator those sales made into states in which the taxpayer is not jurisdictionally present, it is just as effective as the conventional UDITPA throwback rule in preventing "nowhere" income. It has, however, the clear advantage of keeping the sales factor free of supply-side influences.

Finally, there is the matter of sales to the federal government which, under UDITPA, are thrown back to the state of origin. The motivation for this appears to have been the goal of distributing the profits of federal contractors throughout the fifty states, rather than concentrating them in certain jurisdictions where the federal government happens to have supply depots, or to foreign jurisdictions. If this egalitarian justification is still valid, an approach more in keeping with our demand-supply theory would be to distribute the value of such sales across the sales factor numerators of each state in proportion to that state's contribution to the financing of federal expenditure.[3] (The contribution of states in which the taxpayer is not jurisdictionally present would be thrown out of the calculation.)

CONCLUSION

The major advantage of formula manipulation appears to be political. But formula manipulation does have costs, both in terms of equity and efficiency. From economic and legal standpoints, it therefore seems advisable for all states to once again converge on a uniform apportionment formula and pursue other policy objectives through other means. We would argue, though, that the equal-weighted three-factor formula is not optimal. As we have seen, the three-factor formula represented an evolution from an apportionment concept which focused exclusively on the supply side of the market. However, it gives the demand side only one-third weight. This may have occurred because the originators of the three-factor approach did not think in terms of demand and supply sides of the market but in terms of three factors. With three factors, it seems logical to assign equal weight to each.

As we have observed, however, the effects of two of the factors have already been homogenized via the production function.[4] Consequently, equal weighting embodies an implicit double-counting of the supply side, effectively assigning a two-third weight to supply and a one-third weight to demand. Only a formula that assigns a 50 percent weight to each side of the market avoids the objection of overweighting of one side or the other. We find it ironic that past movements to the double-weighted (i.e., 50 percent) sales factor formula have often been criticized on the grounds that they have represented attempts to distort the fair apportionment of income. It may well have been the case that such motives did underlie some such changes, but we would argue that these changes were actually felicitous. Fundamentally, the double-weighted formula is the superior approach. Implementation motives notwithstanding, the double-weighted sales factor formula has the basic advantage of not biasing the distribution of income toward either the demand or supply side of the ledger.

It is the opinion of the authors that by firmly grounding the apportionment problem in economic theory, the debate and resulting inconsistencies in apportionment across the states can be eliminated. The demand-supply framework offers specific answers to problems which heretofore have been resolved only by the negotiating skills and political strength of competing parties. To the extent that state legislatures desire a different distribution of the corporate tax burden than that which flows from the demand-supply model, they can directly achieve these results through exemptions, subtractions, additions, and so on. This approach allows states to take the moral high ground on apportionment problems and makes visible those legislative redistribution policies that would otherwise be buried in the arcana of apportionment.

NOTES

1. Some economists, most notably those associated with the Austrian School (e.g., von Mises, Hayek) became advocates of a pure subjectivist theory of value.

2. This assertion assumes the absence of so-called "nowhere" income, perhaps due to the use of throwback rules.

3. For practical purposes, prior-year personal income figures as published by the Bureau of Labor Statistics for each state would serve as a workable proxy for federal tax payments by state.

4. An example of this would be the homothetic production function. In this case, output can be written $Y = Lf(K/L)$, which indicates that output is equal to labor times a function of the ratio of capital to labor. If the firm expands labor and capital proportionally, then the change in output can be inferred from the change in labor.

6
Federal Collection of State Corporate Income Taxes

ROBERT P. STRAUSS

This volume reflects a growing interest on the part of business taxpayers, tax researchers, and tax administrators in improving the interstate uniformity of the U.S. state and local tax systems. As a number of observers of the state and local scenes have commented, it is becoming increasingly difficult to justify or afford the heterogeneity of ways that we finance the costs of our 80,000+ state and local governments.[1]

There are several fundamental approaches to reducing the diversity/heterogeneity that results from such a large number of independent taxing authorities. The most dramatic would involve reducing the number of governments by realigning their geographic boundaries. For those willing to consider this possible change, I recommend a foray into the normative geography literature which has speculated on how to redraw state boundaries so they would follow current economic and population patterns, rather than those that were hammered out as our rivers were explored and various colonizing powers argued and fought over territorial rights.

Another approach would be to alter the fiscal concurrency powers of our federal, state, and local governments. This approach would realign the constitutional powers of these 80,000+ governments to define uniformly tax bases, and to specify the manner in which tax rates are set by each level of government.[2] That is, there are a number of constitutional models besides our version of "anything goes" in coming to an agreement on who and what should be taxed.

Recently, I wondered if we might be better off if the states were required to ratify changes in the federal tax base definition; this might restrain federal enthusiasm for tax reform. Although this suggestion makes some sense, to date it has not received overwhelming support from elected officials.

Each of these approaches would require a constitutional amendment with attending difficulties and dangers. An alternative to constitutional remedies would be intergovernmental cooperation to achieve greater uniformity in revenue statutes and practice.

UNIFORM TAXATION OF CORPORATION INCOME IS NEEDED

In the area of corporate taxation, uniform application of revenue rules seems especially meritorious for several reasons. First, the cooperation needed would only be among some forty odd revenue authorities. If we sought, by contrast, to homogenize sales or personal income taxes, there would be many variants of local as well as state taxes to deal with, although all local taxes are pursuant to state law. Second, one can argue that the growing uniformity in other nations' business taxes—for example, European Economic Community initiatives to integrate their value-added taxes—provides competitive impetus here as well.

For the states, there is another motivation to cooperate, and this has to do with what I shall call the corporate tax gap. As every seasoned observer of state business taxes knows, much of the friction between business taxpayers and government revenue officials is due to who one thinks is winning the annual battle between taxpayer and tax collector. On the one hand, business taxpayers argue that they are being exploited and doubly or triply taxed by states which have enormous leeway to hunt for business tax revenues in a post-*Container* world. On the other hand, state governments complain that businesses aggressively plan their state business tax payments by parking corporate profits in "nowhere" tax states like Texas and Washington, taking unfair advantage of state dividend exclusions by translating income into dividends to escape taxation, using transfer pricing mechanisms developed by their accountants and software specialists to move income from high-tax to low-tax states, and concocting filing units to escape paying their fair share of the costs of needed public services.

Undoubtedly both are correct, and, other than providing for the full employment of corporate tax specialists, the inter-state conflict over state taxation of business income leads at a minimum to poorly worded statutes, taxpayer uncertainty, and higher compliance costs, and revenue uncertainty for governments.[3]

Table 6.1 presents evidence that the aggregate of state corporate income tax bases *differs from*, and *is lower* than the federal corporate income tax base as reported by the Internal Revenue Service. If we

TABLE 6.1
Comparisons of Aggregate State and Federal Corporate Income
Tax Bases ($billions)

Year	State Corp Net Income Tax Collected[1]	State Base[2]	Federal Corporate Base[3]	State Base as % of Federal Base
1987	21	300	465	65%
1986	18	265	408	65
1985	18	255	364	70
1984	16	231	349	66
1983	13	201	297	68

[1]Calendar-year corporate net income tax collections from Governments Division, U.S. Bureau of the Census, *State Government Tax Collections*, selected years, divided by top corporate marginal tax rate reported by Commerce Clearing House, *All States Tax Guide*, various issues.

[2]The corporate net income tax base for Washington is based on Strauss (1987), Table 6.4, p. 118; the corporate net income tax base for Michigan is 16 percent of the base of the Single Business Tax; the 16 percent figure is the average share that profits constitute of the Single Business Tax base according to Barlow and Connell (1983), Table 22.2, p. 682. The base for Texas is simply 9 percent of the total federal base. The 9 percent is based on an examination of Texas' share of total industrial and commercial electricity consumption in the United States. Figures for Nevada, South Dakota, and Wyoming are based on U.S.-wide per capita averages from the other states with corporate net income taxes.

[3]Statistics of Income Division, Internal Revenue Service, U.S. Treasury Department, *Statistics of Income: SOI Bulletin*, 10 (Summer 1990), 1, Table 13, p. 121 for 1983-1987. The federal corporate tax base is *before* application of deficits and NOL's.

divide each state's corporate income tax collections by the nominal tax rate,[4] we get a rough estimate of the taxable base in each state. Table 6.1 contrasts the aggregation of this figure for all the states to federal corporate taxable income before deficit. For the years in question,[5] the total state base has been about one-third less than federal corporate net income, which provides some motivation for states to seek greater uniformity. Of related interest is the fact that dividing state collections into the federal base in Table 6.1 yields effective tax rates of from 4.4 percent to 4.8 percent over these five years.[6]

Do these calculations prove that business has been unduly aggressive? I am somewhat agnostic on this, and view the lower state tax base figures as reflecting the high quality of our tax accounting and law programs in colleges and universities, the pragmatic restraint of our state taxing authorities, and the value of shareholder pressures on the tax-minimizing behavior of corporate tax officials. Of course, the differences also reflect the wide variety among the states in the filing unit (from unitary to multiformity), taxable income, apportionment factors, and provisions of incentives/tax credits.

Also, the relative modesty of the state bases reflects the political realities of the skewness of the distribution of such taxes in each state. I would venture that 80 percent of the corporate net income taxes in each state are paid by less than 1 percent of the business taxpayers, and that the Fortune 1000 are far and away the predominant payers of state corporate net income taxes. The reality I speak of is the influence and litigiousness of major business taxpayers, domiciled or with a major presence in a state, on the determination of their final liability.

This state corporate tax gap seems to provide for both elected officials and business taxpayers a rationale for a more systematic approach to imposing and collecting state corporate net income taxes. It may be time for the states to admit defeat in this quarter of the business-tax game, and to suggest that the states move on to a more level playing field for the next quarter.

In particular, I suggest the states level the playing field by forming a new, cooperative alliance with the federal government. The cooperative approach I discuss below is the federal collection of state business income taxes, or piggybacking. The essential bargain to a state government in such an enterprise is the assurance that 100 percent of corporate net income can be taxed at some rate[7] to provide for the financing of needed public services, whereas for businesses it means lower compliance costs and an assurance that only 100 percent of income will be subject to tax.[8] The states may also find renewed interest in federal collection of state taxes as a result of several recent Supreme Court decisions which create, for the first time, meaningful exposure to the states for payment of retroactive claims in disputed business tax cases.

This chapter examines federal piggybacking of state corporate income tax as an option/alternative to uniform state statutes, (e.g., UDITPA) from various perspectives: tax administrator, taxpayer, and elected officials. It is my hope to breathe some new life into an old idea here in the United States and to convince these communities that the mutual benefits outweigh any costs of such centralized tax collection.

Below, I work through some of the issues that would invariably arise with federal collection, and rely on the existing provisions of federal piggybacking of personal taxes which have laid dormant for so long. Optional federal collection of state personal income taxes was enacted in 1972 as part of the general revenue-sharing legislation and amended in 1976 to assure that it would be free to any electing state and that any state could "trigger" the system. Due to a staff error, Internal Revenue Code Sections 6361-6365 were eliminated in the 1990 Budget Agreement; however, HR 1555, the Technical Corrections Act of 1991, pending as of May 1991, reinstates IRC Sections 6361-6365 as they stood before this error, as well as provides for joint federal-state tax administration as well as bilateral cost reimbursement.

To those who think such a form of intergovernmental cooperation to be as theoretical as the geographic or constitutional remedies alluded to before, I remind you that the Canadian model of "tax rentals," or piggybacking, has been in operation in various forms since World War II,[9] and that the piggybacking of provincial corporate net income taxes on the central government is something that both government and business have learned to live with.

PIGGYBACK COLLECTION OF STATE CORPORATE TAXES

The essential feature of any federal collection of state corporate income taxes involves a notification process and definition of what constitutes an allowable form of piggybacking in terms of conformity with federal definitions, nature of the state tax to be imposed, and provision for turnover of funds and resolution of disputes.

With respect to the definition of taxable income, there are two adjustments I would suggest. First add state corporate income taxes to the base to avoid a double deduction in a fashion that does not require solving simultaneous equations.[10] Second subtract or prorate interest on federal securities.

With respect to the filing unit, I suggest the adoption of the federal filing unit for state purposes, for example, the federal consolidated return using an 80 percent ownership test of subsidiaries at the water's edge.

With respect to the amount of tax that a state could impose, the next step in the process would be the application of a state tax based either on a surcharge on the federal liability before various federal credits, or based on a state system of tax rates. Given the growing importance at the federal level of minimum taxes based on book income, there might be some merit in allowing the states to decide how to deal with this as well.

Estimated state taxes and final payments for state corporate taxes collected by the IRS through the Federal Reserve System would be turned over promptly to the states, and some sort of provision would need to be made for under- and overpayments that result from taxpayer error and the audit and compliance work of the IRS.

Essential to any system of federal piggybacking would be the construction of unambiguous apportionment rules which would supersede nexus issues, and the authority of the states to examine the apportionment factors to ensure that corporate income was not being "booked " in low-tax or no-tax states. Below, several aspects of this basic model are elaborated on with the objective of finding particular policy proposals that serve the respective interests of taxpayers, tax collectors, and state governments.

Protection of State Interest

Under Section 6363 of the Code, the federal government was authorized to represent any piggybacking state in all civil and criminal proceedings in the federal courts, whereas the states were required to represent state interests in state courts. The net result of this process is for personal income tax disputes to first go through the state systems.

In order to protect taxpayers from initial double administration of the piggybacking process, administrative determinations made by the secretary of the Treasury on personal tax liabilities or refunds would not be subject to review by any officer or employee of a state; however, tax returns would be available for supplemental audits by state revenue authorities with the usual safeguards as to confidentiality of returns, for example, IRC Section 6103.

It should be noted that every state currently has in place an information exchange agreement with the IRS which provides for the exchange of state and federal return information that would help promote the audit process.

Under piggybacking the information flow would be reversed in that the federal government would have the primary authority and responsibility to audit state returns, and the states would be able to audit further. Were a state to reach a determination that differed materially from that of the IRS on an audit question, final authority would remain with the IRS.

Given the importance of the apportionment factors in the determination of state business tax liability, there would probably be a need to amend the Section 6363 process to give state audits of the numerators of the apportionment factors special standing in the administrative process. As will be discussed below, the current federal return contains the denominators of a reasonable three-factor formula (payroll, property, and sales), so that the only point of conflict would be over the attribution of the numerators of each factor among the states.

It is difficult to evaluate whether federal primacy in the determination of state business tax liability would be a cause of chronic conflict between the states and IRS. Given the greater ambiguity in business taxation as contrasted with personal taxation, especially at the state level, the alternative of dual authority on such complex matters would seem to unduly muddy the waters, leading to long delays for taxpayers and creating long-term budgetary uncertainties for the states.

Revenue Stability and the Federal Corporate Tax Base

It is well known that corporate profits, as measured for the gross national product (GNP) accounts, are quite volatile, and that the taxes derived by the federal government are equally if not more volatile. There are two tax reasons for the volatility of federal corporate tax receipts: the continued unpredictability of the foreign tax credit due to taxpayer control of timing, and the existence of very long carryforward periods (and shorter carryback periods) for net operating losses. Historically, other credits such as the general business tax credit and the investment tax credit have been sources of volatility; however, they no longer are provided at the federal level. For example, from 1985 through 1989, refunds of the federal corporate income tax averaged 17 percent of *gross* collections and better than 22 percent of *net* collections after credits.

Also, the federal provision of very accelerated depreciation schedules in 1981, in response to the inflation of the late 1970s, had the effect of generating net operating losses which are only now being fully used up. Since 1986, depreciation has become closer to economic depreciation so that some of the volatility we experienced in the 1980s will slowly filter out of the tax system.

These considerations are important to the states because of their constitutional obligation to balance their budgets in some fashion. Two sorts of policies would seem to protect the states' interest in minimizing the variability of corporate tax receipts. First, piggyback taxes stated as a surcharge on the federal liability should be before the application of various federal tax credits with attending adjustments in the definition of income. Second, the piggyback tax stated as a rate or system of rates applied to the federal taxable base should not allow the federal net operating loss (NOL) deduction, or, alternatively, the NOL deduction should be somehow limited. Perhaps the easiest way to limit the states' exposure to unanticipated refunds would be to provide only NOL carryforwards, and not provide NOL carrybacks.[11]

Revenue Stability and Transfers to States

Revenue stability can also be enhanced by the prompt turnover by the IRS of cash flows to the states. Only Montana does not periodically require an estimated tax payment, and only Ohio requires less than a quarterly payment of taxes. Most of the states follow the federal pattern of quarterly estimated tax payments by the middle of the third month.

Revenue Stability and the Filing Unit

Adoption of the federal consolidated filing unit could easily represent a source of tax stability to taxpayers currently filing on a unitary basis in some of the more aggressive states. As is well known, the sands of a unitary filing unit can shift from year to year. In the minds of some, state tax auditors move the definition of the filing unit away from those portions of a large firm that are losing money to those that are profitable.

Several years ago, I examined the filing unit issue for the State of Washington and contrasted the size of a net income tax base for consolidated units to those portions that could be sorted out into a unitary group. For the 275 corporations for which the experiment could be performed, the tax base of the unitary groups' returns, based on ownership and Washington State business activity, was 16 percent larger.[12] This could reflect a current behavioral response of firms to be relatively more profitable within Washington State because the state does not have a profits tax. For taxpayers, using just the federal consolidated filing unit should eliminate concerns about the alleged predatory tactics of some of the more aggressive states and ensure that only 100 percent of domestic income is potentially subjected to tax.

The agreement to use the federal filing unit is comparable, under the federal personal income tax piggybacking provisions, to accepting the federal personal income tax filing unit and the underlying relationships among household members. Up until the Tax Reform Act of 1986, major states such as New York and California required two-earner households to file *separately*. However, both states moved to adopt the federal filing unit for state purposes. This was a material change for California in view of its common property laws. As states move toward federal entities for personal income tax purposes, they may find it more attractive to do the same for business income tax purposes.

Relationships Among Piggybacking and Nonpiggybacking Taxes

Under the current federal personal income tax piggyback provisions, an essential feature of the piggybacking state income taxes is the agreement to automatically accept revisions of the Internal Revenue Code and to follow the procedures of the IRS. When the piggybacking procedures were enacted, there was concern about how individual income taxpayers with multiple residences during a taxable period in piggybacking states would relate to nonpiggybacking states. Much of the complexity of the individual income tax provisions involve how to relate the personal taxes due under a piggybacking state to those due to a nonpiggybacking state.

For a business, the problem is somewhat different but also more prevalent. Multistate businesses are undoubtedly a more prevalent phenomena than individual taxpayers who work and live in more than one state in one year. Were all states to opt for federal collection, then the interrelation among their taxes could be made identical across states. The effect of an add-back to federal taxable income of all states' corporate income taxes is to argue that the tax payment to states A and B by a company does not reduce its ability to pay to either states A or B.

If the piggyback states have identical tax rates, then 100 percent of income is taxed at the same rate. Both states have agreed to the proposition that the company's ability to pay is neither affected by payments of state taxes nor by payments of the federal tax. It is possible, but unlikely, in this situation for a firm to not be taxable at the federal level but taxable in both states because it has positive income.

At the federal level, there is recognition through deductibility in the determination of taxable income (or ability to pay) that state taxes have a priority or precedence. Thus, state taxes can be viewed as "coming off the top." When tax rates vary, but both states piggyback, only 100 percent of income is taxed, but the sacrifice will vary in accordance with the rate structure. Again, there is the possibility of not being taxable at the federal level but being taxable in both states in varying amounts.

To a large extent the use of formulary apportionment obviates the need for systems of reciprocal agreements among taxing jurisdictions, because the apportionment process, already in existence in one form or another in every state, has the effect of recognizing each state's partial claim on multistate business income.

Another issue that can arise in the design of a piggyback system is whether or not states want to limit the range of tax rates they can impose. If one believes in the maintenance of fiscal autonomy and simply views piggybacking as an administrative convenience, then there should be no restraints on the amount of a surcharge or the system of tax rates. On the other hand, if one believes that centralized collection is a part of an overall federal-state tax policy toward business, then one may wish to set maximum tax rates that the federal government can collect as a way to try to diminish interstate tax differentials and, in effect, discourage tax-induced migration of capital.[13]

Apportionment and the Federal Return

Federal Form 1120 already contains the essential ingredients for administration of the three-factor apportionment formula. Sales less returns are reported in the determination of federal taxable income on page 1, while the denominator of the property factor can be found, at least measured at book value, on the balance sheet. The payroll factor shows up in pieces, and as a result there would be a need to isolate payroll and benefits included in costs of goods sold. As a matter of recordkeeping, however, I do not believe that backing these items out of costs of goods sold poses any difficulties for business; the other items such as wages and salaries, executive compensation, and so on, are already shown separately on the return.

By the same token, creating geographic specificity with regard to payroll and property should not pose substantial recordkeeping difficulties for business. As a matter of refining definitions, there already is significant experience in each state that can be used for statutory guidance. Also, the work of the Multistate Tax Commission should provide more detailed guidance on matters of traveling salesmen, independent contractors, and the like.

The definition of the sales factor, presumably on a destination basis, would probably prove the most challenging issue to resolve. Again, there is significant experience with general mercantile corporations to allow the development of a single statute which business and the states could subsequently, with the Service, look to for administrative guidance.

Undoubtedly, there will remain difficult technical issues to adjudicate. For example, to the extent that Texas and Washington continue to decline to impose a net income tax, there remains a question of whether to favor throwback or throwout of sales made into such states in the denominators and numerators for the other states, as well as how to treat sales to the federal government vis-à-vis the denominator of the sales factor. There will be significant revenue consequences of varying treatment, and I do not have any particular solutions to offer. However, to the extent that the filing unit is defined uniformly, and all the income tax states use the same apportionment formulae, the problems associated with each solution of "nowhere" income are significantly decreased.

Geographic attribution rules for services, telecommunications, the airlines, and financial institutions will continue to be problematical, and space limitations preclude discussions here of each. However, the prospect that the solutions to each problem area would be nationally discussed in the Congress and analyzed by the Treasury, the Service, and interested states, would mean that workable rules would be hammered out and the revenue implications better understood than is often the case at the state level. Indeed, one can argue that the federal corporate tax base would be much better analyzed, and less frequently changed, if both state and federal revenues depended on the same definition of taxable income and examined its attribution to specific geographic areas.

Assuring State Participation

Perhaps the most vexing issue with respect to piggybacking is how to encourage the states to participate. It is difficult to envisage within our current constitutional structure how the federal government could *require* federal collection of state business income taxes. It is also difficult to imagine that the federal government would find piggybacking sufficiently meritorious to use indirect pressure, such as the threat of the possible withdrawal of various federal grants-in-aid, to get the states to participate.

Absent a direct requirement or indirect pressures, it would seem clear that, at a minimum, the states should not be charged for federal collection. Perhaps it is within reason for the federal government to provide a positive set of incentives for state participation. In other areas of shared federal-state responsibilities, the federal government pays for part of the administrative costs of running federal programs, and in effect uses the states as its fiscal agent to provide various public services. It might be desirable to consider federal payment for part of the administrative costs of state tax collection and to consider the employment of state revenue officials to assist in part of the administration of the piggyback system. In this way state agencies would benefit budgetarily, but hopefully in a way that would still allow the presumed economies of scale which piggybacking might provide to be of some overall budgetary benefit.

Another more ambitious form of inducement by the federal government would be the construction of a system of hold-harmless grants to the states who piggyback, should there be unforeseen fiscal consequences of federal corporate tax changes. There is Canadian precedent in this area to learn from. Or, the federal government might construct the equivalent of UI (unemployment insurance) drawing rights for piggybacking states, which might obviate the need for states facing deficits to go to the capital markets in times of duress. Presumably, securities that might be used to capitalize such an insurance pool of rainy day funds would benefit from some form of federal guarantee.

Several points seem obvious from the historical lack of utilization of the existing piggyback statute: States need some form of assurance as well as incentives that greater reliance on the Internal Revenue Code and the Internal Revenue Service will not disadvantage them. One can imagine new institutional relationships as well as financial incentives that could prove effective in the business tax area; however, one must also be mindful not to use such incentives to the point that they exceed in value the benefits of greater uniformity.

PIGGYBACKING COMPARED TO OTHER APPROACHES

Whether piggybacking is the best way to reduce interstate conflict over how to tax business depends on what one compares it to. So far, I have implicitly compared piggybacking to the vagaries of current state business tax law. Three other approaches deserve mention as benchmarks: (1) the spreadsheet approach negotiated some years ago by a task force appointed by President Reagan; (2) the related approach taken by West Virginia in 1985; and (3) a surcharge on the federal corporate income tax and pure revenue sharing of the proceeds to the states on some formulary basis. Below I provide some comments on each of these approaches and compare them to the proposed federal collection.

The Worldwide Unitary Taxation Working Group Proposal: The Federal "Spreadsheet"

As is well known, after the U.S. Supreme Court issued the *Container* decision in June 1983, the business community expressed itself forcefully to President Reagan and the Congress with the objective of limiting the spread of worldwide unitary taxation among the states.

Reagan, formerly the governor of California, where he was both the beneficiary of the geographic reach of the unitary principle in terms of supporting the costs of California public services and a friend of the business community, was in a fairly awkward position. Faced with choosing sides, he elected instead to refer the issue to a committee, and asked Treasury Secretary Donald Regan to chair a committee to address business and state concerns. The "Working Group," as it became known, met through 1983 and 1984. It wrestled with a variety of proposed compromises that would

- limit the states' taxation of business income to the water's edge;
- treat foreign activities of domestic corporations, and domestic activities of foreign corporations, on a level playing field;
- define the business entity subject to tax variously as the federal consolidated group per the Internal Revenue Code—therefore measured on an ownership basis[14]—or that entity that contains groups 80 percent or more of whose *activities* occurred at the water's edge;
- develop an acceptable tax treatment of foreign source dividends;
- and established federal assistance to the states in terms of informing them of the multistate income tax payments of corporations.

If this list of desiderata seems overly ambitious, the reader is correct. The best the Working Group could agree on before it disbanded was to enunciate some principles of what water's edge meant, agree on information sharing, and outline what they disagreed upon.[15]

In the summer of 1985, the Treasury issued draft legislation it felt reflected the efforts of the Working Group and submitted it for public comment. Commentary was extensive, and in December 1985 Representative Duncan and Senator Wilson introduced the Unitary Tax Repealer Act, respectively S 1974 and HR 3980, which reflected the active comments of the domestic and international business communities.

Because California had already provided optional water's-edge treatment and several other states had also withdrawn to the water's edge, much of the impetus for restrictive federal legislation disappeared, so both bills were never acted on by the tax committees of the Congress.

Of interest here is the so-called spreadsheet portion of the two bills. This section was viewed by the states at the time as a way to achieve greater uniformity in their state business taxes. Under the spreadsheet proposal, a multinational company would be required to file an information return annually with the IRS. The information return would contain the income tax liability to each state, its income subject to tax in each state, the method of calculation by which the corporation computed and allocated its income subject to tax, and a list of subsidiaries, owned 50 percent or more, directly or indirectly, which were contained in the information return.[16]

The second important part of the spreadsheet proposal was to loosen up Section 6103 of the Code, the nondisclosure provisions, so that state agencies or "common state agencies" such as the Multistate Tax Commission could have access to this new information return. Moreover, 6103 was proposed to be amended so that such information returns could be shared *among* the states.[17] Currently, federal tax return information about a corporation that a state obtains can not be shared with other states under 6103.

At one level the prospect of a company providing a Lotus 1-2-3 spreadsheet with each row being the states it pays income taxes to, and the columns being taxable income and taxes paid, respectively, might seem to improve the ability of the states to administer their own business income taxes; however, because the states' rules with regard to apportionment, allocation, and filing unit differ in good measure, it is not clear what would be gained, vis-à-vis system uniformity. It would seem that there would have to be fifty-one spreadsheets for a company that did business in every state—with one that reflected what its taxes would be if it filed in all states as it did for state A, state B, and so forth. Given a heterogeneous set of state tax rules, the problem of reconciling differences (the missing one-third of the tax base noted above, if you will) remains.

It does seem that a new sort of federal Form 851 would help the states understand who was doing business in their state, and who was not.

In terms of taxpayer privacy, the passing around of spreadsheets among the states and to common tax agencies undoubtedly would weaken existing privacy relations between any state tax agency and a business. These considerations explain in part why the bills were never acted on.

West Virginia's Information Requirement

In 1985, West Virginia rewrote its business taxes and required that the taxpayer append to its state return, which could be filed on any basis, a copy of its bona fide federal tax return, and a written, signed statement of explanation of the relationship between the federal return and the state return.[18] In effect, this information requirement maintained historical filing practices and maintained historical privacy relationships between the business and the state. But it created an information base—the statement of consolidation that underlies each federal return and the assertions by the signatory of the return of the relationship between the federal statement of consolidation and the state data contained on the state return. This provided more information to the tax authority, but obviously did nothing to ensure greater interstate uniformity for the taxpayer.

Simply Surcharge the Federal Tax and Provide Revenue Sharing

Another approach to making state taxation of business more systematic is to eliminate state corporate income taxes, impose a federal surcharge, and distribute the surcharge back to the states in the form of revenue sharing.[19]

Although this approach would eliminate the thorny issue of what goes into an apportionment scheme, it raises instead the issue of what revenue-sharing distribution formula to use with what variables. Based on the general revenue-sharing experience, I would conjecture that the first enactment of such a formula probably would be the last, and the only remaining issue the Congress would have to face was whether or not to change the surcharge tax rate. It is interesting to ponder the implications of taking business taxes at the state level off the policy debate agenda at the state and federal levels. Whether taxpayers, tax administrators, or elected officials favor this or not depends of course on whether or not one does "better" than under current law.

Comparisons Among Options

With respect to avoiding under- or overtaxation, the piggybacking approach would definitionally have the effect of guaranteeing that 100 percent of corporate income would be taxed, and only once overall. If tax rate limitations were imposed, then greater certainty for taxpayers would result in terms of their contribution to pay the costs of needed public services. However, the revenue-sharing approach would be superior to piggybacking in terms of taxpayer certainty, and inferior from the point of view of state governments because they would lose control over a decision variable, the tax rate. Neither the spreadsheet approach nor the West Virginia approach addresses over- or undertaxation or ensures greater uniformity in state-by-state tax treatment of a business taxpayer.

With respect to privacy, the taxpayer is better off under piggybacking, the West Virginia approach, or current law than under the spreadsheet approach, because the spreadsheet would necessarily lead to multilateral negotiations and the disclosure of not only the fractions but also the aggregate income base because there could easily be as many different tax bases as states a company was doing business in. Moreover, because potentially there will be a different spreadsheet for each state for one taxpayer, given the possibilities of differing definitions of the filing unit, taxable income, and so on, the possibility of disclosure of nonuniform information with widespread confusion seems quite real to me.

Under piggybacking, the essential disclosure is to the IRS alone, with its strong record of confidentiality. State audits of the numerators of the apportionment fractions constitute a far smaller disclosure risk to taxpayers than does the disclosure of elements beyond just the apportionment items. Moreover, any state audits would have to be federally supervised with the result that the overall standards of privacy in the system, compared to current law, would have to increase.

With respect to taxpayer compliance and ease of administration, piggybacking would represent a clear advantage over current law or a spreadsheet approach because there would be one, enforced set of tax laws that defined the filing unit, taxable income, and apportionment factors. Also, one set of regulations, case law, and administrative procedure would constitute clear gains to both taxpayers and administrators in terms of clarity, certainty, and cost of administration and compliance.

The revenue-sharing approach, in lieu of state determination of rates and state-by-state apportionment, might be favored by business as it would focus debate on the tax rate for state business taxes, in one place, Congress, rather than in each state capitol. On the other hand, this would create additional budgetary uncertainties in state capitols because the Congress might intentionally or unintentionally fiddle with the base or rate with surprising effects outside of Washington, D.C. Also, to the extent that the variables in the revenue-sharing formula changed rapidly, this might move revenues around more than current law, piggybacking, or the West Virginia approaches.

CONCLUSION

Any system of corporate taxation involves a confidential relationship between taxpayer and collector, necessarily imposes some compliance costs on the taxpayer, and creates administrative/budgetary costs on the tax collector. From the perspective of financing the budgetary costs of government, corporate taxes are a portion of a portfolio of revenue streams and need to be considered in terms of their stability, efficiency effects, and the underlying budgetary problems/constraints of the governments. Any movement from the independent application of corporate taxes by each state to a centralized system of collection must deal not only with the these various financial interests, to ensure that they are protected, but it also must provide for the protection of state interests in the application of the statutes (e.g., in the courts).

This review of where the states are in terms of their aggregate corporate income tax base, and what would be involved in federal piggybacking of the state corporate income taxes, leads me to conclude that federal collection is not only technically workable but would do much to improve tax administration in our federal system.

Compared to state adoption of federal piggybacking of personal taxes, the federal collection of state business income taxes has much to recommend it. It would eliminate a major source of friction between the business community and the states that has been growing in the past decade, and yet provide a flow of revenue at least as predictable as in the past. Moreover, the number of taxpayers affected by this is far fewer than under the personal income tax. For business, it strengthens many of the procedural guarantees in the tax process by applying federal procedures to the states as well as guaranteeing continued confidentiality.

Pending federal tax legislation (HR 1555) which provides for cooperative state-federal tax administration represents an important first step toward achieving greater uniformity in tax collection and could readily lead to the sort of voluntary piggybacking contemplated in this chapter.

To be sure, state tax administrators and elected officials will have difficulty in delegating to the IRS the first line of tax collection from businesses. However, if the states were to audit the numerators of the apportionment formulae as a part of this piggyback process, and the states were paid by the federal government to do so, much of the historical resistance to piggybacking should subside.

NOTES

1. See, for example, Rivlin (1990) and Strauss (1990).

2. For example, one might imagine a two-thirds majority vote to allow tax rates and/or tax bases to be altered.

3. For a different perspective on the efficacy of at least the California approach to the state taxation on business, see Sheffrin and Fulcher (1984) who seek to ascertain how *different* state corporate income taxes would be if the states used different apportionment schemes or followed unitary practices.

4. I use the top marginal rate where progression is in place.

5. Federal data for 1988 and 1989 are not yet available.

6. During the presentation of this paper, there was an active discussion of the federal corporate base in Table 6.1, column (4). It was argued that the federal base *should* exceed the aggregate of state bases because it includes foreign source income. Several points are in order. First, for states such as California which go beyond the water's edge, inclusion of federal foreign source income makes sense in order to compare like tax bases. Second, because most states have taxed Domestic International Sales Corporations as well as Foreign Sales Corporations, foreign source income is therefore in the state as well as the federal figures. Third, if one examines the SOI corporate income data closely, one finds they include only $19-$22 billion in income from related foreign corporations for 1985-1987. Subtracting this foreign source corporate income from column (4) would thus not change the conclusions, alone. Finally, several state tax officials have observed to me privately that they find the figures in Table 6.1 to be persuasive and indicative of their own audit and litigation experience.

7. This could also include a zero rate, of course, although this would then raise the issue of "nowhere" income.

8. The aggregates mask winners and losers under current state law from changing to a federal piggyback approach. For example, it has been recently reported in the *Wall Street Journal* that California may lose $3 billion per year in revenues if it loses *Barclays Bank International v. the Franchise Tax Board*. At a 9.6 percent tax rate, this means that the aggregate estimate of the state tax bases in Table 6.1 would have to decline almost 10 percent.

9. See LePan (1984), Smith (1976), and Thirsk (1980) on various aspects of the Canadian experience with piggybacking.

10. Interestingly, the Canadian practice in the determination of federal taxable income is to add back deductions for provincial balance sheet taxes or capital taxes, but to allow deductions for provincial corporate net income taxes. At the provincial level, for both piggybacking provinces and those that impose their own corporate income tax (Alberta, Ontario, and Quebec), income for provincial tax purposes includes the deduction for provincial corporate net income taxes. In the United States, virtually all the states that impose a net income tax add back state corporate income taxes paid.

11. As of 1990, twenty-two jurisdictions provided a three-year carryback; however, only a handful of major corporate net income tax states—Illinois, Indiana, and New York—were among them, while California, which has no carryback, limits the amount of carryforward fifteen years to 50 percent of the net loss.

12. See Strauss (1987), Table 7.5.

13. See Papke (1991) for evidence supporting the conjecture that effective tax rate differentials affect business location decisions.

14. Essentially, subsidiaries that are owned 80 percent or more are part of the consolidated return, and subsidiaries owned less than 80 percent file separately).

15. See McLure (1984) for a personal account of what transpired in 1983 and 1984, and the Working Group's documents reproduced in Appendix 1 of McLure (1986).

16. See the proposed Section 6039 of the Senate version of the bill (*Congressional Record,* December 18, 1985, p. S17976).

17. See Section 4 of the proposed legislation.

18. See HR 1693, West Virginia House of Delegates, enacted on April 8, 1985.

19. I believe this approach was suggested at one point by Charles McLure, Jr.

7
The Impact of State Corporate Income Taxes on the Economic Condition of the United States

ROBERT N. MATTSON

State corporate income tax systems and practices, especially those dealing with U.S.-based global corporations, have a major effect on the economic strength of the United States. This is a major reason that states increasingly recognize tax competition with sister states as a formidable opportunity to attract in-state investment by large corporations.

In Chapter 8, Bill Brown traces the political realization by the states that discriminatory taxes affect economic expansion and limit the creation of jobs and welfare of their citizens. It is now fairly well accepted that state tax incentives and disincentives influence business decisions. As Schoettle (1991, p. 1152) keenly observes "Businesses are continually reallocating their physical and human resources, adding to their physical plant here, adding or subtracting an employee there, and generally responding to the market. Each week, thousands of decisions are made that involve taxes in one way or another. The effect of taxes on any one of these decisions may be quite small. However, over a decade or so, the cumulative effect of a particular tax system entering into millions of decisions will be to make the world a different place than if some different tax system had been in effect."

An illustration of Schoettle's observation is how states have expanded their tax bases to include non-U.S. income. While the worldwide unitary tax approach is virtually extinct[1] as a method of state corporate income taxation, the same attempt to reach income earned outside the water's edge is still in existence in a few states that tax foreign source dividends. Probably no other provision is so universally distasteful to American business because it provides such an obvious competitive tax advantage to foreign-based companies.

As to the question of equity between large and small businesses, replacing U.S.-owned large company investment with foreign investment (e.g., Honda in Ohio versus General Motors in Michigan) will not necessarily benefit local small businesses. This is because foreign-owned investors often replace the purchase of parts and materials from local small businesses with imports from business suppliers in their home countries.[2] Thus, when one uses as a standard of equity the local taxpayer's position, one needs to understand that local taxpayers benefit greatly from a friendly business and tax climate for U.S.-owned global companies.

STATE TAX INCONSISTENCIES

George Break (1991, p. 517) at the 1990 NTA Conference said that improvements in the efficiency of state revenue systems would contribute directly and significantly to the performance of the U.S. economy. States do not tax corporations at uniform rates nor do they utilize similarly defined tax bases. Most states use allocation and apportionment methods to source income, especially for global corporations, in totally uncoordinated and inconsistent ways.

Break further comments that the state corporate income tax is subject to interjurisdictional tax competition which is likely to intensify during the 1990s for two reasons. First, technological developments are making more businesses more mobile. Second, states operate in an increasingly competitive global market environment. Break reaches the same conclusion as Brown—that sales taxes at the state level are a far superior state revenue source and are less economically distortive than state corporate income taxes.

UNITED STATES ECONOMIC CONDITION

The United States position in the world economy has weakened considerably in the last two decades. The United States was the largest supplier to the world's capital markets. But, today, the United States is the world's largest debtor. United States investment abroad has grown nine times since the mid-1960s, but foreign direct investment in the United States has grown forty times. Our exports twenty-five years ago doubled our imports. Now we have the largest deficit in balance of trade in the world. You might think that deficit results from oil imports. It doesn't. The percentage of oil imports relative to total imports has remained stable throughout the period.

International trade was a small part of our total GNP back in the 1960s. We almost ignored the foreign aspects of business and the tax law. U.S. multinationals had more than 70 percent of their entire business in the United States. But, today, U.S. corporations conduct more than 50 percent of their business outside the this country. IBM, for example, has almost two-thirds of its business outside the United States. In the 1960s, eighteen of the world's top twenty industrial corporations were American companies. Today, only nine are American.

That's the bad news. The good news is that most economists say that we have a very good chance of returning to outward investment at a greater pace than inward investment by the end of the decade. But state tax laws, unless amended to take into account the reality of international business today, will make it difficult for U.S. business to achieve that objective. Thus, when states overreach by taxing dividends from foreign operations, they provide a competitive advantage to foreign-owned competition.

As we move into the twenty-first century, U.S. outward direct investment and U.S.-owned global companies can regain their strong positions—but not if crippled by punitive, discriminatory and inconsistent state corporate income taxes.

STATE TAX RATES

It is startling to realize that the state portion of both federal and state corporate income taxes has more than doubled in the last two decades. It should not be surprising, then, that today the state corporate income tax has become a greater focus of business investment decisions. The state corporate tax is a more important factor because the federal subsidy has been significantly reduced—now one-third down from nearly one-half. For this reason state tax incentives are also more important and will have a greater impact on interstate competition in the future. This is because businesses are able to retain more of the state tax incentive.

Nineteen states have raised their corporate income tax rates since 1986, whereas eight have reduced those rates. Also, it is important to realize that whereas, currently, only four states have double-digit rates,[3] a number of other states are nearing the double-digit columns.[4] Also, "temporary" corporate surtaxes are beginning to appear as a state revenue solution.[5]

FEW STATES TAX DIVIDENDS FROM FOREIGN OPERATIONS

Under the unitary concept, there are currently twelve states[6] that tax a significant portion of dividends from foreign operations (excluding states that tax 20 percent or less in lieu of expense attributions). Although the percentage taxed and the methods used to include the dividends in taxable income vary, the results are universally punitive.

For example, although California's water's-edge provision permits the exclusion of up to 75 percent of foreign dividends, the tying of that exclusion to historical employment and dividend factors creates enormous distortions because of fluctuating exchange rates (see the example in Table 7.1).

As the example demonstrates, with no change in the payroll or job factor or the local currency dividend amount, the weakening of the U.S. dollar by 75 percent increases the amount of dividends taxed by California from 25 percent to over 40 percent. Comparing the U.S. dollar value of the German mark and the Japanese yen, the exchange rate increases from January 1, 1984 (a base year, for purposes of California computation) to January 1, 1991, were 81.5 percent and 70.6 percent, respectively.

Because there is no mechanism for the offset against state taxation of foreign dividends for taxes paid on the underlying income from which the dividends are paid, the increasing level of double taxation is a serious problem which must be addressed.

In his editorial in the January 16, 1991, *Tax Notes International*, Michael McIntyre discusses this problem and the necessity for national governments to take responsibility for providing a solution. It would appear more reasonable to attempt to alleviate the problem through a state approach to the elimination of the double taxation of foreign dividends similar to what Colorado has provided by recognizing that foreign taxes have already been assessed against the income from which the dividend was paid. For example, companies with excess foreign tax credits on their federal returns should be able to use a portion of the excess credits to reduce the state tax on the foreign dividends. States would then be able to collect taxes on the dividends when the state plus the federal rate exceeded the foreign tax burden. This would alleviate the existing double tax problem for U.S.-owned global companies and "level the playing field" vis-à-vis their foreign-owned competitors. Two

TABLE 7.1
Example of Calculation of Dividend Deduction

	Base Period	Current Period
Exchange Rate[1]	1.00	1.75
Dividends Received		
(in foreign currency)	1,000	1,000
(in dollars)	1,000	1,750
Foreign Payroll		
(in foreign currency)	200	200
(in dollars)	200	350
U.S. Payroll (in dollars)	200	200
Total Payroll (in dollars)	400	550
Foreign Payroll as % of U.S. Payroll	50	63.6

Computation of foreign dividend deduction (per Part V, California Form 2411):

1. Largest base period dividends	1,000
2. 75% base period dividends	750
3. Current year foreign payroll (%)	63.6
4. Largest base period payroll (%)	50
5. Foreign payroll increase (%)	13.6
6. Current-year foreign payroll (%)	63.6
7. Fully taxable percentage (line 5 ÷ line 6)	21.4
8. Current-year foreign dividends	1,750
9. Balance (line 7 x line 8)	375
10. Amount from line 8	1,750
11. Amount from line 1	1,000
12. Balance (line 10 - line 11)	750
13. Smaller of line 9 or line 12	375
14. Balance line 12 - line 13	375
15. Line 14 x .75	281
16. Line 2	750
17. Construction project dividends	0
18. Dividend deduction (sum of lines 15-17)	1,031
Dividend deduction percentage	58.9

[1]Dollars per unit of foreign currency.

recent U.S. Supreme Court decisions, *Allied-Signal* and *Kraft General Foods*, will reduce this double tax problem, since they will significantly restrict state taxation of dividends from foreign operations of U.S.-owned corporations.

CONCLUSION

As states become aware of the damage done by discriminatory and inequitable tax structures, to their economic climate as well as to that of the United States, action must be taken to cure the ills that exist in those structures. Two major steps will signal to industry the recognition by the states of their need to maintain and increase investment. First, corporate state statutory tax rates must be lowered to a point that is significantly below the double-digit level. Second, discriminatory state corporate income taxation of dividends from foreign operations received by U.S.-owned global corporations must be eliminated through a rational relief mechanism.

NOTES

1. Effective with tax years beginning after December 31, 1991, no state mandates use of a worldwide unitary method of taxation. The last state to eliminate that requirement was Alaska, which in May 1991 enacted a law that abolished the worldwide method (for companies other than oil companies) and replaced it with a mandatory water's-edge system. Five states (California, Idaho, Montana, Utah, and North Dakota) permit the election by the taxpayer of the water's-edge method. In addition to Alaska, the water's-edge method is mandatory in New Hampshire. California's Supreme Court, by reversing the Court of Appeal decisions in *Barclays Bank International* and *Colgate-Palmolive*, has found the worldwide combined reporting method to be unconstitutional. These cases may be appealed to the U.S. Supreme Court.

2. The National Association of State Development Agencies reports that forty-three states maintain offices in foreign capitals. California has a tax system that is more advantageous to foreign-owned firms than to U.S.-based entities.

3. Pennsylvania (12.25), Connecticut (11.5), Iowa (12.0), North Dakota (10.5).

4. Massachusetts (9.5), Minnesota (9.8).

5. Surtaxes on basic rates are shown below:

State	Rate	Surtax	Total
New York	9.00	15.00	10.35
Rhode Island	9.00	11.00	9.99
Connecticut	11.50	20.00	13.80
Maine	8.93	10.00	9.82
North Carolina	7.75	4.00	8.06

6. Hawaii, Iowa, Mississippi, Missouri, New Hampshire, New Mexico, Rhode Island, and Vermont plus partially in California (25% plus), North Dakota (50%-70%), Utah (50%) and Maine (100%, declining 10% per year to 50% in 1993). Colorado provides a foreign tax credit similar to the federal credit to effectively eliminate significant foreign dividend taxation for most companies.

III
Exporting of State Taxes

This part examines the techniques, consequences, and constitutionality of tax exporting. Both Brown (Chapter 8) and Stanley (Chapter 9) point to and decry the political popularity of tax exporting, as they describe how states attempt, not always successfully, to shift tax burdens from in-state to out-of-state taxpayers. They focus on tax exporting that states bring about as they manipulate their formulas for apportioning corporate income. When a state gives greater weight to the sales factor than to payroll and property factors, corporations that sell within the state but produce mainly in other states face a greater tax than they would face with an equally weighted three-factor formula. The result is that outsider corporations—those with relatively little payroll and property within the state—are taxed disproportionately. Stanley explains that *local* corporate and noncorporate business, those that sell primarily within a state, may suffer *higher* taxes as a result of a state's efforts to export taxes by over-weighting the sales factor. The reforms and changes recommended in Part II, especially the adoption of a uniform three-factor formula, would, of course, reduce if not eliminate this form of tax exporting.

Despite its economic effects and the door that it opens to tax competition among the states, this form of tax exporting is constitutional according to the Supreme Court's 1978 ruling in *Moorman Manufacturing Company v. Bair*. Schoettle (Chapter 10) argues that inappropriate tests and doctrines have clouded the Supreme Court's rulings on commerce clause challenges such as *Moorman*. He explains the conditions under which a state tax statute, such as Iowa's single-factor (sales) apportionment formula, should be subject to commerce clause challenge. He argues that the key test is whether it gives a cost advantage to in-state businesses (taxpayers)—that is, whether it places interstate commerce at a disadvantage. He further explains that the Supreme Court's approach to commerce clause challenges may prevent its decisions from turning on the outcome of this test.

8
Techniques of State Tax Exporting

WILLIAM R. BROWN

> Proposals to generate $50 million in additional taxes do not hit consumers, but do affect people living outside West Virginia, Gov. Gaston Caperton said Thursday...."This has been a carefully put together revenue program in which approximately 70 percent of the revenues we get from this package are exported outside the state, paid by others, and 100 percent of the dollars coming in are going to go to the children of West Virginia and the school system," Caperton said.
>
> (AP story appearing in the Martinsburg, WV,
> *The Morning Journal*, August 24, 1990)

Exporting tax burdens to out-of-state companies or individuals is politically popular, and states try their best to do so. Various strategies are employed. Most common is altering the weighting of the corporate income tax apportionment formula. The normal method involving three equally weighted factors (the percentages of property, payroll, and sales) has been replaced in a growing number of states by one that double-weights the sales factor. The effect is to shift taxes to firms that produce out of state and away from those with in-state production facilities. Several states have gone so far as to use a single sales factor, and unfortunately such formulas have been upheld by the U.S. Supreme Court as not being in violation of the commerce clause (*Moorman Manufacturing Company v. Bair*, 1978).

Another method, worldwide combination, attempts to export taxes not only to other states but to the rest of the world. This method, pioneered by California, requires multinational corporations to combine the worldwide income of their affiliated corporations, including those with no operations in this country. When President Reagan appointed the Worldwide Unitary Taxation Working Group in 1983, there were a dozen states requiring worldwide combination. Today, all of these states allow a water's edge option for most companies; Alaska, in 1991, was the last to do so.

Other strategies include aggressive attempts to tax foreign source dividends, taxing services performed out of state, and applying different taxes or different tax provisions to out-of-state firms as compared with those located in-state.

Although states employ these strategies in an effort to force nonresidents to bear part of the taxes they impose, they are not always successful. In an open competitive economic system, market adjustments limit the extent to which taxes can actually be exported. For example, a state that imposes discriminatory tax burdens on firms that export their products would make these firms less competitive in national and international markets. To maintain market share these firms may be forced to pay lower wages or accept lower profits. Land values in the high-tax state might even be depressed as firms shift activities to escape discriminatory taxation. Especially in the long run, incidence of taxes is likely to remain in-state to a far greater extent than is generally appreciated.

Nevertheless, legislatures tend to focus on the short run. And in the short run the strategies outlined in this chapter at least give the appearance of exporting tax burdens.

CONSTITUTIONAL CONSTRAINTS ON TAX EXPORTING

One of the basic purposes of the Constitution was to provide for the free flow of commerce. These constitutional principles were well stated in the *amicus* brief that the Committee on State Taxation of the Council of State Chambers of Commerce, the National Association of Manufacturers, and the Chamber of Commerce of the United States filed in the *Amarada Hess* case:

The central concern of the Framers in adopting the Commerce Clause was to prevent "economic Balkanization of the states. [*Hughes v. Oklahoma,* 441 U.S. 322, 325-26 (1979)]. The Framers were aware of the "drift toward anarchy and commercial warfare between [the] states" under the Articles of Confederation. [*H.P. Hood & Sons, Inc. v. DuMond,* 336 U.S. 525, 533 (1949)]. In sound reaction to the "mutual jealousies and aggressions of the States, taking form in custom barriers and other economic retaliation" [*Baldwin v. G.A.F. Seelig, Inc.,* 294 U.S. 511, 522 (1935), *quoting* 2 Farrand, *Records of the Federal Convention* 308 (1911)], the Framers formulated the Commerce Clause to "provide for the harmony and a proper intercourse among the states." [The

Federalist No. 41, at 291-92 (J. Madison), H. Dawson ed. (1863)]. Among other things, the Commerce Clause was intended to restrain "the desire of the commercial states to collect, in any form, an indirect revenue from their uncommercial neighbors." The regional rivalries of our time—Sun Belt versus Rust Belt, oil-producing versus oil-importing states—would be foreign to the Framers, but the spectacle of states using natural advantages and disadvantages to extract benefits from their sister states would be depressingly familiar and would readily be recognized as part of the class of conduct it was the purpose of the Commerce Clause to eliminate. [See the *Federalist* No. 22, at 140 (A. Hamilton), H. Dawson ed. 1863)].[1]

The equal protection clause of the Fourteenth Amendment, the commerce clause, and the due process clause all provide some protection against state exporting of tax burdens to the extent the courts choose to apply them. Although the commerce clause is an affirmative grant of power to Congress under the so-called "negative" commerce clause, the courts have held that, by its own force and without national legislation, it places restrictions on state authority. Although the negative commerce clause has been accepted by the U.S. Supreme Court for 150 years, Justice Scalia is now challenging it (Hellerstein, 1990, pp. 332-333).

The importance of the courts' application of the commerce clause is seen when it is recognized how reluctant the Congress is to accept its responsibilities to protect interstate commerce from state tax discrimination. The failure of the courts to provide adequate protection from state taxation of out-of-state businesses without business location in the states led Congress in 1959 to enact PL 86-272, which provides protection from state corporate taxes for those businesses whose only connection with a state is solicitation of sales without any employees, payroll, or property in the state. PL 86-272 also provided for the five-year study of interstate taxation by the Willis Subcommittee of the House Judiciary Committee (*State Taxation of Interstate Commerce,* 1965). Despite repeated efforts, Congress has not enacted any interstate tax legislation of general application since the Willis Subcommittee reported in 1965.[2] However, it has enacted legislation applicable to specific industries such as the railroads and the airlines.[3]

EXPORTING THROUGH INCOME APPORTIONMENT

The weights assigned to sales, property, and payroll factors in a state's formula for apportioning corporate net income can affect the extent of exporting of that state's corporate income tax. Such actions are apparently constitutional. Jerome Hellerstein (1983, para. 4.8-4.9) has gone so far as to say the following: "The principle that state taxes on interstate commerce must be fairly apportioned has been largely reduced to a piece of unenforceable rhetoric by the Court's determination in the *Moorman Manufacturing* case that it is beyond its province to invalidate state apportionment methods, even though they may result in duplicative taxation."

Justice Stevens, writing for the majority upholding the Iowa single-factor (sales) apportionment formula for corporate income taxes, took the position that this was not a matter for which the Court should assume responsibility, but rather a matter for congressional determination (*Moorman Manufacturing Company v. Bair*, 1978, p. 230):

While the freedom of the States to formulate independent policy in this area may have to yield to an overriding national interest in uniformity, the content of any uniform rules to which they must subscribe should be determined only after due consideration is given to the interests of all affected states. It is clear that the legislative power granted to Congress by the Commerce Clause of the Constitution would amply justify enactment of legislation requiring all States to adhere to uniform rules for the division of income. It is to that body, and not this Court, that the Constitution has committed such policy decisions.

Hellerstein (1983, pp. 357-358) asserts that the Supreme Court did not properly apply its own guidelines in the *Moorman* decision, as the single-factor (sales) formula is "inherently arbitrary," and there is no warrant for it in fiscal policy. Further, he considers the Court to be in error in believing that Congressional action was necessary, as virtually all other states at that time were using an equally weighted three-factor formula.

Unfortunately, even though there is considerable agreement between state and business interests that a uniform, equally weighted three-factor formula is desirable, there has been no congressional action primarily because of the inability of business and state groups to agree on other issues which are generally considered more important to each group, such as requirements for worldwide combination in reporting corporation income, tax treatment of foreign source dividends, and collection of sale/use taxes on interstate direct mail sales.[4]

Spread of the Weighted Formula

The Committee on State Taxation (COST) of the Council of State Chambers of Commerce, in an *amicus* brief filed in support of the taxpayer's Petition for Rehearing in the *Moorman* case (which the Supreme Court rejected), correctly forecast the impact of the decision:

The combined effect of this congressional paralysis and the present decision, leaving state taxing power untrammeled in the absence of congressional preemption, will inevitably be to encourage the emerging reversion toward parochial and protectionist state taxation of interstate commerce. The present opinion here will be viewed as permitting, even requiring, the states to change their taxing statutes to give a discriminatory advantage to in-state businesses.... It appears virtually certain that the Court's opinion will serve as an impetus for the adoption of disparate apportionment formulae by various states, thus terminating the substantial movement over the past fifty years toward, and near achievement of, uniformity of state apportionment formulae. The actions of the states to enhance in this manner what they perceive as their individual interests may well present the Court with the very type of controversy over state apportionment formulae that the majority here seeks to avoid.[5]

There has been a slow but fairly steady spread of unequally weighted apportionment formulae since the Supreme Court sanctioned them in its 1978 *Moorman* decision. Twenty-one states currently give disproportionate weight to the sales factor to some extent (Table 8.1). Fifteen states—Arizona, Connecticut, Florida, Illinois, Kentucky, Maine, Maryland, Massachusetts, Michigan, New York, North Carolina, Ohio, Oregon, West Virginia, and Wisconsin—double-weight the sales factor; three of these states—Arizona, Maine, and Michigan—enacted double-weighting in 1991. Minnesota gives sales a 70 percent weight. Nebraska started phasing in a single-factor (sales only) formula in 1990 with the sales weight at 60 percent in the first year, rising to 80 percent in 1991 and 100 percent in 1992. Colorado employs a two-factor (sales and property) formula, but also allows a three-factor option. Kansas has a two-factor (sales and property) formula, but it is available only to qualifying taxpayers whose payroll factor exceeds 200 percent of the average of the property and sales factors.

TABLE 8.1
Weighting of the Sales Apportionment Factor

Double Weighting	Sales Only	Other
Arizona	Iowa	Minnesota: 70% Sales
Connecticut	Missouri	Colorado: Optional Two-Factor (sales and property)
Florida	Nebraska	Kansas: Restricted Two-Factor
Illinois		
Kentucky		
Maine		
Maryland		
Massachusetts		
Michigan (SBT)		
New York		
North Carolina		
Ohio		
Oregon		
West Virginia		
Wisconsin		

The Case for the Equally Weighted Three-Factor Formula

The Willis Subcommittee on State Taxation of Interstate Commerce recommended a uniform division of income apportionment formula composed of property and payroll factors *without the use of a sales factor*. A major reason for the subcommittee's recommendation against use of a sales factor was ease of compliance, but the subcommittee's report also made several other points. First, the existence of property and labor activity indicates that the company is performing its most fundamental activities within the state. Second, enforcement is easiest when taxpayers have property and payroll in the state. Third, companies are most concerned with the conduct of state government in those states where they have business locations—that is, property and payroll. It is in these states that the company is best able to make its needs and interests known through the political process.

Conversely, if there is not property and payroll; "The state, as a unit, has little immediate concern with the firm's continued operation—and, in fact, may at times view the company as an unwelcome outsider, competing with local companies....In summary, the restriction of income attribution to those states where the interstate company has its property and employees yields a system of taxation which conforms to the long-held view in the United States that taxation and representation should go hand-in-hand (*State Taxation of Interstate Commerce*, 1965, pp. 1144-1150)."

Despite the above advantages to interstate business of an apportionment formula with no sales factor, a major portion of the business community sided with the states in supporting an equally weighted three-factor formula in the 1969 Hearings on the Willis Interstate Taxation Bill (HR 11798). Testifying in behalf of the Chamber of Commerce of the United States, Leonard Kust stated:

It is the position of the chamber that whatever additional benefit to interstate commerce from reduction in compliance cost may be achieved through a two-factor formula it is achieved at too high a cost of interference in the impact of the state's present tax systems by shifting burdens significantly among taxpayers....The chamber believes that the imposition of uniformity in the method of apportionment is more important in relieving interstate businesses of unnecessary compliance burdens than is the specific nature of the formula. Thus, a very significant reduction in compliance costs and improvements in the climate for interstate business which are the purposes of HR 11798 can be achieved through use of a uniform three-factor formula, and they can be achieved using this formula with a minimum of interference with present state systems (*State Taxation of Interstate Commerce*, 1965, pp. 1144-1150).

WORLDWIDE COMBINATION

Worldwide combination is a requirement that multinational corporations report income of all affiliated corporations from operations throughout the world and pay taxes on an apportioned fraction of that worldwide income. Tax exporting results if the state, through its apportionment formula, can impose tax on income from overseas activities. At one time as many as a dozen states sought to apply their corporate income taxes to combined worldwide income.

In a 1978 report for the U.S. Department of Commerce, Blough and Wagner (1978, pp. 28-34) pointed out the limitations of formula apportionment of corporate income as applied in a worldwide context:

...within the common market of the United States, the three-factor formula, when uniformly applied by different states to multistate enterprises, will give reasonably acceptable results....When the unitary method is applied to multinational business, however, the errors of the three-factor apportionment formula are raised to unacceptable levels, for the following reasons: (1) In multinational business, one phase of the operation, e.g., sales, may take place in one country while another phase, e.g., production, may take place in another country. The three-factor allocation formula must assume that each of the factors bears the same relation to profit in each of the countries, which obviously is often not the case. (2) The widely differing wage rates in relation to profit in different countries make the payroll factor likely to unfairly skew toward the jurisdictions that have relatively high payrolls. (3) A wide divergence of profit margins in different countries will mean that some of the income from a country with a high profit margin on sales will be attributed instead to a country or state with a low or even negative profit on sales. (4) As in the case of sales and payrolls, the ratio of profits to property investment can vary widely from country to country. Moreover, the different accounting methods used in the valuation of property investment, e.g., undepreciated original cost, undepreciated cost of reproduction, depreciated cost after deducting straight-line depreciation, depreciated cost after deducting accelerated depreciation, the treatment of investment subsidies or credits, the determination of salvage value or obsolescence, etc., can produce an unfair apportionment of property value and therefore of income under the three-factor formula.

Over the past decade, worldwide combination has become less popular. All of the states that had at one time insisted on worldwide combination of income for corporate tax purposes now allow a water's-edge option. In California, because of unreasonable restrictions placed on the water's-edge option, worldwide combination still is effective to some extent as a means of exporting taxes.[6] Other states have not generally made the water's-edge option as unattractive as California. In fact, many American companies that now file on a worldwide basis do so because they save on taxes, as their overseas operations are not as profitable as their domestic operations.

Nevertheless, as far as the U.S. Supreme Court is concerned, worldwide combination remains a perfectly constitutional method of exporting taxes if the state chooses to utilize it. But that situation may be changing. The decision, in *Container Corp. v. Franchise Tax Board* (1983), which upheld California's worldwide combination procedures as applied to American companies, specifically excluded foreign-owned corporations.[7] A California Court of Appeal, in *Barclays Bank International Ltd. v. Franchise Tax Board* (1990), held unconstitutional the state's application of worldwide combination to a foreign parent corporation and its foreign subsidiaries, one of which did business in California and was subject to California tax. In *Colgate-Palmolive Company v. Franchise Tax Board* (1988), a California Superior Court rejected the application of worldwide combination to an American multinational. The California Court did in this case what the U.S. Supreme Court failed to do in the *Container* case—it recognized an overriding federal interest in speaking with "one voice" on foreign policy.[8] Thus, the U.S. Supreme Court may still have an opportunity to rectify the major error it made in the *Container* case. The California Supreme Court has ruled against the commerce clause arguments in *Barclays* (May 11, 1992) and *Colgate* (June 18, 1992). *Barclays* is expected to appeal to the U.S. Supreme Court.

STATE TAXATION OF FOREIGN SOURCE DIVIDENDS

State taxation of foreign source dividends is another Supreme Court-sanctioned method of exporting taxes. How state taxation of foreign source dividends results in state exportation of the tax burden was spelled out by Ernest S. Christian, Jr., in testimony in 1980 to the House Ways and Means Committee in behalf of the Committee on State Taxation (COST) of the Council of State Chambers of Commerce:[9]

A good case can be made that foreign source dividends should not be taxed by States at all; and a particularly good case can be made that those dividends should not be apportioned and taxed by a nondomiciliary State. The theory of the three-factor apportionment formula is that it is a reasonably accurate way of measuring that portion of a corporation's income which was attributable to activities in the State and a reasonable measure of the contribution of that State's economy in earning the particular income. But where dividends represent income earned by activities by another corporation carried on solely outside the United States, what contribution has the state made to earning that income? The answer is none.

As was noted earlier, how a state treats foreign source dividends is much more important to American companies than is worldwide combination. Again, the U.S. Supreme Court, in upholding Vermont's taxation of foreign source dividends, failed to see the importance of the issue to our international competitive situation. In the *Mobil Oil Corp. v. State Commissioner of Taxes of Vermont* (1980) decision, the U.S. Supreme Court upheld Vermont's right to tax an apportioned share of

Mobil's worldwide foreign source dividends even though the only investments Mobil had in Vermont were gas stations.

Mobil agreed that Vermont was entitled to tax a share of its operating income because this was related to its gas station operations, but it unsuccessfully contended that Vermont had no right to tax foreign source dividends which had no connection whatsoever with Vermont. Mobil also conceded that the state of commercial domicile, New York, had a right to tax the foreign source dividends. The Supreme Court in effect ruled that both states could tax the foreign source dividends under its unitary business concept.

Some observers felt at the time that Mobil should have argued that no state had the right to tax the foreign source dividends. In hindsight, they may have been right. This theory has yet to be tested because no case arguing this point has been heard by the Supreme Court.

Ten states completely exempt foreign source dividends (Table 8.2). Twenty-two additional states conditionally or partially exempt such income. The five states that allocate foreign source dividends to the state of commercial domicile largely, in effect, exempt foreign source dividends because there are very few corporations with substantial foreign source income that also have commercial domiciles in these five states. This leaves only seven states (Hawaii, Iowa, Mississippi, New Mexico, Pennsylvania, Rhode Island, and Vermont) and the District of Columbia that continue to insist on taxing their full apportioned share of foreign source dividends.[10] A challenge in the U.S. Supreme Court to the Iowa discrimination against foreign source dividends (*Kraft General Foods, Inc. v. Iowa Department of Revenue and Finance*, No. 90-1918, October Term, 1991) has been decided in favor of *Kraft*.

OTHER METHODS OF TAX EXPORTING

Florida-Type Service Tax

Application of the sales tax to services is not necessarily a device for exporting the tax to out-of-state companies if the tax is applied only to services performed within the state. However, this was not the case with the service tax enacted by Florida.[11] Florida attempted to apply the state's now repealed tax to many services performed outside the state and to use its income tax apportionment formula with its double-weighted sales factor to tax what it claimed was Florida's share. The state also overreached politically by applying the tax to advertisers, who

TABLE 8.2
Taxation of Foreign Source Dividends

Exempt	Conditional Partial Exemption	Allocate	Largely Tax Apportion
Alabama	Alaska	Alabama	Hawaii
Connecticut	Arkansas	Louisiana	Iowa
Delaware	California	N. Carolina	Mississippi
Florida	Colorado	Oklahoma	New Mexico
Georgia	Idaho	S. Carolina	Pennsylvania
Kentucky	Illinois		Rhode Island
Nebraska	Indiana		Vermont
Ohio	Kansas		Dist. of Col.
Virginia	Maine		
W. Virginia	Maryland		
	Massachusetts		
	Minnesota		
	Missouri		
	Montana		
	New Hampshire		
	New Jersey		
	New York		
	N. Dakota		
	Oregon		
	Tennessee		
	Utah		
	Wisconsin		

were able to enlist the support of the state's newspapers and other media in generating strong public opposition to the tax.

Different Taxes Applied to In-State vs. Out-of-State Companies

Applying one tax or rate to out-of-state companies and a different one to in-state companies, as in the following examples, would seem to be a clear violation of the commerce clause prohibition on discriminating against interstate commerce. While these strategies for exporting taxes are more likely to be restricted by the courts than are the techniques discussed previously, it is not a sure thing. Also, even if the violation is so flagrant that it is held unconstitutional, the state may not be required to refund the taxes that it collected unconstitutionally.

Washington and West Virginia Gross Receipts Taxes. Prior to court decisions that overturned them, Washington's and West Virginia's gross receipts taxes discriminated against out-of-state businesses. Washington imposed a "selling" tax on both local and out-of-state manufacturers. However, local manufacturers were exempt from the state's "manufacturing" tax. Out-of-state manufacturers were not allowed that exemption. The West Virginia gross receipts tax was a mirror image of that of Washington's.

The U.S. Supreme Court held that both states were taxing out-of-state businesses in an unconstitutional manner.[12] In both cases the states resisted paying refunds for the unconstitutional taxes they collected, and it appears that the U.S. Supreme Court is going to let Washington at least get away with it.

Following the 1987 decision in *Tyler Pipe Industries v. Washington* (1987) to strike down this discriminatory scheme, Washington repealed the multiple-activities exemption and replaced it with a credit system that in effect achieves the same discriminatory result. Technically, both in-state and out-of-state manufacturers are entitled to the credit, but as a practical matter few, if any, out-of-state manufacturers will be able to qualify for the credit.

Alabama Franchise Tax. Under Alabama law, an out-of-state corporation is subject to a net worth tax on "the actual amount of...capital employed" in the state [Alabama Code, Section 40-14-41(a)]. The term "capital" includes the par value of outstanding stock, surplus, including paid-in surplus, capital surplus, retained earnings, long-term debt, certain other debt, and accelerated depreciation [Alabama Code, Section 40-14-41 (b)]. Alabama domestic corporations are not subject to the same or a comparable tax. Rather, the tax base for a domestic corporation is limited to the par value of the corporation's stock [Alabama Code, Section 40-14-41)].

The U.S. Supreme Court has declined to review Alabama Supreme Court cases upholding this discriminatory scheme.[13]

Alabama Tax on Out-of-State Waste. On July 15, 1990, Alabama imposed an additional tax of $72 per ton on waste generated outside the state. The basic rate is $40 per ton, but out-of-state waste disposers pay $112 per ton. Five generators of out-of-state waste who dispose of their waste in a hazardous waste facility in Alabama brought suit in federal court claiming, among other things, that the Waste Tax violates the commerce clause because it discriminates against interstate commerce.[14] On June 1, 1992, the U.S. Supreme Court ruled that the Alabama fee is unconstitutional (*Chemical Waste Management Inc. v. Hunt*, No. 91-471).

Disallowance of Deductions by Out-of-State Businesses. New Jersey has found a unique way to try to export tax burdens by denying oil companies a deduction from the New Jersey Corporation Business Tax for the 1980 Federal Windfall Profits Tax. The U.S. Supreme Court has ruled that this does not discriminate against interstate commerce because there is no explicit discriminatory design to the tax.[15] The federal tax is triggered by removal of crude oil from the vicinity of the well. Because there are no wells in New Jersey the state is adding an element to net income that cannot burden in-state activity.

Favoring an In-State Product or Service Over Out of State. The U.S. Supreme Court has struck down state efforts to favor local products over out-of-state products, most recently a Florida liquor excise tax scheme (*McKesson Corp. v. Division of Alcoholic Beverages and Tobacco*, 1990). In this case, Florida again demonstrated why it deserves the title of the state that tries the hardest to export its tax burdens, although not necessarily with the most success.

In 1984, the U.S. Supreme Court indirectly struck down Florida's earlier attempt to discriminate against out-of-state products in the case of *Bacchus Imports v. Dias* (1984) which involved similar Hawaiian legislation.[16] The Florida legislature reacted to this decision by making only cosmetic changes to its taxing scheme instead of removing the underlying discrimination against out-of-state products. The legislature simply replaced the specific preference for "Florida-grown" products with a preference for products made from specified citrus, grape, and sugarcane products, all of which are commonly grown in Florida and not in most other states. The Florida Supreme Court saw through this subterfuge and struck down the change, but it refused to grant the taxpayer a refund. McKesson appealed this decision to the U.S. Supreme Court which ruled that it was entitled to a refund under these circumstances.

Florida is still attempting to favor in-state finance companies over out-of-state companies. Its attempt to provide such favoritism was unsuccessfully challenged in the U.S. Supreme Court.[17] The case involved an intangibles tax imposed on all accounts receivable, "wheresoever situated, arising out of, or issued in connection with the sales, leasing, or servicing of real or personal property in the state." The

COST *amicus* brief which was filed jointly with the American Financial Services Association states the following:

Clearly, the Florida tax on intangibles is structured to discourage out-of-state businesses from engaging in financing transactions in the state, thereby favoring local finance companies, since an out-of-state business risks multiple taxation that the local business avoids....Florida's intangibles tax is structured to provide a disincentive for non-Florida financial corporations to do business in the state, creating a monopoly for Florida businesses. It is just such commercial advantage to local business that the commerce clause is intended to prevent.[18]

Taxing Products or Services Primarily Exported Out of State. The quote from West Virginia Governor Caperton at the beginning of this chapter referred primarily to his proposal, subsequently enacted, for a tax on electricity generated in West Virginia. Because more than 70 percent of the electric power generated in the state, utilizing its coal resources, is sent outside the state, it was presented as a plan to export the tax burden. The tax was not completely perfect from a political viewpoint, however, because some of the electricity is consumed in the state, and the tax on this electricity is being passed on to the in-state consumer. At the time the proposed tax was under consideration by the legislature, state officials were reported as estimating that the average in-state electricity user's bill would increase by 50 cents a month.

Special Industry Rules Focusing on Out-of-State Businesses. One of the most popular approaches to exporting taxes today is to apply special nexus and apportionment rules to certain industries that happen to be largely headquartered outside the state applying the rules. Current approaches being taken by some states, and under consideration by many states in this category, involve taxation of interstate activities by financial institutions and the media industries.

The Multistate Tax Commission (MTC) and the Committee on State Taxation (COST) of the Council of State Chambers of Commerce have become involved in the controversy on taxation of financial institutions and the media industries. The MTC has proposed special regulations for the states to adopt on these industries and is developing a National Nexus Program. COST, on the other hand, had adopted position papers on both *The Taxation of Financial Institutions* and *The Taxation of Media Industries* that supported traditional nexus standards and equally weighted three-factor apportionment formulae so as to avoid discrimination against out-of-state businesses.

This is an area where the traditional conflict between headquarters states and market states comes clearly into play. The conflict is illustrated by a letter to the editor by Roger S. Cohen of the New York State Finance Committee. Cohen (1990, p. 631) objected to McCray's (1990, p. 1229) criticism that it is "surprising that of all the new state laws the New York law pays the least heed to new developments in banking." Cohen states the following:

Revenue considerations are the crux of McCray's proclamation that states should broaden their tax jurisdiction. She has tried to craft a method whereby states could export their tax burden to other states with impunity. Although these states may violate the spirit of the interstate commerce clause of the Constitution or its philosophical underpinnings, nevertheless, they do not violate current constitutional interpretations—or rather, McCray's interpretation of those interpretations.

EXPORTING TAXES CONFLICTS WITH CREATING JOBS

The West Virginia Legislature gave little consideration to the fact that by imposing a tax on electricity it was making it less attractive to generate that electricity in the state rather than in some other state that did not impose such a tax. Thus, it further penalized its coal miners and other West Virginians whose jobs depend on this activity. Historically, West Virginia has not paid much attention to such matters, especially when compared to other states such as its next-door neighbor, Virginia, and it has paid a high price in lost jobs, income, and population.

The pressure that state legislators are under to export tax burdens to out-of-state companies is described in the *amicus* brief filed by the Committee on State Taxation of the Council of State Chambers of Commerce, the National Association of Manufacturers, and The National Chamber Litigation Center in *Amarada Hess Corp. et al. v. Director, Division of Taxation, New Jersey Department of the Treasury* (1989):

The American public continually puts it elected representatives in a no-win situation: everybody wants more public services, but nobody wants to pay for them. The legislator who balks at expanding increasingly expensive public services is vilified as lacking in compassion. If the same legislator raises taxes to pay for those services, he or she is certain to encounter voter hostility at election time. Faced with these twin pressures, state representatives inevitably welcome methods of raising revenue that impose a disproportionate share of the tax burden on businesses and voters that are safely out of state.

Many of the most obvious routes to extraterritorial taxation have been closed off by this Court. For example, the New Hampshire "commuter" income tax imposed exclusively on nonresidents was invalidated in *Austin v. New*

Hampshire, 420 U.S. 656 (1975), and New York's allowance of personal exemptions for residents only was invalidated in *Travis v. Yale & Towne Mfg. Co.*, 252 U.S. 60 (1920). In the corporate area, states have been precluded from assessing facially neutral, "flat" taxes that have the effect of imposing disproportionate burdens on interstate corporations, *American Trucking Assn. v. Scheiner*, 107 S. Ct. 2829 (1987), and from selecting apportionment formulas that attribute an intrinsically disproportionate share of corporate income to the taxing state. [*Hans Rees' Sons, Inc. v. North Carolina*, 283 U.S. 121 (1931)].

States' efforts to export tax burdens to out-of-state companies not only conflict with the also politically attractive economic development objectives of creating more jobs, markets, and income, they also conflict with the need for greater state tax uniformity to help American companies compete more effectively in the world market. Strauss (1990) has emphasized that state governments must increase the uniformity of their tax bases and tax administration systems in order to both attract investors and encourage U.S. exporters while European countries harmonize their fiscal systems and worldwide competition grows.

CONCLUSION

The above discussion constitutes an introduction to some of the ways states attempt, not always successfully, to export tax burdens to out-of-state taxpayers. New schemes seem to rear their heads every year. Discriminating in favor of in-state businesses is so natural politically that in many cases it probably does not even occur to a state legislator, or even a state tax administrator, to consider whether or not the procedure is constitutional—or fair!

NOTES

1. *Amarada Hess Corp. et al. v. Director, Division of Taxation, New Jersey Department of the Treasury*, No. 87-453, decided April 3, 1989, pp. 11-14.

2. The author has compiled a comprehensive *Chronology of Federal Interstate Tax Legislation 1959-1990* which was presented to the 1990 Great Issues Conference, sponsored by the Committee on State Taxation and the Colorado Association of Commerce and Industry, Beaver Creek, Colorado, August 1-2, 1990. See also Brown and Cahoon (1973) and Brown (1979).

3. The 1976 4-R Act (49 U.S. C. 11503) and the airline provision in the 1982 TEFRA responded to state discriminatory application of property tax classification against railroads and airlines. See Rosner and Derus (1990).

4. One of the principal business groups interested in interstate tax legislation, the Committee on State Taxation (COST) of the Council of State Chambers of Commerce would have been willing to support legislation overruling the *Bellas Hess* decision, thus permitting states to require direct sellers to collect sales tax for them if the states had been willing to include provisions resolving the worldwide combination\foreign source dividend problem, but the states have adamantly insisted on no linkage. There was an agreement on a federal interstate income tax bill worked out in 1974-1975 between COST and the Executive Committee of the National Association of Tax Administrators (now known as the Federation of Tax Administrators) which would have provided for an optional equally weighted three-factor formula, but there was too much state opposition to other provisions in this compromise bill to even justify it being introduced in Congress.

5. Motion of the Committee on State Taxation of the Council of State Chambers of Commerce for leave to file brief *amicus curiae* and brief *amicus curiae* in support of appellant's petition for rehearing, *Moorman Manufacturing Company v. Bair*, Supreme Court of the United States, October Term, 1977, No. 77-454.

6. The major problems with the California's water's-edge election, which is causing many major taxpayers to continue to file worldwide combination include: (1) so-called 80/20 American-incorporated companies with more than 80 percent of their operations overseas are not permitted to elect water's edge; (2) election fees are imposed; (3) full-disclosure spreadsheets are required; and (4) intercompany foreign source dividends are not fully excluded as they are under a worldwide combination. 7 Justice Brennan's majority opinion (*Container Corp. v. Franchise Tax Board*, 1983, p. 26), stated "We have no need to address in this opinion the constitutionality of combined apportionment with respect to state taxation of domestic corporations with foreign parents or foreign corporations with either foreign parents or foreign subsidiaries."

8. In the majority opinion (*Container Corp. v. Franchise Tax Board*, 1983, p. 34), Justice Brennan stated, "We note, however, that in this case, unlike *Japan Line*, the Executive Branch has decided not to file an *amicus* brief in opposition to the state tax....The lack of such a submission is by no means dispositive. Nevertheless, when combined with all the foreign policy of the United States—whose nuances, we must emphasize again, are more the province of the Executive Branch and Congress than of this Court—is not seriously threatened by California's decision to apply the unitary business concept and formula apportionment in calculating appellant's income."

9. Hearings Before the Committee on Ways and Means, House of Representatives, Ninety-Sixth Congress, on HR 5076, pp. 161-163.

10. For a detailed state chart with specific statutory and regulatory citations, see *State Tax Report*, No. 254, October 25, 1990.

11. Florida has the distinction of being the state that tries the hardest to export its taxes to outsiders. However, it has had mixed success in this effort because it tends to enact extreme legislation without sufficient legislative consideration as to its broader impact. Then it flipflops with complete repeals. This was the case with worldwide combination and the service tax, but it had better success in double-weighting the sales factor, perhaps to some extent because this was favored by some major out-of-state companies with big investments in the state.

12. *Tyler Pipe Industries, Inc. v. Department of Revenue*, 483 U.S. 232 (1987). The U.S. Supreme Court has ruled unanimously that its 1984 decision (*Armco v. Hardesty*,

467 U.S. 638) striking down West Virginia's Business and Occupation (Gross Receipts) Tax, as discriminatory against interstate commerce, applies retroactively (*Ashland Oil, Inc. v. Michael E. Caryl, Tax Commissioner of West Virginia,* U.S. Supreme Court, No. 88-421, June 28, 1990).

13. *General Motors Corp. et al. v. Department of Revenue,* U.S. Supreme Court No. 89-1574 and *Reynolds Metals Company v. Sizemore,* U.S. Supreme Court No. 89-1587.

14. *Clean Harbors of Braintree, Inc. v. Sizemore,* No. CV-90-P-00826 (filed april 25, 1990).

15. *Amarada Hess Corp., et al. v. Director, Division of Taxation, New Jersey Department of the Treasury,* No. 87-453, Decided April 3, 1989. An *amicus* brief filed in this case by the Committee on State Taxation of the Council of State Chambers of Commerce, the National Association of Manufacturers, and The National Chamber Litigation Center argued that, "The factors that make the New Jersey scheme locally attractive make it dangerous from the perspective of the nation. If all it takes to export a state's tax burden is to identify some resource that the state does *not* have, then most states can do that, and more surely will. The specter of state government being financed by increasingly unrepresentative taxes is a serious one: our constitutional system presumes that those taxed are represented in the taxing authority. To the extent that presumption is invalid, the legitimacy of the system breaks down."

16. In this decision the Court adopted a more limited view of the Twenty-first Amendment impact on the commerce clause than in *McKesson.* In that case it held that the Amendment did not empower states to favor local industries by erecting barriers to competition—that is, it removed commerce clause restraints from state taxation only for purposes of promoting temperance or other objectives of the Twenty-first Amendment.

17. *Ford Motor Credit Company v. Department of Revenue, State of Florida,* U.S. Supreme Court, October Term 1990, No. 88-1847.

18. Brief of the Committee on State Taxation of the Council of State Chambers of Commerce and the American Financial Services Association submitted August 10, 1990 as *amici curiae* in support of appellant, *Ford Motor Credit Company v. Department of Revenue, State of Florida,* U.S. Supreme Court, October Term 1990, No. 88-1847, pp. 8-9.

9
The Role of Corporations in Tax Exporting

BURNS STANLEY

There is nothing conceptually new about tax exporting. It results from the intentional or unintentional collection from multistate or multinational taxpayers of a disproportionate share of taxes imposed by a state or local government. This practice has existed at least since allocation and apportionment of income and franchise tax bases came into use. That we hear more of tax exporting now than in the past is largely a matter of degree and emphasis—there is steady movement toward extremes. It is certain that schemes are proliferating for disproportionately increasing the tax load of outsiders (multistate and multinational corporations). Exporting taxes is good politics: voters are advantaged; outsiders are disadvantaged.

Most targets of tax exporting are multistate and multinational corporations, but some exportation schemes impact intrastate corporations and other businesses as well. Although corporations are the principal victims, there has been no monolithic front of corporate resistance, for reasons that will now be discussed.

There is no end to the ingenuity of those proposing to lighten the burden on in-state taxpayers at outsiders' expense. While manipulation of apportionment formula factors is the most fertile medium for tax exportation, it is by no means the only one. For example, a state's granting of tax credits may result in tax exporting. If an investment tax credit of 10 percent is allowed by a state for capital expenditures within its borders, the corporation engaged only in making sales within the state from outside inventory pays correspondingly more in taxes than the competitive in-state recipient of credits. William Brown, in Chapter 8, mentioned several operatives schemes. The possibilities are numerous.

Businesses operating solely within an offending state may be injured indirectly by its tax exporting practices. For example, any state with a dominant industrial economy will probably suffer revenue loss from enactment of a double-weighted sales apportionment factor, because its largest corporate taxpayers consequently will employ sales double-weighting to attribute a greater share of their tax base to out-of-state activity. Nevertheless, many states engender this loss in exchange for compensating benefits—often increased tax rates—which effect a new revenue gain. These increased rates, however, usually extend to exclusively in-state businesses as well. Thus, the in-stater becomes a net loser, taking heavier rates without an offsetting apportionment formula advantage. Out-of-state corporations without significant capital investment within the taxing state whose principal activity is selling within the state also will lose.

THE PROTAGONISTS

Those promoting and resisting tax exporting schemes may be identified generally as follows.

First are state and local legislators. ("State" is used hereafter to include both state and local.) These protagonists are motivated principally by political and fiscal considerations. They want to please voters, and they want to raise as much revenue as possible with the least possible burden on voters. Whether their legislation is constitutional is of secondary importance, at least while they capitalize on the publicity from initial enactment.

Second are state tax administrators. Their principal duty is to administer the laws enacted by the legislators, but administration of tax laws is a remarkably flexible and creative activity. It includes statutory interpretation and issuance of rulings, activities that often approach the force of law. The fisc may be enhanced or reduced by administrative decisions. Many administrators try to conduct their administration evenhandedly and in accordance with a fair interpretation of statutory and constitutional laws. Decisions of others, however, may be influenced by desire for professional advancement, by bias against certain taxpayers—often multistate corporations, by determination to collect the greatest possible amount of revenue, and by pressure to satisfy political masters.

Third is a combination of legislators and administrators. Legislators and administrators usually function in real but informal tandem. There exists a significant degree of interdependence among the parties which often exerts strong influence on both the legislative and administrative products.

Fourth are corporations and other businesses. The quantitative bulk of business is conducted in the corporate form. How, then, is corporate tax policy formulated? It is generally conceded that most of American corporate management is motivated primarily by the short-term bottom line. Shareholders constantly press for increased dividends. Executive compensation is significantly influenced by quarterly earnings reports, and emphatically by annual results. This places vast pressure on CEOs and other executives to make decisions with an eye sharply focused on the near term. This pressure, in turn, is passed on to the chief corporate tax executive, because his or her recommendations and decisions have a direct and immediate effect on financial results. This chief tax executive may be an ethical, influential, and relatively independent tax policymaker; or he or she may be a corporate lackey who has readily adopted the congressional philosophy, "To get along, go along."

Fifth are combinations of legislators, tax administrators, governors, and other state officials, and a meaningful part of the corporate business community. A number of corporations will always be aligned with the state combination in support of all but the most extreme tax exporting schemes. If, for example, the project is to secure enactment of a double-weighted sales factor, corporations with significant capital investment in the state, and geographically widespread sales, are likely to be supportive of the state's efforts. Indeed, they may well have initiated the project, because they stand to gain in the short term even though the state may suffer diminished revenue from double-weighting, as mentioned above and explained more fully later.

CONTESTING DOUBLE-WEIGHTING OF THE SALES FACTOR

To illustrate the interplay among the protagonists in a meaningful tax situation, assume that the state is indeed attempting to enact a double-weighted sales factor. The effect of double-weighting is, of course, to apportion a greater share of the corporate tax base of a multistate, multinational business to its sales locations, thereby reducing the tax base available to the state of manufacture or production.

Thus, a state with little capital investment, but many consumers, would profit from double-weighting of the sales factor, whereas a state with large industrial concentrations would tend to lose revenue from double-weighting of sales because of the consequent dilution of its property and payroll factors.

How, then, are industrial states persuaded to enact such a double-weighted sales factor? Often, it's plain old-fashioned horse trading.

Frequently, a key component of a state's agreement with corporate movers is that the latter will support a hike in tax rates (or some other compensating tax change) sufficient to make the state whole, or, indeed, to enhance its revenues. Another argument is that the benefit from double-weighting the sales factor is likely to attract the location of manufacturing activities to sites within the state.

Corporations opposed to double-weighting of sales may argue that sales have no legitimate role in an apportionment formula, and certainly not an enhanced role. Prominent tax economists have argued that because capital and labor are the dominant elements of production, property and payroll should alone comprise the apportionment formula. In this regard, PL 86-272 of 1959, the only meaningful general congressional interstate tax enactment in over 30 years, provided for a congressional committee to study interstate taxation. This group, the Willis Subcommittee, reported to the Congress after five years of study. One of its key recommendations was that sales *not* be included, and that a two-factor formula of property and payroll be substituted for the traditional three-factor formula. But Congress did not act on the Willis Subcommittee recommendations, and, while many broad interstate tax bills were introduced over the past 30 years, none became law.

Whatever the pros and cons of a sales factor in economic theory, there is no probability, as a practical matter, that it will be dropped. States without significant industrial facilities rely principally on the sales factor for corporate revenue. Congress heeds their anguished cries!

In Chapter 8, Brown reviewed how a combination of judicial abnegation *(Moorman Manufacturing Company v. Bair,* 1978) and Congressional paralysis (over 30 years of nonaction) have led inevitably to the widespread distortion of apportionment formulas, which has resulted in twenty-one states now having some form of disproportionate sales weighting. Fifteen states have double-weighting.

Corporations often have collaborated with state legislators and administrative officials to secure enactment of double-weighting of sales in the fifteen states that have it. Other corporate businesses have vigorously opposed this business-government combination, at times successfully. California, for example, hardly known for its reticence to impose stringent and unfair business taxes, has not yet adopted a distorted sales factor. Corporate proponents are usually multistate companies with significant industrial installations within the adopting state. Corporate opponents are principally those companies without such significant industrial sites and wholly intrastate businesses that fear a general tax increase to compensate for any revenue loss attributable to double-weighting. Many corporate tax officers on both sides of the issue understand that in the long term the proponent corporations, if successful, may nevertheless end up losers. This could result primarily from higher compensating tax rates, retributive enactments of double-weighting of sales by states in which they have no significant industrial operations, or by enactment of some other form of tax unfavorable to them. Notwithstanding, the corporate proponent reasons that those probabilities likely will not occur before the end of the quarter, and perhaps never—so let the short-term bottom line reign supreme!

It should be noted, however, that there are occasional instances when, as a matter of principle or from a grasp of the long view, corporate tax executives do base their position objectively on the merits, even when the merits cost their companies short-term profits. These executives are a decided minority and are destined to remain so.

ETHICS, CONSTITUTIONAL LIMITATIONS, AND THE PROFIT MOTIVE

Ethics

As previously explained, the crux of exporting taxes is to concoct a scheme that will shift to multijurisdictional taxpayers a disproportionate share of taxes imposed by the state. Depending on the sagacity and drafting skills of the state's legislators, administrators, and cooperating corporate tax lawyers and accountants, the contrivance may meet constitutional tests. Notwithstanding its legality, is a scheme to be abjured as unethical which shifts a disproportionate share of a state's taxes to those beyond its state or national boundaries?

Being neither philosopher nor instructor in morality, I cannot speak to the good or evil embraced by the question. I can speak to the reality of the situation. The issue will generally not be perceived in terms of right or wrong. Consider the old chestnut that states in effect: Smart taxation consists of plucking the most feathers from the other fellow's goose—and never mind the squawking! Have you ever heard that without smiling? And wasn't your smile empathetic? Was yours, then, an unethical smile?

Constitutional Limitations

Corporations and other businesses exploited by states and allied corporations and other businesses, by being on the short end of the enactment, or enforcement, of an exported tax, can, of course, go to court. But litigation is both risky and expensive, especially since chances in state courts are very hazardous. This makes the necessity of an appeal to the U.S. Supreme Court probable, and the possibility of even being heard there is scant at best, particularly since Congress recently relieved the Court of its mandatory acceptance of taxpayer appeals from state courts. While I chose not to align state court systems with the pro-export tax forces previously specified, it is not unusual to detect a distinct air of confidence in even a neophytic assistant attorney general assigned to a tax case in state courts.

Nevertheless, there exists a highly complex body of decisional law regarding the commerce, due process, and equal protection clauses that has accumulated in kaleidoscopic staggers over the two-century history of the Supreme Court. The cases offer a modicum of guidance, at least until the next decision day, a day made more exciting by such initiatives as Justice Scalia's persistent, albeit lonely, disavowal of such precedent as 150-plus years of the "dormant" commerce clause, the doctrine that prohibits action by states to tax interstate or foreign commerce even in areas where Congress has been silent (see dissenting opinion in *Tyler Pipe Industries, Inc. v. Washington* (1987)).

But whatever the risk of losing, it is essential that injured corporate taxpayers continue to test the waters in the Supreme Court. Justices come and go, and new law—sometimes favoring the taxpayer—is made. Note, for example, the explicit overruling of *General Motors Corp. v. Washington* (1964), a startling decision, by *Tyler Pipe*. For twenty-three years, the *General Motors* case had imposed virtually insurmountable conditions on taxpayers attempting to prove multiple taxation of interstate sales. So anything is possible! Justice Stevens authored the *Tyler Pipe* opinion; obviously, he is not blindly dedicated to precedent. One can but wonder, then, how he feels about his majority opinion in the *Moorman* case, without which today's program on tax exporting would be devoid of much of its significance, because, in *Moorman*, the Supreme Court validated Iowa's use of an apportionment formula comprised of a single factor of sales. It was hard enough to context apportionment formulas after Justice Black's opinion in *International Harvester Company v. Evatt* (1947), in which he wrote:

This Court has long realized the practical impossibility of a state's achieving a perfect apportionment of expansive, complex business activities such as those of appellant, and has declared that "rough approximation rather than precision" is sufficient....Unless a palpably disproportionate result comes from an apportionment, a result which makes it patent that the tax is levied upon interstate commerce rather than upon an intrastate privilege, this Court has not been willing to nullify honest state efforts to make apportionments. (at 422-423)

Apparently the Iowa legislature, which enacted the single sales factor apportionment formula at issue in *Moorman*, was populated by members who saw this objectively distorted formula as an honest state effort at fair apportionment, at least in the honest opinion of the Nine Wise Men.

Moorman threw wide the doors, thereby making possible rampant abuse by apportionment-factor manipulations.

Multistate corporations must take the lead in challenging constitutionally suspect legislation and administrative actions for imposing tax exportation schemes, which are proliferating at an unparalleled pace. If an issue is of broad significance, multistate companies should join in initiating litigation. Such corporate tax organizations as the Committee on State Taxation of the Council of State Chambers of Commerce (COST), the Tax Executives Institute (TEI), the U.S. Chamber of Commerce, the National Association of Manufacturers, and various trade organizations, have had broad experience in this area, and often have common ground for taking appropriate action. Of course, there always are members of such large organizations whose interests are adverse to joining in a given judicial challenge. But where a consensus clearly exists, it has been amply demonstrated that collective action can be taken.

Profit Motive

Finally, what role does the keystone of capitalism, the profit motive, play in the tax exporting process? I'm sure the answer is apparent from my viewpoint, because the profit motive has either overtly or implicitly been the controlling force in much that I have addressed.

I regret that I cannot look into the future with anticipation that worthy long-term objectives will prevail if the cost of prevalence is the negation or diminution of short-term profits. So long as shareholders place a premium on dividends now, and corporate officers rise or fall by this quarter's—or this year's—bottom line, so long will most corporations fight shortsightedly for tax exporting schemes that contribute to short-term gain, and oppose those that reduce it.

Thus, tax exporting is not a simple matter of states against multistate corporations, for if corporate America were not driven by the short-term syndrome, states would be hard put to enact tax exporting schemes over united corporate opposition. "Divide and conquer" remains a potent state formula for legislative tax success.

Especially in our acutely antitax political climate, states will continue to accelerate tax exporting legislation, and a shifting but predictable body of corporations will aid and abet their efforts. The larger corporate community will nevertheless prevail in many legislative battles.

We must hope that the Supreme Court ultimately will provide restraint against extremes of tax exporting efforts.

10
Economic Analysis and Expert Testimony in Commerce Clause Challenges

FERDINAND P. SCHOETTLE

United States courts, both federal and state, traditionally hear disputes in which a complainant alleges that a state or local tax creates barriers to free trade that violate the agreement to have a common market.[1] Some jurists and scholars argue that courts should grant the states greater freedom from commerce clause regulation. Most scholars of the commerce clause believe that commerce clause challenges to state taxes present a different problem than commerce clause challenges to other state laws, and consequently they require a different analysis. Commerce clause challenges to state taxes are, in fact, unique. Unlike most commerce clause disputes, tax challenges neither involve complicated regulatory issues nor require judicial value judgments that arguably should be left to the legislature.

The most important consideration in determining the constitutionality of a state tax is the relative tax cost for in-state and out-of-state taxpayers. In deciding a commerce clause challenge to a state tax, courts should ask the following question: Does the challenged tax have effects that place interstate commerce at a disadvantage?[2] To answer this question, courts should implicitly or explicitly generate factual findings such as those that economists make concerning the effects of challenged taxes on interstate commerce.[3] In particular, courts should compare marginal costs that, according to economists, guide economic actors.

Formal doctrine should not be so influential as to limit, rather than enhance, a court's ability to view the effects. For example, in considering challenges to state taxes, the U.S. Supreme Court has asked such doctrinal questions as whether the tax under scrutiny was direct or indirect;[4] whether the tax created a multiple burden[5] or the risk of a multiple burden;[6] whether the tax rested on the "privilege" of engaging in interstate commerce;[7] whether the tax was fairly related to services;[8]

and whether the tax was internally consistent.[9] None of these tests, however, should be dispositive. None directly relate to relative tax costs and to the ultimate goal of keeping markets free of unwarranted government interference.

WHY SHOULD THE COURTS PROTECT THE FREE MARKET?

The free market attempts to increase consumer welfare by allowing unfettered exchange to present the consumer with the widest possible choice of goods and services. The general equilibrium competitive market paradigm of exchange and production postulates that, given initial endowments, free trade results in a Pareto efficient market equilibrium. A Pareto efficient market equilibrium is one in which one actor's economic welfare cannot be improved without disadvantaging another economic actor. State tax systems threaten this market equilibrium when taxes impede free market goals. The following sections describe situations when state tax systems threaten the free market. An understanding of these points provides guidance in selecting an appropriate legal strategy for resolving commerce clause challenges to state taxes.

Taxes Should Not Change Relative Marginal Costs

The basic free market philosophy requires that out-of-state taxpayers incur the same marginal tax costs as in-state taxpayers. States should provide a level playing field, rather than an exemption, for interstate commerce. As Adam Smith (1963, pp. 29-30) stated, foreign goods should bear an equal tax to "leave the competition between foreign and domestic industry, after the tax, as nearly as possible upon the same footing as before it."[10] Smith's comments contain more economic thought than might be apparent initially to readers who are not economists. One rationale of the free market is to allocate society's resources to their most efficient use, thus satisfying consumers' wants at the least cost. To ensure that taxes do not interfere with an efficient economic order, taxes should disturb a pretax economic order as little as possible. Pretax relative efficiencies and marginal costs of in-state and out-of-state taxpayers should prevail in the posttax environment. Only by attempting to keep relative real economic relationships intact can the tax system lower the losses it imposes on society.

From an economist's point of view, a tax that subsidizes interstate commerce by imposing higher marginal costs on in-state producers than out-of-state producers is as undesirable as a tax that does the opposite.[11] Justice Frankfurter's belief that the tax system should err on the side of favoring interstate commerce—a belief partially, if not completely, accepted by the Supreme Court from 1946 to 1977—is undesirable from an economic perspective.[12]   Economic theory does not support Frankfurter's basic tenet that "revenue serves as well no matter what its source" (*Freeman v. Hewit*, 1946, p. 253). A tax that imposes higher marginal costs on in-state producers disturbs the efficient economic order as much as a tax that imposes higher marginal costs on out-of-state producers.

The discussion above has focused on marginal costs, which are the costs incurred as a result of a specific sale. Marginal costs do not include other costs not incurred as a result of that specific sale. For example, the marginal costs of production are the costs of producing the last unit of output. Thus, costs incurred regardless of whether the last unit of output is produced are not included as marginal costs of production. The standard economic model of the firm postulates that firms sell as long as the sale price is the same as or greater than the marginal costs incurred on account of the sale.

Taxes can be considered a type of marginal cost incurred by a seller. A firm's selling price must equal or exceed its normal marginal costs plus any taxes incurred on account of the sale. A tax that increases the marginal costs of out-of-state firms without imposing a similar cost on local firms favors local firms and thus has protectionist effects. Such a tax wastes resources when items that were relatively more expensive pretax become less expensive posttax because competing items bear a tax. The key to appropriate analysis is to focus on marginal costs rather than total costs or the overall tax bill. Even if an out-of-state firm bears lower overall taxes, higher marginal taxes can have protectionist effects. The following section considers who might desire protectionist taxes.

The Risk of Protectionist Taxes

Despite the Pareto efficiency of the new equilibrium, the move from a closed to a free trade economy does not necessarily result in an improvement in the welfare of all households. Consumers benefit, but factory owners may not. Thus, a state might impose taxes that discriminate against out-of-state businesses to protect local factors of production from competition (the anticompetitive effect). Alternatively, a state might impose such a tax to generate revenue (the impost motive).

State governments are frequently subject to pressure to discourage interstate competition. Despite the arguments that may have influenced a society to choose a free trade economy, producers may lobby governmental officials to limit freedom of trade for items that are important to particular workers or owners of capital. Such demands for protectionist taxes have a long history. Indeed, Adam Smith (1963, p. 30) noted that, in Great Britain, when the government imposed a tax on a domestic industry, the clamorous complaints of the local merchants and manufacturers that they might be undersold caused the sovereign to increase its tax levies on similar foreign goods.

Protectionist taxes have solid political support. As pointed out above, such taxes assist local producers. Even if the local community does not lobby for protectionist taxes, political pressures against such taxes may be unlikely because they do not obviously fall on resident businesses and constituents.[13]   Because the political process may produce a result contrary to collective interstate goals, a judicial role in reviewing challenges to state taxes seems warranted (*Raymond Motor Transportation Inc. v. Rice,* 1978, p. 444).

Impact of State Taxes

Some judges and other policymakers believe that state taxes have little relation to business growth and locational decisions.[14]   Such a belief may be based on opinion polls in which businesses have responded that taxes were not a primary factor influencing their business decisions. Courtroom observations—especially in the Supreme Court—may enforce a belief that taxes do not matter. The taxpayers who appear in court tend to be very large firms with significant market shares, and it is difficult to believe that taxes matter at all to them.

There are two responses to this perception. First, only large businesses have sufficient tax liability to justify incurring legal and other fees to contest tax liability. Thus, the litigant before the court serves as a "private attorney general" representing smaller businesses that cannot justify the costs of tax litigation. Second, although the effects of taxes may not be apparent in the short run, they are apparent in the long run and matter for everyone, including large businesses.

The key to thinking properly about tax incidence is recognizing that although taxes may contribute relatively insignificantly to each individual decision, they make a significant difference over the long term.

Businesses continually reallocate their physical and human resources when they add to a physical plant, add or subtract an employee, and genèrally respond to the market. Each week, businesses make thousands of decisions involving taxes. The tax impact on any one of these decisions may be quite small. The cumulative effect of a particular tax system entering into millions of decisions, however, makes the world a different place than if some other tax system had been used.[15]

Expert Testimony on the Effects of Taxes

Before turning to the substance of commerce clause challenges to state taxes, we need to deal with an evidentiary issue. Can an expert appropriately testify concerning tax accounting matters or do disputes concerning tax accounting involve questions of law about which testimony would be inappropriate? In the title of this chapter I refer to "expert testimony" in order to emphasize the point that rules governing the appropriate accounting for income by a multistate taxpayer mostly speak to factual issues, not pure questions of law. In my opinion, particularized facts, not abstractions concerning the nature of income, should be the central focus of most disputes concerning the appropriateness of particular methods of reporting income to a state. The statutes governing accounting to the states for income generated in interstate commerce are replete with references to factual findings. Article IV, Section 18 of the Uniform Division of Income for Tax Purposes Act (UDITPA), for instance, allows an alternative accounting for income to a state if "the allocation and apportionment provisions of this article do not fairly represent the extent of the taxpayer's business activity in this state." Allowed by UDITPA are such alternative methods of accounting for income that are "reasonable," that "fairly represent the taxpayer's business activity" in the state, or that "effectuate an equitable allocation and apportionment of the taxpayer's income." All of these factual predicates are appropriate subjects for proof in a tax dispute.

As to the admissibility of expert testimony concerning accounting for interstate income, courts should admit such testimony if the experts direct their testimony to questions of fact, as opposed to questions of law. Rule 702 of the *Federal Rules of Evidence*, which allows testimony by experts, states that:

If scientific, technical or other specialized knowledge will assist the trier of fact to understand the evidence or to determine a fact in issue, a witness qualified as an expert by knowledge, skill, experience, training, or education, may testify thereto in the form of an opinion or otherwise.

In a recent case, the Minnesota Tax Court considered a challenge to my testimony as an expert witness in a case concerning the appropriate accounting to Minnesota for the income of a resident multistate taxpayer (*Commonwealth Leasing Corporation v. Commissioner of Revenue*, 1991 Minn. Tax Lexis 119). Tax Court Judge Arthur Roemer confirmed the factual basis of the accounting dispute. The judge noted:

These [income tax] statutes use such words as "unjust to the taxpayer" or "fairly reflect such net income" which involve questions of fact rather than a legal issue. It is these factual issues that appellant's expert witness seeks to address.

Even if the "fact" about which the expert seeks to testify is an "ultimate fact," the testimony will most likely be admitted. Ultimate facts are "facts essential to the right of action or matter of defense" (*Black's Law Dictionary*, 1979, p. 1365). Historically, courts did not allow witnesses to give opinions on ultimate facts in issue. The courts were concerned that admitting such testimony might usurp the function or invade the province of the jury because the jury might then "forego independent analysis of the facts and bow too readily to the opinion of the expert." Since the 1940's, the trend has been to allow testimony concerning ultimate facts. Currently the majority rule is that expert testimony on ultimate facts is admissible (*McCormick on Evidence*, 1979, § 12). This rule has been codified in Rule 704(a) of the *Federal Rules of Evidence*, and it has also been adopted by many states (e.g., *Minnesota Rules of Evidence*, Rule 704). Rule 704(a) provides that:

... testimony in the form of an opinion or inference otherwise admissible is not objectionable because it embraces an ultimate issue to be decided by the trier of fact.

With the evidentiary matter out of the way, we turn now to consider the substance of this chapter.

A MARGINAL COST ANALYSIS OF HOW TAXES AFFECT THE FREE MARKET

In this section I offer examples to support the following two major propositions: (1) commerce clause challenges to state taxes should resolve questions of fact concerning relative tax costs for in-state and out-of-state taxpayers; and (2) the doctrinal "tests" that the Supreme Court has used to resolve commerce clause challenges to state taxes have been more confusing than helpful in advancing the constitutional goal of safeguarding out-of-state taxpayers from protectionist taxes. The first proposition is illustrated with three examples involving an income tax, a property tax, and a compensatory tax. The second proposition is illustrated with several cases involving flat taxes.

The following analysis does not involve tax incidence analysis but a much simpler analysis of marginal costs as they might appear to a business taxpayer. Tax incidence analysis asks who bears the real burden of taxation and involves computations of supply-and-demand elasticities and similar calculations. Such incidence analysis can be studied at various levels of abstraction. At one level, it is relatively accessible to those untrained in economics (McLure, 1983). At a higher level, however, it is understandable only to those who both are comfortable with mathematical expressions and have a reasonable amount of time for study (Schoettle, 1985). This work presents an analysis at the lower level and involves no complex computations in determining marginal tax cost.

Income Taxes: The State of Source Should Tax Income

An income tax that taxes out-of-state taxpayers on income not earned in the taxing state can impose marginal costs on nonresident taxpayers that are not shared by resident taxpayers.[16] If one of a nonresident's costs of doing business in a state is payment of a tax not only on income earned in that state but also on income not earned in that state, that nonresident faces a higher marginal tax cost than does a resident. The following hypothetical, based on *Mobil Oil Corp. v. State Commissioner of Taxes of Vermont* (1980) illustrates this situation: A lawyer lives and practices law in Alpha, a state with no income tax, and also represents clients in Beta. The lawyer has had several long trials in Beta. Beta taxes the income of the out-of-state lawyer by employing a percentage-based formula that uses the number of hours billed in Beta as a numerator and the total billable hours in both Alpha and Beta as the denominator. This factor is then multiplied by the lawyer's total income to determine the percentage of taxable income in Beta. May Beta use the same formula to tax some of the lawyer's income from dividends, capital gains, or book royalties? Answer: No, because such a tax would have both impost and anticompetitive effects. If Beta taxed peripheral income, an out-of-state lawyer considering whether to accept a trial in Beta would need to consider not only taxes on the income earned at the trial but also taxes on the lawyer's dividends, capital gains, and royalties. In-state lawyers, however, would only consider taxes imposed on the income earned at the trial because they would already be paying taxes on their other income.

If Beta did tax peripheral income, the economic impact would clearly be protectionist. If a nonresident's cost of doing business in a state is payment of a tax not only on income earned in that state but also on income not earned in that state, then the tax is protectionist. Such a system also has impost effects in that it raises revenue from out-of-state taxpayers.[17]

Despite these adverse effects, however, applying a rule that only the source jurisdiction may tax the income may prove impossible because of the difficulty in some cases of determining where income is earned.

Property Taxes: Double Taxation Is Not Necessarily Protectionist

The Supreme Court has traditionally expressed concern that state taxes may impose double taxation on out-of-state businesses. This appears on the surface to be a valid concern. Yet, from the viewpoint of advancing free market goals, the Court should instead focus on the impost and anticompetitive effects of a challenged tax. For example, the following hypothetical, based on *Japan Line Ltd. v. County of Los Angeles* (1979), shows that double taxation does not always result in protectionist effects.[18] A company, Widgets, owns personal property and leases it to users. Widgets' home state levies a property tax on the personal property, wherever situated, of all its resident taxpayers. The basis for such taxation is ownership by a resident. Widgets also leases property to users in another state, "the state of market." The state of market levies a personal property tax on all business personal property used in the market state regardless of where the owner resides. Does the double taxation of the leased property—once by the home state and once by the state of market—have impost or anticompetitive effects? Answer: No, such double taxation has neither impost nor anticompetitive effects. The marginal cost for all taxpayers bidding to lease property to users in the market state includes the property tax of the market state. If Widgets were not required to pay the property tax of the market state, its marginal costs of doing business in the market state would include no tax costs. Furthermore, because Widgets must pay the property tax to the home state regardless of where it leases the property, that tax is not a marginal cost of doing business in the market state.

The rationales supporting the free market suggest that the state of market should impose its property tax on leased property owned by out-of-state lessors. Double taxation in this situation is efficient. Exempting the property of the out-of-state lessor from property taxation results in lower marginal tax costs for the out-of-state lessor than the in-state lessor, and thereby violates the free market goal of allowing real costs, not tax costs, to determine relative prices.

Complementary Taxes: Focus on Marginal Costs, Not the Total Tax Bill

Complementary taxes provide a good example of the need to focus on marginal costs rather than the total tax bill.[19] Suppose that a state has very high property and sales taxes. The sales taxes apply to sales of machinery and equipment. Suppose further that the state is concerned about its local producers of machinery and equipment, who must pay both the high sales and property taxes. The state therefore enacts a complementary tax scheme: It charges local firms sales tax on in-state sales of machinery and equipment, but it simultaneously gives local firms a rebate on property taxes for the amount of sales tax incurred. The state gives no rebate to out-of-state producers who have not paid a local property tax. Is this complementary tax scheme protectionist? Answer: Yes, it is protectionist. An out-of-state firm selling its products must recover both costs of production and of sales tax. In contrast, a local firm, which receives credit against its property taxes for its sales taxes, effectively pays no sales tax and therefore incurs no marginal tax costs on an in-state sale. The key to analyzing a complementary tax system, therefore, is to focus on marginal costs. Because of the credit arrangement, the local firm incurs no marginal tax cost on new in-state sales, regardless of the overall tax liability of the two firms.

Flat Taxes: Doctrinal Tests Are Confusing

Flat taxes, which are in the form of fixed fees, include license taxes and annual activity taxes. Such taxes can advance both impost and protectionist goals by raising revenues from out-of-state taxpayers and by resulting in some anticompetitive effects. For example, a resident producer might allocate a license tax to domestic production throughout the year and thereby incur a relatively low per unit cost. On the other hand, such a tax may result in a greater per unit cost for out-of-state producers because they do less business in the state. Thus, such a tax may convince the least profitable producers to forego doing any business in the state.[20]

It is important to recognize that after an out-of-state producer pays the fixed fee, the marginal tax costs are the same for in-state and out-of-state taxpayers. The higher marginal cost for the out-of-state taxpayer arises when the out-of-state taxpayer decides whether to do business in the taxing state. After the out-of-state taxpayer decides to do such business in the state and pays the fixed fee, the out-of-state taxpayer and the in-state taxpayer incur equal per unit marginal tax costs.

The U.S. Supreme Court has decided many cases involving fixed fees. I discuss three: *Case of the State Freight Tax* (1873), *Robbins v. Shelby County Taxing District* (1887), and *American Trucking Associations v. Scheiner* (1987). In each case the majority invalidated a state tax because the tax had forbidden protectionist effects. Furthermore, in all three cases, rather than basing its opinion on the straightforward ground that the effects of the tax rendered it a forbidden "regulation of commerce," the Court either gave no explicit ground of decision or announced a subsidiary test or rule of decision. Most often, the announced rule, such as "no regulations can be made directly affecting interstate commerce,"[21] had no commonly understood application. In each case, however, the dissenters focused on the majority's announced rule, not the tax facts, and interpreted the majority opinion to hold that a particular type of tax was valid or invalid, not that the challenged tax had forbidden effects. Although the Court correctly decided the three cases, the Court's failure to explicitly rely on a tax's forbidden effects on interstate commerce deserves criticism.

Case of the State Freight Tax (1873). The U.S. Supreme Court first invalidated a state tax for violating the commerce clause in this case. The challenged tax, which Pennsylvania levied on all freight carried in the state, varied from two cents per ton for mined products to five cents per ton for most other freight. The Reading Railroad Company presented evidence of the percentage of total tax revenues collected from freight passing through Pennsylvania, which showed disproportionate effects on interstate commerce. According to the uncontroverted facts, $46,520 of $84,881 in taxes paid by the Reading Railroad to the state for three-quarters of a year was for freight exported to locations outside Pennsylvania. Pennsylvania argued that the tax was facially neutral and a fair charge for the use of Pennsylvania's public works.

The challenged tax was more of an impost than a protectionist tax. Pennsylvania occupies a key position because most freight shipped from the mid-Atlantic or New England states must pass through Pennsylvania on its way west. The challenged tax in effect charged a toll for such passage, and the toll had no relationship to the use of Pennsylvania's public facilities. Emphasizing the disadvantageous effects of this flat tax on interstate commerce, the Court compared the tax to a customs duty and invalidated it. Two dissenting justices focused on the facial neutrality of the tax.

In a similar case decided the same day as *Freight Tax,* the Reading Railroad challenged another Pennsylvania tax. In *State Tax on Railway Gross Receipts (1873),* the Court reviewed Pennsylvania's unapportioned tax of three-quarters of one percent on the Reading Railroad's gross receipts. The Court's opinion, written by Justice Strong, who also wrote the *Freight Tax* opinion, upheld the tax. Justice Strong easily could have distinguished the *Gross Receipts* gross receipts tax from the flat tax in *Freight Tax* by explaining that the former did not have as great a deterrent effect on interstate commerce as the latter. In contrast to the flat tax, the gross receipts tax did not single out interstate commerce and treat it disproportionately. Instead, Justice Strong's *Gross Receipts* opinion referred, inter alia, to taxes on transportation and to taxes on its fruits.[22] His opinion is confusing and has received well-deserved criticism.

Three dissenting justices in the *Gross Receipts* case added to the confusion already created by the majority opinion. They described *Freight Tax* as setting forth the rule that taxes on transportation are unconstitutional.[23]

Robbins v. Shelby County Taxing District (1887). This case held that the Shelby County Taxing District, which included Memphis, Tennessee, could not constitutionally require all those offering goods for sale in the taxing district and not having a regular licensed house of business, to pay a $10 per week or a $25 per month tax before offering goods for sale. The majority opinion, written by Justice Bradley, emphasized the tax's deterrent effect on out-of-state sellers. Justice Bradley stated that "to say that such a tax is not a burden upon interstate commerce, is to speak at least unadvisedly and without due attention to the truth of things."[24]

The Court, rather than relying on a finding of fact that the challenged taxes were a sufficient impediment to out-of-state vendors to constitute an unjustifiable regulation of commerce, cited *Freight Tax* for the rule that "interstate commerce cannot be taxed at all."[25] As a marginal cost analysis demonstrates, the tax challenged in *Robbins* had a highly protectionist effect. The marginal costs of attempting to make a sale in the jurisdiction were zero for those already there, but they were substantial for those who had no permanent place of business and had not paid the tax. In his dissent, Chief Justice Waite emphasized, as had the dissenters in *Freight Tax,* the facial neutrality of the statute. He argued that the tax was not discriminatory because the fee was required from all taxpayers without a permanent place of business.

American Trucking Associations v. Scheiner (1987). This case, resolved a commerce clause challenge to an annual axle tax imposed on all trucks using Pennsylvania's highways. Although the industry was different—trucking, instead of railroads—the facts of the 1987 case were similar to the facts of the 1873 *Case of the State Freight Tax.* Pennsylvania imposed an annual marker fee or axle tax of $36 per axle on trucks weighing more than 26,000 pounds operating on Pennsylvania's highways, and it delivered a rebate to trucks traveling less than 2,000 miles. Evidence indicated that tax revenues for the fiscal years 1982-1983 and 1983-1984 were about $136,000,000, with $107,000,000 derived from trucks registered in states other than Pennsylvania. The cost per mile for out-of-state trucks was approximately five times more than the cost per mile incurred by local trucks.

The challenged Pennsylvania tax scheme had both impost and anticompetitive effects. The impost effects were substantial. As was the case with railroad freight more than 100 years earlier, most freight shipped by truck from the mid-Atlantic or New England states had to pass through Pennsylvania on its way west. The Pennsylvania tax also had visible protectionist effects. An out-of-state trucker who considered using Pennsylvania's highways faced higher costs for the first few uses of those highways—$180 for a five-axle truck.

A divided Court held the challenged tax unconstitutional. As in the earlier 1873 and 1887 cases, neither the majority opinion by Justice Stevens nor the dissenting opinions by Justices O'Connor and Scalia analyzed the challenged tax in terms of its effect on interstate commerce. Instead, the majority applied the "internal consistency" test, which asks whether a tax would impermissibly interfere with free trade if every state applied the tax.[26] The challenged tax failed the test. Justice O'Connor contended that precedent supported the flat tax. As did the dissenters in *Freight Tax* and *Robbins,* Justice Scalia argued that the tax should be upheld because it was facially neutral. He also argued that there was no constitutional support for the internal consistency test.

American Trucking should not have been a difficult case; the Court should have invalidated Pennsylvania's tax for the reasons advanced by Alexander Hamilton in *The Federalist,* No. 7, in which Hamilton warned of "the opportunities which some states would have of rendering others tributary to them by commercial regulations." He pointed to New York as his example of a state which could impose duties that would ultimately be borne "by the inhabitants of the two other states in the capacity of consumers of what we import."[27]

ANALYSIS AND PROPOSAL: THE ROLE OF COMPARATIVE TAX COSTS IN SUPREME COURT DECISIONS

The free market ideas espoused by Adam Smith, James Madison, Alexander Hamilton, and other intellectuals have guided the Court's consideration of constitutional challenges to state taxes. Although the Court discusses formal tests and rules, free market ideas provide a better basis for understanding and predicting those decisions. Economic ideas have always been the basis for the holdings of these cases. The question then is whether the Court should explicitly, rather than implicitly, rely on free market ideas in its decisionmaking.

The Court's Traditional Consideration of Economic Effects

In commerce clause cases, the Supreme Court has repeatedly written inexact opinions, with inexplicit grounds of decision, while actually relying on economic arguments. This characterization has practical significance because a lawyer who uses economic arguments and relative tax cost analysis in commerce clause challenges to state taxes has a better chance of winning cases. Even if a court applies a doctrinal test in its opinion, it will nevertheless announce a holding that advances the societal interest in the free market. Therefore, a lawyer should always introduce evidence comparing tax costs for in-state and out-of-state taxpayers and emphasize that comparison in the litigation strategy. As the following comments demonstrate, a lawyer who does not make this comparison risks losing a good case.

Thomas Reed Powell (1918, pp. 917-918) recognized that the Supreme Court implicitly relies on economic effects:

If we discard all the doctrinal disquisitions of the opinions and look only to the results of the decisions, we find that the controlling motive of the Supreme Court has been the desire to prevent the states from imposing on interstate commerce any peculiar or unusual burden. Where the court has been assured that the state did not have a device which might be operated to discriminate against interstate commerce, taxation of that commerce has been allowed. When it imposes license or franchise or occupation taxes, or adopts any other revenue devices which are not certain to fall equally on all enterprise within the state, then it runs the risk of disappointment whenever it seeks to lay its hand on interstate commerce. What the court is insistent upon is that there must be adequate safeguards against subjecting interstate commerce to heavier taxation than local commerce. It does not require the states to confer a bounty upon interstate commerce by exempting it from burdens which competing business must bear.

Supreme Court Justice Stone also recognized the importance of a challenged tax's effect on interstate commerce. Dissenting in *Di Santo v. Pennsylvania* (1927, p. 44), he criticized the majority for basing its decision on whether the state tax was a prohibited "direct" tax on interstate commerce or a permitted "indirect" tax:

In this case the traditional test of the limit of state action by inquiring whether the interference with commerce is direct or indirect seems to me too mechanical, too uncertain in its application, and too remote from actualities, to be of value. In thus making use of the expressions, "direct" and "indirect" interference with commerce, we are doing little more than using labels to describe a result rather than any trustworthy formula by which it is reached.

Stone's insight was not new to him and had been recognized by others. For example, the editors of the 1927 *Texas Law Review* stated that "probably the result reached by a majority of the Court in applying the test...depends not so much on the application of the tests as such as on their opinion of the ultimate effect of the decision on the free flow of interstate or foreign commerce."[28] Surprisingly, when Justice Stone later wrote a majority opinion in *Western Livestock v. Bureau of Revenue* (1938), he did not adopt a factual approach but instead announced a new test. He emphasized protecting against multiple burdens and ensuring that the challenged tax was not susceptible of replication in other states, thereby imposing a cumulative burden on interstate commerce.

The risk-of-multiple-burdens test was not a significant improvement on previous tests. It did not completely reflect the judicial decisionmaking process, and the Court continued to implicitly rely on economic factors. For example, two years after *Western Livestock,* in *McGoldrick v. Berwind-White Coal Mining Company* (1940), the Court upheld New York's two percent sales tax on coal shipped from Pennsylvania. Because both states could tax the transaction—although Pennsylvania did not do so—the risk-of-multiple-burdens test dictated invalidating New York's tax. Nevertheless, Justice Stone, writing for the Court, upheld the tax and reached the correct result. Free market doctrine dictated upholding New York's tax so that the New York buyer's choice would depend on the relative cost of the coal, not on saving taxes. As far as doctrine and tests are concerned, Chief Justice Hughes's dissent in *McGoldrick* more faithfully applied Stone's risk-of-multiple-burdens approach than Stone's opinion for the Court.

Several years later, Justice Frankfurter, writing for the Court in *Freeman v. Hewit* (1946, p. 252) expressly recognized the importance of specific facts and effects in previous decisions: "To attempt to harmonize all that has been said in the past would neither clarify what has gone before nor guide the future. Suffice it to say that especially in this field opinions must be read in the setting of the particular cases and as the product of preoccupation with their special facts." Justice Rutledge, concurring in the same case, made a similar observation (*Freeman v. Hewit,* 1946, p. 270):

Judgments of this character and magnitude cannot be made by labels or formulae. They require much more than pointing to a word. It is for this reason that increasingly with the years emphasis has been placed upon practical consequences and effects, either actual or threatened, of questioned legislation to block or impede interstate commerce or place it at practical disadvantage with the local trade.

All of the above quotations were made by "experts"—jurists or scholars who were knowledgeable of and interested in commerce clause issues. They recognized that the Court's motivation for a decision did not always expressly appear in an opinion. The following section considers whether the Court should abandon such "judicial dishonesty" and explicitly state the basis for its decisionmaking.

A Proposal for Future Decisionmaking

The Supreme Court should adopt a more direct approach to deciding commerce clause challenges to state taxes by studying free market goals and analyzing whether a challenged tax interferes with those goals.[29] This approach is simpler and more straightforward than the traditional indirect approach. Furthermore, the established legal doctrine concerning constitutional challenges to state taxes cannot be managed well in briefs and opinions. Too many doctrines, old cases, and opinions that obscure, rather than illuminate, the real grounds of decision occupy the shelves of legal libraries. Justice O'Connor's dissent in *American Trucking*

Associations v. Scheiner illustrates—as detailed elsewhere—the general misunderstanding of Supreme Court precedents.

CONCLUSION

Historically, tests and doctrines have clouded the Court's vision in its analysis of commerce clause challenges to state taxes. Recently, the clouds have been getting darker. The lawyers who should provide some of the light in their briefs are not as well trained as their predecessors. Furthermore, the academic community offers little help. Few academics consistently teach, research, and write in the area of commerce clause challenges to state taxes. Among those who do write in this area, many only study the subject for a short time and have little training in taxation, case law, and the economics of the free market.

Guidance in the area of commerce clause challenges to state taxes seems needed. I propose the following test. When deciding such a case, a court should ask one question: "Does the challenged tax have effects that place interstate commerce at a disadvantage?" In answering this question, the court should implicitly or explicitly generate factual findings concerning the effects of challenged taxes on interstate commerce, such as comparisons of marginal costs. Expert testimony and a well-prepared factually presented case can help a court in making such a finding. The court should attempt to view the economy from a taxpayer's perspective and not involve itself with higher-order mathematical economics.

NOTES

This chapter is an edited, and shorter, version of "Commerce Clause Challenges to State Taxes," *Minnesota Law Review*, 75, 907 (1991).

1. Challenges to state taxes often receive their first hearing in a state, and not a federal, court because the Tax Injunction Act, 28 U.S.C. §1341 (1988), bars the federal courts from enjoining the collection of state taxes "where a plain, speedy and efficient remedy may be had in the courts of such state."

2. The Supreme Court on occasion does say that it regards a commerce clause issue as a question of fact. For instance, in *Interstate Busses Corp. v. Blodgett* (1928, pp. 245, 251), Justice Stone said: "To gain the relief for which it prays appellant is under the necessity of showing that in actual practice the tax of which it complains falls with disproportionate economic weight on it....The record does not show that it made any attempt to do so." This chapter attempts to do something that the Court has not done; that is, to give general methodological content to Justice Stone's remarks. This

approach differs from that of other articles because it focuses on the variables of economics.

3. Collins (1988) shares with this work a focus on the free market aspects of the commerce clause.

4. *Ozark Pipe Line Corp. v. Monier* (1925).

5. *Moorman Manufacturing Company v. Bair* (1978).

6. *Western Livestock v. Bureau of Revenue* (1938).

7. *Spector Motor Services, Inc. v. O'Connor* (1951).

8. *Complete Auto Transit, Inc. v. Brady* (1977). The test has not been applied as written. See *Commonwealth Edison Co. v. Montana* (1981).

9. *Armco, Inc. v. Hardesty* (1984).

10. Adam Smith's ideas found expression in Article IV of the Articles of Confederation which seemed to provide for the level playing field that Smith envisioned.

11. In Schoettle (1990), I argue that small out-of-state vendors with no physical presence in the market state should be spared collecting a use tax and that a requirement for such collection would violate the commerce clause because of the high administrative costs for the vendor.

12. The period runs from *Freeman v. Hewit* (1946) to *Complete Auto Transit, Inc. v. Brady* (1977).

13. Scholars who write about the nontax aspects of the commerce clause can be grouped according to whether they favor judicial review because of their concerns about economic efficiency and free trade, or whether they favor such review because of their concern with the political process that produced the result the court is reviewing. Pomper (1989) does an excellent job of reviewing and explaining these and other aspects of the commerce clause literature. As to the instant subject, I believe that both economic and political concerns support judicial intervention to hear challenges to state taxes.

14. See, for example, Pomp (1984, p. 943).

15. See, for example, Feldstein (1974).

16. Some of the ideas presented here are related to the Uniform Division of Income for Tax Purposes Act, which is discussed generally in Schoettle (1980).

17. The Supreme Court has from time-to-time embraced the territorial principle (*Wallace v. Hines,* 1920).

18. The California property tax against which the Court provided protection appeared to have no protectionist effects. The Court struck down the tax because of the international ramifications of its application (*Japan Line Ltd. v. County of Los Angeles,* 1972, p. 451-53).

19. Recent examples of complementary tax cases are *Armco, Inc. v. Hardesty* (1984), and *Tyler Pipe Industries, Inc. v. Washington State Department of Revenue* (1987).

20. To maximize the yield from the tax, the state must select a tax rate that causes some potential taxpayers to withdraw from the state. Not until the base starts to decrease does the state have an incentive to lower its tax rate.

21. *Robbins v. Shelby County Taxing District* (1887, p. 494).

22. *State Tax on Railway Gross Receipts* (1873, p. 295). Justice Strong, writing for the Court, stated that: "While it must be conceded that a tax upon interstate transportation is invalid, there seems to be no stronger reason for denying the power

of a state to tax the fruits of such transportation after they have become intermingled with the general property of the carriers, than there is for denying her power to tax goods which have been imported, after their original packages have been broken, and after they have been mixed with the mass of personal property in the country."

23. *State Tax on Railway Gross Receipts* (1873, p. 298). (Miller, Field & Hunt, JJ., dissenting). The dissenters characterized the holding in *Freight Tax* as follows: "And it is there declared that any tax upon the freight so transported, or upon the carrier on account of such transportation, is within the prohibition."

24. *Robbins v. Shelby County Taxing District* (1887, p. 495).

25. *Robbins v. Shelby County Taxing District* (1887, p. 497).

26. See Hellerstein (1988b, p. 187) who concludes that adoption of this doctrine was unnecessary because the case in which it was invoked could have been decided by "a straightforward application of the venerable fair apportionment requirement." Instead, the Supreme Court "has embraced a doctrine of 'internal consistency' that may introduce confusion and uncertainty in an area of the law that has had more than its fair share of both."

27. *The Federalist*, No. 7, at 63 (A. Hamilton) (J. Cooke ed. 1961). The two other states that Hamilton used in his example were Connecticut and New Jersey.

28. "Recent Cases: Constitutional Law—Foreign Commerce—License Tax Placed on Persons Selling Steamship Tickets from or to Foreign Countries," *Texas Law Review, 5,* 318, 319 (1927).

29. Robert Nagel (1985, p. 211) criticizes the Court for adopting a "cumbersome formulaic style."

IV
State Taxation of Telecommunications

Hellerstein and Nugent argue in Chapters 11 and 12, respectively, that changes in the technology and the organization of the telecommunications industry mean that traditional approaches to establishing nexus and apportioning income are no longer applicable. The industry is no longer dominated by a regulated near-monopoly. The technology of telecommunications has moved from poles and wires to microwaves and satellites.

The result of these changes is not only a poor fit between the industry and the statutes designed to tax it. Apportionment patterns have also been dramatically altered. Some state and local governments have seen their revenues shrink as a result of both the restructuring of the Bell System and the changing technology of communication.

In Chapter 11, Hellerstein details the main tax issues that have arisen because of these changes. He concludes that important questions of nexus and apportionment involved in taxing corporate income, sales, and gross receipts remain unresolved. Nugent further analyzes apportionment issues in Chapter 12. He explains that whereas apportionment is always approximate, at best, a different formula will be required for apportioning each tax base. Apportionment for income taxation should measure the extent to which the profits of a business can be attributed to its presence in a state. Apportionment for sales taxation should reflect the locus of the transaction. Both authors urge policymakers to arrive at informed, credible, and rational solutions to the problems that must be faced in determining nexus and apportioning tax bases of the telecommunications industry. But their description of these problems leaves a clear impression that any tax regime cannot escape being arbitrary to a significant degree. Further, reducing the arbitrary element is likely to entail a nontrivial cost in terms of complexity.

11
Critical Issues in State Taxation of Telecommunications

WALTER HELLERSTEIN

The unprecedented legal and technological changes affecting the telecommunications industry in recent years have had significant state tax implications. With the breakup of the Bell System and the replacement of a telecommunications network based on poles and wires with one based on microwave, fiber optic, and satellite technology, many of the assumptions underlying the states' traditional approach to taxation of telecommunications have been undermined. The states can no longer reasonably assume that the objects of their telecommunications taxes are regulated utilities enjoying a legal monopoly in the provision of telecommunications services. Nor can they reasonably assume that the definitions of "telephone" and "telegraph" companies typically employed in their taxing statutes even begin to describe the contemporary telecommunications industry. As a consequence, application of the states' conventional taxing regimes to today's telecommunications industry has become awkward at best and chaotic at worst.

The poor fit between the structure of the industry and the statutes designed to tax it is, however, only a piece of the picture. The metamorphosis of the telecommunications industry has also had dramatic fiscal implications in many states and localities. For example, many localities faced large losses of revenue because of the restructuring of the Bell System that had the effect of removing substantial receipts or property from the local utility tax base. In other states, changes in the telecommunications industry promised large increases in tax revenues because formerly nontaxable transfers of revenues between members of the Bell System resurfaced as separately taxable charges (e.g., access fees) in the transformed telecommunications environment.

These developments have forced the states to reevaluate their telecommunications tax policies. In so doing, they have struggled with a number of broad policy problems, which reflect the concerns identified above: (1) how to accommodate their tax structures to the telecommunications industry's reshaped environment; (2) how to preserve the preexisting telecommunications tax base insofar as it is threatened by the industry's restructuring; and (3) how to redefine the telecommunications tax base in order to capture additional revenue that may be escaping taxation under existing taxing schemes.

At a more mundane level, the transformation of the telecommunications industry has spawned a wide variety of legal issues that are as complex as the underlying technological and regulatory changes themselves. Is an out-of-state company that owns no tangible property in a state but provides long-distance telephone service to in-state customers by leasing circuits from a local operating company a "telephone company" subject to the state's property tax as a public utility; and, if so, how is its property to be assessed?[1] May a state tax a share of a satellite communications company's income derived from the company's ownership interest in satellites that never even pass over the taxing state; and, if so, how should such income be apportioned to the state?[2] Although space limitations preclude a detailed analysis of these and scores of other questions raised by state taxation of telecommunications, it will nevertheless be instructive to examine some of the more significant controversies that have been the focus of recent judicial and legislative attention because they provide a window into the critical issues that are emerging in this area.

TAXATION OF ACCESS CHARGES

Most states impose either sales or gross receipts taxes on telecommunications services. Variations in the scope of these taxes abound, and the legal questions they raise are legion. What is a taxable telecommunications service? What receipts—intrastate, interstate, or some combination thereof—does the state seek to tax? What are the constitutional limitations on the taxation of interstate receipts?

Perhaps the most controversial issue involving sales and gross receipts taxes of telecommunications services is the taxation of access charges. Broadly speaking, access charges are the charges that long distance (interexchange) telephone companies or resellers of telecommunications services pay to local telephone companies for "access" to telephone users through the local exchange network. Prior to the AT&T divestiture, carriers that provided long distance communications in competition with AT&T were required to pay to connect with local exchange companies. No such charges, however, existed within the Bell System, which generated the lion's share of interstate telephone revenues. Reimbursement of the Bell operating companies and independent telephone companies by AT&T for access to the local network was handled through a division of revenues known as "separations and settlements," and was treated essentially as the sharing of toll charges for the joint provision of long distance service. After divestiture, however, the Bell operating companies were required to provide "equal access" to all long distance carriers, including AT&T. As a result, the preexisting system was replaced by one of tariffed access charges paid by all long distance carriers on the same basis and at the same rates.

The appropriate treatment of access charges has been the subject of both judicial and legislative attention. In a number of cases, the essential question was whether the tax should apply to the access charges received by the local exchange company from the long distance carrier in light of the fact that the long distance carrier would ultimately include the access charges in bills to its customers—a service that is itself taxable by the state. Taxation of access charges paid by the long distance carrier would thus result in "double taxation" of the same service and would, in the context of retail sales taxation of telephone services, violate the antipyramiding objective that underlies the sale for resale exemption.

The New York State Tax Commission embraced these views in holding that the state's tax on furnishing of utility services measured by 3 percent of the utility's gross income should not include the local exchange company's receipts from access charges. The statute was intended (like a retail sales tax) to apply only to amounts received for services rendered for "ultimate" consumption by the purchaser, and the Commission construed the levy in light of that intent:

The access service provided to the long distance carrier constitutes a "critical element of the final product sold to customers." Granted, the sale of the access service by NY Tel is not a sale for resale as such, but a resale as a component part of the service sold by the long distance carrier. This is a transaction of the type envisaged by the sales tax regulation which states that the [sales tax] resale exclusion is applicable "where a person, in the course of his business operations, purchases...services which he intends to sell...as a component part of other...services."[3]

The Wisconsin Department of Revenue issued a similar ruling declaring that Wisconsin Bell's sale of access charges to long distance carriers was not subject to the retail sales tax because the long distance carriers would resell the service to the ultimate consumers.[4] The Wisconsin legislature, however, faced with a revenue shortfall for 1985-1986, statutorily reversed the ruling by explicitly extending the state's sales tax of access charges to interexchange carriers.[5] But the Wisconsin Supreme Court held that this provision violated the equal protection clause because the tax was imposed only on local access charges to interexchange carriers but not on similar charges to other local exchange carriers or to resellers of telephone services.[6]

The treatment of local access charges has also been the subject of controversy in Michigan. In 1984, the Michigan Court of Appeals, without specifically addressing the sale for resale question, upheld the application of the state's use tax to access charges paid by MCI to Michigan Bell in an opinion that was concerned largely with federal constitutional issues.[7] In a subsequent decision, however, the same court took a somewhat narrower approach to the scope of a taxable telecommunications service in Michigan:

We believe that §3a of the Use Tax Act treats a taxable communication as a complete, end-to-end communication. Under that section, telephone calls can be grouped into three categories: a local telephone call, an intrastate long-distance call, and an interstate long-distance telephone call. Under §3a, the first two items are taxed and the third is not.[8]

The case therefore held that the purchase of access services by an interexchange carrier from a local telephone company was not subject to the use tax.

A number of states have dealt with the issue of access charges under their sales and gross receipts taxes by specific legislation. For example, Ohio exempts from its sales tax on telecommunications services sales of telecommunications to a provider of telecommunications services, including access services.[9] Tennessee's sales tax on telecommunications services likewise exempts access charges from the levy.[10] And Texas's sales tax on telecommunications has been construed not to apply to charges for access services.[11] On the other hand, Washington specifically provides for the taxation of access services under local business activities taxes.[12]

TAXATION OF INTERSTATE SERVICES

Taxation of interstate telecommunications services has emerged as another controversial issue in the state tax field. For much of our constitutional history, it was thought that interstate commerce could not be taxed at all, and therefore the revenues derived from interstate telecommunications were immunized from state taxation.[13] In recent years, however, as the Supreme Court has broadened the states' authority to tax interstate commerce, the question of the states' power to tax interstate telecommunications services has been raised anew.

In *Goldberg v. Sweet*,[14] the Supreme Court addressed the question whether Illinois' Telecommunications Excise Tax Act violated the commerce clause. The tax was imposed on the "act or privilege" of "originating" or "receiving" interstate telecommunications in the state at the rate of 5 percent of the gross charge for the telecommunications. The tax applied only to calls charged to an Illinois service address, which the Court understood to mean the address where the telephone equipment was located, regardless of where the telephone call charge was billed or paid. An identical 5 percent tax was also imposed on intrastate telecommunications by another section of the Act. To avoid multiple taxation of the call by more than one state, the Act provided a credit to any taxpayer upon proof that the taxpayer had paid a tax to another state on the same interstate telecommunication taxed by Illinois. The tax was collected by the retailer of the taxable telecommunication (i.e., the telecommunications provider) from the consumer whose service address was charged.

The critical issue in the case was whether the Illinois tax was fairly apportioned to the taxpayer's activities in the state. The requirement that a tax affecting interstate commerce be fairly apportioned to the taxpayer's activities in the taxing state is a venerable one. It has acquired greater significance, however, as the Court's decisions have broadened the states' taxing powers. With the abandonment of the formal criteria that once created an irreducible zone of tax immunity for interstate commerce, the Court's emphasis has shifted from the question of whether interstate commerce may be taxed at all to the question of whether interstate commerce is being made to bear its fair share—or more than its fair share—of the state tax burden. If a tax is fairly apportioned to the taxpayer's activities in the taxing state, there is no risk, at least in principle, that a tax will subject a taxpayer engaged in interstate commerce to more than its fair share of the tax burden and expose it to a risk of multiple taxation not borne by local commerce.

In *Goldberg*, the taxpayers[15] contended that Illinois' telecommunications tax violated the commerce clause's fair apportionment requirement because it was levied on the gross charge for each telephone call. They argued that the fair apportionment requirement compelled Illinois to include within its tax base only that portion of the gross charge for each interstate telecommunication that reflected the ratio of in-state activity to total activity associated with the telecommunication. They pointed to the apportionment formulas that the states have developed and the Court has approved for apportioning the tax bases of other instrumentalities of interstate commerce engaged in land, water, and air transportation, based on such factors as track mileage,[16] barge line mileage,[17] and revenue tons.[18] By analogy, they claimed, Illinois was required to apportion taxable gross receipts from interstate telecommunications by some equivalent ratio, such as the miles the electronic signals traveled within Illinois to the total miles traveled.

The short answer to the taxpayers' claim was that Illinois *did* apportion its tax. By taxing only the receipts from calls originating or terminating in Illinois that were charged to an Illinois service address, Illinois effectively taxed only half the universe of interstate telecommunications originating or terminating in Illinois. This assumes, quite reasonably I believe, that roughly half of the calls originating or terminating in Illinois are charged to an Illinois service address with the other half charged to the service address of the caller in the other state in which the call originated or terminated. Because only states of origination or termination have the power to impose a tax on an interstate telecommunication—a fact made clear elsewhere in the Court's opinion—Illinois' "charged-to-an-Illinois-service-address" limitation on its tax effected a 50 percent apportionment of the tax base to Illinois. Such an apportionment ought to satisfy constitutional strictures in a domain in which "rough approximation" rather than "precision" is the controlling standard.[19]

The Court, however, took a more circuitous route to the same conclusion. Invoking the language of *Container Corp. of America v. Franchise Tax Board*,[20] the Court viewed the fair apportionment requirement as triggering an inquiry into the question of whether a tax is "internally and externally consistent." The Court's "internal consistency" test, which the Court has recently grafted onto the body of its commerce clause doctrine (Hellerstein, 1988), requires that a tax "be structured so that if every State were to impose an identical tax, no multiple taxation would result."[21] The Illinois levy plainly satisfied this standard. If every state confined its telecommunications tax levy to receipts from interstate telephone calls that were charged to an in-state service address, only one state would tax the receipts from each interstate call.

The Court then turned to the "external consistency" standard, which reflects familiar commerce clause doctrine requiring fair apportionment. Here the Court confronted a thornier problem. The Illinois tax was clearly unapportioned, in the sense that the tax applied to the gross charge of an interstate activity, and there was no formulary apportionment of the tax base to reflect in-state activity. The Court responded to this objection on several—not wholly consistent—grounds. The tax was like a sales tax and did not need to be apportioned; the tax was fairly apportioned because it created little risk of multiple taxation; the tax created some risk of multiple taxation, but provision of a tax credit eliminated the possibility of actual multiple taxation; and true apportionment of the tax base, on a mileage or other geographic basis, was administratively and technologically impossible in light of the complexity of contemporary telecommunications networks.

As indicated above, the Court's conclusion that the Illinois tax was fairly apportioned was justified. It is unfortunate, however, that the Court failed to embrace the most straightforward response to the fair apportionment claim. Each of the justifications the Court advanced for its conclusion that the Illinois tax was fairly apportioned has weaknesses,[22] and they may come back to haunt the Court in other contexts.

In any event, the Court's decision in *Goldberg* sustaining Illinois' tax on the receipts from interstate telecommunications services has opened the door for other states to follow suit, and a number have done so. Moreover, the Multistate Tax Commission has promulgated a Model Telecommunications Excise Tax, which imposes a tax on interstate telecommunications services, and this will undoubtedly provide added impetus for the states to tax interstate telecommunications services. It remains to be seen whether the states' widespread adoption of taxes on interstate telecommunications will lead to the multiple taxation of such services about which some taxpayers have warned.

GROSS RECEIPTS TAXES ON INTEREXCHANGE CARRIERS

More than half the states impose selective gross receipts taxes on telecommunications companies, usually as part of a tax imposed on utilities doing business in the state. The historical rationale for many of these levies was that they constituted a quid pro quo for the special rights and privileges that the states granted to utilities, such as monopoly power within a defined service area, the power of eminent domain, and the right to use public rights-of-way. For many years, this rationale justified the imposition of utility gross receipts taxes on the telecommunications industry, which was essentially a regulated monopoly protected from competition by the states. With the dramatic changes that the telecommunications industry has undergone in recent years, the justification for applying utility gross receipts taxes to the competitive segment of the telecommunications industry has been brought into question.

There can be little doubt that changes in the regulatory and technological environment of the telecommunications industry have eroded the historical rationale for including the competitive segment of the telecommunications industry—the long-distance or interexchange carriers—within a utility gross receipts tax. Interexchange carriers are no longer protected from competition by the state, so the argument that they should be subject to special taxes in exchange for the grant of a monopoly franchise no longer applies. Other special privileges, such as eminent domain and the uncompensated or subsidized use of public rights-of-way, are today largely confined to the local operating companies and thus provide no continuing justification for subjecting interexchange carriers to a special tax regime. Nor (with the exception of AT&T in approximately half the states) do interexchange carriers conduct their business within the framework of pervasive economic regulation designed to ensure the delivery of telecommunications services to all of a state's residents at reasonable cost in return for a reasonable return on investment. In short, interexchange carriers no longer have the essential characteristics of public utilities that would justify taxing them under a scheme designed for public utilities.

A number of studies have concluded that interexchange carriers should no longer be subjected to utility gross receipts taxes. In 1985, the Florida Telecommunications Task Force in its Final Report to Governor Graham "acknowledged that the traditional quid pro quo for the state subjecting an industry to gross receipts taxation is some form of state protection for that industry from market competition." It went on to observe that "recent technological change has served to increase substantially competitive market forces in the telecommunications industry during the same time that regulatory agencies have realized a reduced role in industry protection."[23] Although the Florida Task Force recommended retention of the gross receipts tax on interexchange carriers, it did so not because this represented sound tax policy but rather because revenue concerns overrode other considerations.

In 1986, the Minnesota Tax Study Commission issued a final report in which it considered all aspects of the state's tax structure. With respect to the taxation of the telecommunications industry, which has long been subject to a gross receipts tax in Minnesota, the report (Minnesota Tax Study Commission, 1986, p. 53) recommended that the legislature "maintain the gross receipts tax on telephone and telegraph companies for one or two years to permit planning for replacement of the tax with a property tax that treats telecommunications business as other commercial/industrial activities are treated."

A Touche Ross & Co. report considered various alternatives to Pennsylvania's existing system of taxing the telecommunications industry, which includes a utility gross receipts tax. The report recognized the general inappropriateness of applying a utility gross receipts tax to competitive segments of the telecommunications industry, and three of the four proposed alternatives eliminated the gross receipts tax on interexchange carriers (Touche Ross & Co., 1986, pp. 69-87).

A 1985 report of the staff of the Texas Lieutenant Governor and the Comptroller of Public Accounts considered four options relating to the state's then-existing gross receipts tax on the telecommunications industry. In evaluating the advantages and disadvantages of each option, the report recognized that substituting a sales tax for the gross receipts tax on interexchange carriers would treat competing services more uniformly (Texas, State of, 1985, pp. 20-22). The advantages of retaining the gross receipts tax on the telecommunications industry included familiarity, simplicity (because no legislative action would be required), and uncertainty over the impact of changing the existing system, because the telecommunications industry is in a state of flux.

Case (1986, p. 58) observed that the historical justification for imposing gross receipts taxes on the telecommunications industry had "eroded." He noted that "differential taxes on telecommunications firms are not neutral with respect to economic choices; they distort both consumption and investment decisions leading to a misallocation of society's valuable resources." And he concluded that the justification for special tax treatment of the telecommunications industry has ended, and that "the time has come for states to treat telecommunications firms like other businesses."

Wassall and Sullivan (1988, pp. 342-47) addressed state taxation of telecommunications and concluded that "the present system of state telecommunications taxation could be improved upon with respect to equity, efficiency, and ease and cost of administration if the gross receipts tax on telecommunications were eliminated."

In short, there is no tax policy justification for including interexchange services within the scope of a utility gross receipts tax base. The conclusion is supported by the erosion of the historical rationale for applying a utility gross receipts tax to the contemporary telecommunications industry; by widely accepted principles of tax policy, which militate against subjecting interexchange carriers to a special tax on their gross receipts; and by the findings reached by a number of independent studies that have examined this question.

OTHER SIGNIFICANT ISSUES

One could multiply the length of this paper many times, if one were to treat in any depth the myriad issues that are arising today in the field of state taxation of telecommunications. Although constraints of time and space preclude such treatment, a brief summary of some of these issues gives one a taste of the questions that we are likely to be confronting well into the twenty-first century.

The Florida Department of Revenue has ruled that its utility gross receipts tax applies to an information service company's communication charge for telephone network hook-up but not to its charges for equipment rental and service.[24] A New York tribunal has ruled that a long distance telephone company was not subject to a sales tax on the intrastate components of its interstate service.[25]   Kansas has adopted a method of apportioning the business income of telecommunications companies to the state by multiplying such income by a fraction whose numerator is the information-carrying capacity of wire and fiber optic cable available for use in Kansas and whose denominator is the information-carrying capacity of wire and fiber optic cable available for use everywhere during the tax year.[26]   In Vermont, a company providing operator-assisted long distance telephone service by directing calls to one of the long distance carriers available to transmit the call is not subject to gross receipts tax if it does not own or operate any telephone lines or transmission facilities in the state.[27]   In Alabama, telephone toll resale carriers were not subject to the gross receipts tax, which was held to apply only to those companies providing local exchange service.[28]   In Illinois, on the other hand, persons who resell telecommunications (including hotels that charge guests for telephone calls and universities that sell services to students living in dormitories) must collect and pay the Illinois telecommunications excise tax based on the gross charges, that is, the amount charged to customers for sending or receiving telecommunications in Illinois. In Wisconsin, a telecommunications company that provided long distance telephone service in conjunction with other telephone companies was entitled to exclude its local "access service" costs from gross revenues in determining its telephone license tax.[29]   And in Texas, a taxpayer's rentals of radio repeaters were telecommunications services subject to tax under Texas' sales tax, despite the taxpayer's claim that the Federal Communications Commission prohibited the taxpayer from providing common carrier telecommunications services.[30]

CONCLUSION

This brief survey of the critical issues emerging in the field of state taxation of telecommunications demonstrates above all else that there is a pressing need for continuing policy and legal analysis of these issues. State policymakers and lawmakers must familiarize themselves with the reshaped economic and regulatory environment in which telecommunications companies operate so that they may create fair and rational regimes for taxation of the telecommunications industry.

NOTES

1. See *United States Transmission Systems, Inc. v. Board of Assessment Appeals,* 715 P.2d 1249 (Colo. 1986), answering the first question "yes" and sustaining an assessment based on a unitary system valuation.

2. See *Communications Satellite Corp. v. Franchise Tax Board.,* 156 Cal. App. 3d 726, 203 Cal. Rptr. 770 (1984), *appeal dismissed,* 469 U.S. 1201 (1985), answering the first question "yes" and sustaining an apportionment formula that assigned receipts and extraterrestrial property California based on the relative amounts of in-state terrestrial activity.

3. Advisory Opinion, New York State Tax Commission, Petition No. C840627B (1985, September 20).

4. Declaratory Ruling SR-1, Wisconsin Department of Revenue (1985, May 2).

5. See Wis. Stat. §77.51(14)(m).

6. *GTE Sprint Communication Corp. v. Wisconsin Bell, Inc.,* 155 Wis. 2d 184, 454 N.W.2d 797 (1990).

7. *MCI Telecommunications v. Department of Treasury,* 136 Mich. App. 28, 355 N.W.2d 627 (1984).

8. *GTE Sprint Communications Corp. v. Department of Treasury,* 179 Mich. App. 276, 445 N.W.2d 476, 480 (1989).

9. Ohio Rev. Stat. §5739.01(AA)(4).

10. Tenn. Code Ann. §67-7-6-342.

11. 34 Tex. Admin. Code §3.344(f).

12. Rev. Code of Wash. §35.21.715.

13. See *Cooney v. Mountain States Telephone & Telegraph Co.,* 294 U.S. 384 (1935).

14. 488 U.S. 252 (1989).

15. The named plaintiff, Goldberg, was a taxpayer whose liability arose out of the telephone calls charged to his service address. However, GTE Sprint Communications Corporation, whose challenge to the Illinois tax was also before the Court in a companion case (*GTE Communications Corp. v. Sweet*), was technically a tax collector rather than a taxpayer. For sake of simplicity, all challengers to the tax will be referred to as taxpayers.

16. See *Pittsburgh, C., C. & St. L. Ry. v. Backus,* 154 U.S. 421 (1894).

17. See *Ott v. Mississippi Valley Barge Line Co.,* 336 U.S. 169 (1949).

18. See *Braniff Airways, Inc. v. Nebraska State Board of Equalization,* 347 U.S. 590 (1947).

19. See *Illinois Central R.R. v. Minnesota,* 309 U.S. 157, 161 (1940).

20. 463 U.S. 159, 169-70 (1983).

21. *Goldberg,* 488 U.S. at 261.

22. In Hellerstein (1988a), I have explained the weaknesses of each of the four justifications advanced by the Court. .

(1) "The tax was like a sales tax and did not need to be apportioned." It is true that the tax had many of the characteristics of a retail sales tax in that it was assessed on the individual consumer, it was measured by the price of the service sold, and it was collected by the retailer. It is also true that retail sales taxes generally are not apportioned. Our tolerance of unapportioned sales taxes is largely a creature of administrative necessity and represents no more than a second-best solution to the fair apportionment of receipts from an interstate transaction over which more than one state may legitimately exercise taxing power. Moreover, the Court has unjustifiably extended its tolerance of unapportioned retail sales to unapportioned business gross receipts taxes.

Because the line between retail sales taxes and general business gross receipts taxes is not always clear (at least to the Court), and because there is a risk that the Court may extend its analysis of the retail gross receipts tax in *Goldberg* to the business gross receipts taxes that many states impose on telecommunications and other public service companies, it would have been better if the Court had not put its imprimatur on an unapportioned levy in this context.

(2) "The tax was fairly apportioned because it created little risk of multiple taxation." This is essentially a non sequitur. While it is true that the fair apportionment requirement is designed to prevent multiple taxation, it does not follow that any tax that does not create the risk of multiple taxation is apportioned fairly. Wholly apart from its role in preventing multiple taxation, the fair apportionment criterion serves to limit the territorial reach of state tax power by requiring that the state's tax base correspond to the taxpayer's in-state presence. *Norfolk & Western Ry. v. Missouri State Tax Commission*, 390 U.S. 317, 323-35 (1968). There may be cases in which a state's tax creates no risk of multiple taxation but nevertheless involves unquestioned extraterritorial taxation—for example, if a state sought to tax the unapportioned income of all corporations doing business in the state but granted a credit for other states' taxes. In such cases, it is important that we not lose sight of the fact that there is more to the fair apportionment criterion than avoiding the risk of multiple taxation. The Court's opinion is unhelpful in that respect.

(3) "The tax created some risk of multiple taxation, but provision of a tax credit eliminated the possibility of actual multiple taxation." The provision of a tax credit does not make an unapportioned tax "fairly apportioned," even though it may deal with the multiple taxation issue. The Court's opinion may lead some readers to the opposite conclusion.

(4) "True apportionment of the tax base, in the sense of division of the tax base on a mileage or other geographic basis, was administratively and technologically impossible in light of the complexity of contemporary telecommunications networks." As noted in the text above, this conclusion is essentially untrue in light of the possibility of dividing the tax base on a 50-50 split between the state of the calls' origin and destination. Moreover, it may encourage states to adopt crude approaches to apportionment of technologically complex industries, such as financial services, when in fact more precise ways of measuring in-state presence are feasible. See, for example, the Multistate Tax Commission's Proposed Regulations for Apportioning the Income of the Financial Services Industry, 1989 Multistate Tax Commission Rev. 17 (March 1989).

23. Letter from Co-Chairmen Joseph P. Cresse and Randy Miller to Governor Bob Graham, reproduced in Florida Telecommunications Task Force, *Report of the Florida Telecommunications Task Force*, Tallahassee, Feb. 1, 1985.

24. Florida Department of Revenue, Technical Assistance Advisement, No. 91(B)-001, March 8, 1991.

25. *Southern Pacific Communications Co. v. State Tax Commission*, New York Division of Tax Appeals, Tax Appeals Tribunal, No. 800275, May 15, 1991.

26. H.B. 2492, 1991 Kans. Laws.

27. Vermont Commissioner of Taxes, Formal Ruling 90-4 (1990, July 10).

28. *State Department of Revenue v. Telnet Corp.*, Alabama Civil Court of Appeals, Feb. 27, 1991.

29. *Schneider Communications, Inc. v. Wisconsin Department of Revenue*, Wisconsin Tax Appeals Commission, Jan. 3, 1991.

30. Decision of the Comptroller of Public Accounts, Hearing No. 25,709 (1990, November 8).

12
Apportionment of Telecommunications Interstate Attributes for Income, Consumption, and Property Tax Purposes

PATRICK J. NUGENT

Drawing on NTA's solicitation for membership, its unique contribution in the broad field of tax policy is an opportunity for academicians, tax administrators, and taxpayers to exchange views. The end of that exchange, as I would see it, is an exposure of alternative policy positions, or opportunities to differ in the interest of intellectual growth and policy evolution. So if we say nothing controversial here we have wasted an opportunity and have been unfaithful to the challenge of NTA.

At the outset I must caution you that the views which I will express are entirely my own. They do not necessarily coincide with positions take by my company, the management of the MCI tax department, or even those of my colleagues charged with compliance with myriad tax laws, rules, regulations and practices.

My assigned topic is interstate apportionment in the telecommunications business. Apportionment is required in three areas of taxation: apportionment of net income for income tax purposes; apportionment of revenue for consumption (sales, use, and gross receipts) tax purposes; and apportionment of value for property tax purposes. Apportionment for income taxation is meant to measure the relationship of a taxpayer with a state—that is, to measure the contribution that a presence within a state makes toward achieving profit for the business. Apportionment for consumption taxation is used to identify the source of revenue for both sales and use tax purposes—that is, to establish a locus of the transaction. Apportionment for property taxation assigns a value to the interstate attributes of tangible property for the purpose of local ad valorem taxes.

It is necessary here at the beginning to understand something of the history of the modern, competitive telecommunications business in this country, and of the evolution of its taxation. Hellerstein (Chapter 11) has described enough of the particulars of the current forms of telecommunications taxation to establish a basis from which I proceed to argue in favor of different approaches to apportionment of net income, property values, and taxable revenue for consumption tax purposes.

HISTORY OF THE MODERN, COMPETITIVE TELECOMMUNICATIONS INDUSTRY

The history of the industry really begins in the late 1960s with a number of court decisions allowing new entry into the telecommunications equipment and service businesses by persons in competition with the then-existing monopoly of AT&T. The radical change in the business climaxed in 1983, when AT&T and the Justice Department agreed to the divestiture of the local exchange telephone companies by AT&T.

Leaving aside the many independent local telephone companies and other holding companies, such as United and GTE because they are not broadly relevant, AT&T was the universe for tax policy and practice. The statutes were drawn and the practices established with AT&T in mind.

Further leaving aside the nonservice subsidiaries of AT&T (manufacturing and research), one company with approximately fifty local service subsidiaries constituted the telephone industry. Each AT&T subsidiary was limited to providing local service within one state, and the Long-lines Division of the parent provided long distance, intercity service nationwide. Accordingly, the local companies had no interstate business and no revenue or property to apportion. So the question of apportionment of interstate attributes was concerned solely with the parent, AT&T.

Its interstate business was carried on in a form AT&T has characterized as a partnership among the parent and its subsidiaries. A long distance call originated in a local exchange company, passed through the Long-lines Division, and terminated in a local exchange company. Through an internal process called "division of revenues," the intercity revenue was divided among the participating entities. Because each local company engaged only in an intrastate business, its share of the long distance revenue was fully taxed in its state. The parent apportioned its share of the revenue according to a home-grown formula called the "fifty-state study."

This approach was accepted, I believe, for several reasons. First, there was a rather broad acceptance of the idea that taxing interstate telecommunications could be held to violate the interstate commerce clause of the U.S. Constitution. So challenging the system invited a risk that there was more to lose than to gain. Second, a significant portion of the revenue was taxed by the states, so efforts to disturb the apportionment would have borne little practical fruit. Third, the perceived integrity of the taxpayer and the complexity of its operations made audit of the "fifty-state study" unwarranted and impractical. State tax agencies may also have placed some reliance on the regulatory process for a measure of comfort in the company's reporting.

That was how the industry worked and was taxed when the new, competitive companies, initially MCI and Sprint, entered the business. All intercity calls originated and terminated in a local exchange company, the long distance signal carried by one of the three interexchange companies. The form of the intercompany revenue-sharing has been altered, but it remains essentially unchanged. The local companies report all revenue from interstate business as intrastate access revenue, and the long distance companies apportion.

APPORTIONMENT OF INTERSTATE NET INCOME

To understand the present argument, temporarily put aside your notions of rightness in apportionment theory and disregard the line of court cases which seemingly resolve much historical dispute. Bear in mind, also, that this is not an authoritative legal brief. If I could do that it would not be necessary to suggest a scholarly investigation. The courts do not have appropriate laws to contest. Also, they must labor under antiquated statutes and precedents. Although scattered support for my proposition can be found, if it were substantial and convincing, I'd be in court rather than here.

Purpose of Income Apportionment

The purpose of income apportionment is to measure the relationship of a taxpayer with a state.[1] It is clear that the purpose is not to accurately calculate profit. "[A] 'rough approximation' of the corporate income that is 'reasonably related to the activities conducted within the taxing state'" is good enough.[2] It is the reasonable relationship with the state that determines the measure of tax, that is, "whether the taxing power exerted by the state bears fiscal relation to protection, opportunities, and benefits given by the state."[3] Judicial evaluation of the acceptability of apportionment methods has matured to a rather mechanical analysis of the Court's four-prong test, severely mitigating the element of judgement as to reasonableness. Nonetheless, the Supreme Court decisions provide a reasonable basis from which to begin a rational—as compared to legal—analysis.

Methods in Use

AT&T continues to use its unique apportionment method for income tax purposes, at least in some states. Other long distance companies have been forced to make adaptations of existing apportionment methods. These methods are an amalgam of techniques designed to establish a measure of reasonable relationship for manufacturing and product marketing companies and for personal service companies. They are not designed to establish a relationship for a service that occurs simultaneously in two or more states. The adaptations are the source of inappropriate apportionment methods which neither reflect the nature of telecommunications nor recognize the proper tax reach of state and local governments in an age of high-technology information transfer. Rather than making an effort to understand the industry and develop creative policy to deal with it, tax authorities and taxpayers alike have adapted methods created in an age when the businesses they now influence could not even have been imagined. Voluntary compliance and court confirmation have given historic methods an aura of authority which many have been unwilling to disturb.

Unique Attribute of Interstate Telecommunications

Unlike other businesses, interstate telecommunications can *only* be interstate. By contrast, a purchaser of clothing has the choice of purchasing it from a local store or through a catalogue merchant located out of state. The nature of the product does not dictate either. Moreover, the manufacturer of the shirt can chose to locate a facility in one place and service multiple states through an interstate delivery medium. Alternatively, the manufacturer can choose to service customers by locating distribution points in several states serving many customers "intrastate." In either case, there is a choice. Also, in either case, the location relationships between the seller and buyer are not at all relevant to the nature of the transaction.

Telecommunications customers, however, use long distance services only because they are in both places—that is, only because they are interstate. Were long distance carriers located only where the callers were and not where they chose to call, or vice versa, the long distance companies could not help them. Because we are in both places, and only because we are in both places, we can satisfy their need to communicate. There is a *necessary interstate element* that is lacking in other transactions. In the purchase of a shirt, an interstate element in not necessary. In a call from El Paso to Minneapolis, the interstate element cannot be avoided. This is so obvious, it may seem simple-minded. Its subtlety may escape casual inquiry. But it is a crucial notion. The very nature of an interstate telephone call makes it so dissimilar from other taxable events that it must be evaluated on its own terms. It is neither appropriate nor sufficient to simply adapt a rule designed for some other, fundamentally different, purpose.

Taxation of Interstate Attribute

State income taxes, without exception, attempt to divide the entirety of long distance revenue among the states. What I suggest is that there is some measure of earnings that is exclusively interstate and beyond the reach of any individual state.

An illustration may be helpful. Communications satellites are in an orbit 22,000 miles above the earth. An interstate telecommunication signal transported over a satellite system must physically travel those 22,000 miles to the satellite, and then 22,000 miles returning. Given the most liberal claims to air rights, no state, to my knowledge, will claim jurisdiction up to 22,000 miles. Imagine a triangle connecting the two cities of the call and the satellite. A line parallel to the line between the cities can be drawn somewhere—it matters little where—representing a state's air rights jurisdiction. That line is the base defining a smaller triangle at the top of the original. Assume, further, a mathematical assignment of a portion of the total earnings from the call to each of the two areas—the inscribed triangle at the top and what remains of the original triangle below. Presumably the amount of earnings assigned to the uppermost triangle would be beyond the tax reach of the underlying jurisdictions.

The choice of a satellite to illustrate my argument should not distract from the fact that the same "interstateness" exists in any transmission medium. The fact remains that there is a fundamental attribute in interstate telecommunications that traditional apportionment methods cannot take into account. There is earning in the interstate telecommunications business that should be beyond the reach of state income tax. There is activity that earns income that is not reasonably related to any activities in any states. Devising a solution for eliminating an appropriate amount of exclusively interstate income is beyond the scope of this chapter. Rather, it should be an interesting challenge to scholars to investigate this "interstateness" and to propose a means of recognizing it in income tax statutes.

APPORTIONMENT OF REVENUE (SALES)

If you think about it, apportionment for sales tax purposes almost sounds silly. Sales tax is based on point of sale. Where the sale occurs, the tax is applied. What's to apportion? Point of sale is not one of the more intellectually challenging concepts of tax policy. Even the raging debate surrounding the National Bellas Hess situation avoids this question. That issue is the obligation to collect, not where to collect or remit. If a manufacturer ships a pair of shoes C.O.D. from Maine to Nebraska, the point of sale is Nebraska, and the sale is subject to its tax. If a fur coat is bought in Chicago for delivery and use in Iowa, there is no Chicago tax on it. If a San Francisco lawyer travels to Boston to work on a client matter, he sells himself in Massachusetts.

Yet, *where does a telephone call "occur"?* It can't happen unless the caller dials the number in his or her state. Still, there is no sale, no revenue, unless the phone at the other end is answered. And, save the satellite case, unless it travels through intervening states, there will be no signal over which to communicate. So where does it occur—where is the point of sale? This is a high-tech dilemma, for which there is no answer. *It "occurs" in all places simultaneously.* Yet consumption taxes, including sales taxes, gross receipts taxes, and utility user fees, are transaction taxes. I'll spare you from arguing that there is no transaction, at least in the conventional sense, and consequently no transaction tax. But that does not answer the question of point of sale.

The *Goldberg* Solution

There is no answer to this question, which only further demonstrates that conventional rules simply do not work for many telecommunications issues. But, believe it or not, this is the least challenging question, because in its wisdom, and in counsel with MCI, the Supreme Court has a solution to this dilemma. The Court answered the question in its recent *Goldberg* decision. There *is* no answer, it said. "Such a retail purchase is not a purely local event since it triggers simultaneous activity in several states," but the apportionment method "reasonably reflects the way that consumers purchase interstate telephone calls."[4] The Court supported its decision through an analysis of its criteria in earlier interstate commerce cases. The Court seemed to agree with the Illinois Supreme Court that this is not an apportionable tax, but it found that if it were apportionable, it would meet the standards. So it held that the statute is acceptable.

Application of *Goldberg*

A question remains as to what sorts of tax the *Goldberg* standard will govern. Will it protect a similar "apportionment" under a gross receipts tax? In recent discussions with legislative and administrative staffs in two eastern states, this was a real concern. These staffs would like to recommend a *Goldberg* approach, but they have been counselled by some that it would be subject to constitutional challenge. Hence the question.

The Illinois tax at issue is not a retail sales tax. Illinois statutes contain a retail sales tax, from which this excise is distinct. In fact, the sales tax is a privilege tax on Illinois retailers *required* to be collected from the purchaser. The excise tax is very similar to the retail sales tax, but there are clear differences. The Court noted that although this is not a sales tax, it "has many of the characteristics of a sales tax," and so can be analyzed as though it were.

The Court held that the *Goldberg* apportionment method was valid for a tax other than a sales tax which has "many of the characteristics" of one. Moreover, it accepted the director of revenue's contention that it has the "same economic effect as a sales tax." It would appear, then, that any other tax that has "many of the characteristics" and the "same economic effect" as a sales tax would also be protected from challenge.

The alternative apportionment methods for gross receipts taxes are as many and varied as income tax methods themselves, and with no more sound basis. In one state, until recently, MCI apportioned interstate revenue according to a milage formula, then deducted an amount attributed to traffic which only passed through the state. In another state, the apportionment is based on relative property investment in the state, whereas in still another state apportionment is made according to a formula that attempts to take into account both property and revenue.

Competitive Considerations

One important factor in these apportionment approaches is the effect on competition. When there was only one telephone company, nobody cared whether any inequity resulted. Such apportionment approaches caused no competitive advantage to any carrier, because there was no competition. The costs were simply recovered in the rates charged to customers. With the entry of the competitive companies—whose rates were and are not based on a guaranteed rate of return but solely on competitive pricing—a great difference arose. Companies pay different effective rates of tax depending both on the extent of their deemed presence in a state and on the fact that different apportionment methods are applied to different taxpayers. So under any apportionment method, some companies will be competitively disadvantaged. Because a *Goldberg* approach is not apportioned in the conventional sense, but each dollar of revenue is taxed the same regardless of the service provider, any relative advantages are eliminated.

A typical gross receipts tax is imposed on the provider of telecommunications services for the privilege of exercising its "franchise" in the state. That is, it is measured by revenue. Gross receipts taxes have always been "collected" from consumers in regulated rates for service. In the case of interstate gross receipts taxes, they are passed on to consumers as a surcharge. They look like a sales tax and have the same economic effect, except that the surcharge reflects the different effective rates the companies pay. So they are unlike a sales tax insofar as they are not uniform to the consumer. For example, in one state a long distance carrier's effective tax rate might be significantly higher than some of its competition, resulting in different surcharge rates among the competitors. Because of this competition, the first long distance carrier may be unable to fully recover the tax through the surcharge and as a result it bears a different burden from its competitors.

The Court's acceptance of the Illinois apportionment method for a tax other than a sales tax opens it to any other taxes that bear significant characteristics of a sales tax and have a similar economic effect. The typical gross receipts tax would meet those criteria. They are imposed on the consumer because the legislatures always know that the tax will be borne by the consumer through the regulated rate-making process. They are collected by the retailer and accompany the retail purchase of an interstate telephone call. Finally, because they have the same economic effect as a sales tax, they are appropriately apportioned under the Illinois method accepted by the Court in *Goldberg*. Accordingly, the notion that the Illinois apportionment method does not apply to utility gross receipts taxes should be disregarded.

APPORTIONMENT OF TANGIBLE AND INTANGIBLE PROPERTY

The problem in ad valorem taxation of telecommunications is not so much one of apportionment as one of valuation. But accepted valuation approaches make it one of apportionment.

All valuation methodologies or techniques attempt to establish fair market value or its equivalent, depending on the statute. In some cases it is "real value" or "true value," but they are all tantamount to fair market value, and employ the same criteria in arriving at it. The broadly accepted, and market valid, approach is "comparable selling price."

The competitive telecommunications business suffers from identification with an industry whose valuation practices have evolved to recognize the value of the utility monopoly franchise and a historic difficulty in valuing tangible utility property. Traditionally, assessors have chosen unique practices for telecommunications companies. These fall broadly under the heading of the "unit value" approach. An entire business is valued with some factor applied to ascribe the intangible value of the enterprise to the tangible property. Within the unit value method, there are several techniques. Generally, these include data about historical cost, replacement cost, reproduction cost, depreciation, capitalized earnings, imbedded debt, market value of the capital stock of the utility, and others. In any case, all are employed in an attempt to determine fair market value.

As for establishing the value of competitive telecommunications property for tax purposes, these approaches cannot arrive at an appropriate value. By their very approach they value some intangible, going concern kind of value and assign it to tangible property. That intangible historically represented the monopoly franchise that utilities had been granted. Broadly, although not universally, only utilities are taxed on intangible property. Because they are labelled as utilities, competitive interexchange companies have been taxed as though they possess those valuable monopoly franchises. Of course, the fact is the opposite. Nonetheless, that is the source of the problem. As presently assessed, the tangible property value of interexchange companies such as MCI includes an amount representing an intangible franchise value.

Fallacy of Present Practice

That intangible franchise value, in turn, must be apportioned to the taxing jurisdictions. Although some telecommunications companies are state assessed, apportionment normally is a two-step process. The nationwide value is apportioned to a state, and the statewide value, so established, is reapportioned to local taxing jurisdictions which assess and collect the tax at uniform local rates.

The techniques applied in apportioning values, like with the income tax, simply rely on old, comfortable methods which have never been intellectually scrutinized for adaptability to a fundamentally different taxpayer population. A common method assigns intangible value according to the relative cost of tangible property. Theoretically, the proportion of a company's property located in a state is directly representative of this intangible worth there attributable. Yet there is no conclusive support for relativizing intangible values with property cost.

Even allowing for assignment of intangible value to tangible property, there is little to say that because a company has 3 percent of its property in a state, the same proportion of the intangible value is likewise attributable. It would seem, if cost of property is any measure, there is more intangible worth created by a greater concentration of investment. One would expect that there would be an acceleration dynamic at work when some sort of critical mass level was attained, which would enhance a company's presence beyond its investment. It is only logical that a company's greater presence, represented in part by its property, makes it worth disproportionately more. Investment is more valuable at the margin. If a $1 investment generates $2 of revenue, but a $3 investment will return $8 in revenue, certainly more of the intangible value rests in the concentration of investment. Similarly, if $1 invested in a small state will produce $2 of revenue, but in a larger, more commercial, state the same investment will generate $3 of revenue, the direct cost/intangible relationship is shown to be a myth.

On the other hand, because of technology, this business is locationally transparent. A facility can be placed nearly anywhere with little consequence to the variety of locations. For example, MCI has a major switching facility in Ohio which essentially serves the East Coast. That facility could have been built in Pennsylvania or West Virginia with absolutely no consequence to the system configuration or operations. The facility is one that MCI calls "dark"—that is, the lights are never turned on there because there are no people there. It is an automatic operation. So the public, customers included, really do not know the facility is there. The dynamic I spoke of earlier is absent, and

MCI's Ohio business is no greater than it would have been without the facility. That being the case, presence by property has no effect on the intangible value attributable to a state of higher property concentration.

Current Illustrations

Practices in two states highlight the arbitrariness inherent in the apportionment of value. One state apportions nationwide unit value to itself according to a formula combining property cost and revenue. The combination of the property factor and the revenue factor result in the percentage apportionment of unit value. The property taxes are actually local taxes, based on the state-assessed value which must be allotted to the local tax authorities. In apportioning the state value among the counties, the state abandons its formula and employs a fundamentally different approach. It measures the length of MCI's "lines" in each local jurisdiction as a percentage of the entirety of its system in the state, and then apportions the state value accordingly. This latter device has a subtle redistributive effect. Most of the investment in any telecommunications system is in the central office or switch location. With rare exception, these facilities are located in center cities. The apportionment scheme that uses mileage to assign assessed values among local governments has the effect of distributing value from cities to rural areas, where most of the "lines" are located.

In the other state, a rural state in the West, where MCI has very little property and disproportionately high revenue, MCI serves those customers, by and large, through facilities leased from other long distance companies. Understand that "leased facilities" in this sense means that MCI buys service from them and resells it to customers. That state then apportions nationwide value according to the percentage of revenue in that state versus all states. MCI's property in that state is valued at 16 times its original cost! So the state attributes value in the hands of MCI to property owned by, and taxed to, other companies, whose value is also likely inflated because of the income they earn from MCI. This practice has not been challenged in court because the amount of tax involved does not warrant the likely cost of litigation.

The foregoing argues that *there is no valid means of apportioning intangible values to tangible property of interstate, competitive telecommunications companies.* This fact should demonstrate that any technique that reaches beyond the comparable selling price approach to valuation of tangible property is reaching beyond the bounds of reasonable law.

CONCLUSION

The different purposes of apportionment for income, sales, and property taxation were noted early on. It should be pointed out that those differences make the apportionment methods mutually exclusive. An apportionment method carefully and effectively designed to measure the relationship of a taxpayer with a state cannot measure the point of sale in a retail transaction. Correspondingly, a system established by fiat, in lieu of certitude, to reasonably approximate how consumers purchase long distance telephone service cannot reasonably measure the profit results of the relationship between a taxpayer's activity and the services offered by the state.

Apportionment is always at best an approximation. The further from reality, from facts, from the subject an apportionment exercise moves, its credibility is diminished. The different purposes of apportionment represent differences of character in the matter being taxed. Apportionment methods, to be valid, must reflect the character of the underlying reality as closely as possible. Arbitrary application of one method to facts of a different character discredits the entire system.

NOTES

1. *Mobil Oil Corp. v. State Commissioner of Taxes of Vermont*, 445 US 425 (1980).
2. *Moorman Manufacturing Company v. Bair*, 437 US 267, 273 (1978).
3. *Wisconsin v. J. C. Penney Co.*, 311 US 435, 444 (1940).
4. *Goldberg et al. v. Sweet*, 488 US 252 (1989).

V
State Taxation
of Multistate Banking

Regulatory and technological changes have focused attention on the state taxation of depository institutions, principally out-of-state banks and savings and loan associations. Barriers to interstate banking are gradually falling, whereas innovations in computers and financial instruments have increased the sophistication of banking services and lending practices. Several states have recently changed the way in which banks are taxed. Chapters 13 and 14 take contrasting views on whether the recent enactment by several states of destination taxation of banks results in increased state uniformity and reduced economic distortions.

William F. Fox and Michael Kelsay describe in Chapter 14 the significant changes that have occurred in the banking environment during the past decade. They argue that the current structure of state taxation of banks is based on the out-dated assumption that banks earn their income in a single state.

Banks are generally taxed differently than nonfinancial corporations. Only twenty-three states use the same structure for banks and other corporations. Fox and Kelsay argue that the current structure of bank taxation offers opportunities for banks to engage in tax avoidance by shifting of assets either through loan securitization or through locating wholesale and production activities, such as credit card services, in low-tax-rate states.

Fox and Kelsay make the case for a destination, rather than an origination, tax for financial services companies. They argue that banks and other lending institutions should be taxed on their interest and service income using a single-factor receipts formula based on where the customer is located or the proceeds are used. A destination tax would not be subject to tax avoidance through shifting of assets or production facilities. By reducing tax avoidance, revenues might be increased for both "headquarter" and "market" states.

In Chapter 13, Thomas S. Neubig examines what would occur in the transition to Fox and Kelsay's destination tax. Because most states currently tax domiciled depository institutions on all of their income, irrespective of where it is earned, multiple taxation can result if only a few states enact destination source tax rules. A multistate bank could be taxed twice on the income from a loan—once in its state of domicile, and again in the state of the customer.

Neubig argues that because banks have a choice of where to lend, they can avoid the potential double tax by not lending to residents and businesses in a destination tax state. The higher opportunity cost of lending to borrowers in a destination tax state would reduce the financial services supplied to that state and/or increase the cost of these services. Depending on the structure of the destination tax, capital "importing" states would be the most likely states to be adversely affected.

New data on the extent of cross-border lending and financial services are presented. The four states that have enacted destination taxation of financial institutions are likely to be capital "importers," and thus are maximizing the revenues from out-of-state financial institutions, but they are also most likely to experience reduced or more expensive financial services. Neubig argues that the trend toward destination taxation of financial services is likely to increase differential tax treatment of financial service providers and increase economic distortions.

13
Economic Effects of One State Enacting Destination Source Taxation of Financial Institutions

THOMAS S. NEUBIG

Depository institutions (i.e., commercial banks, and savings and loan associations) generally have been taxed by state governments under the "residence" principle, that is, where the institution is chartered and physically located. Three states have recently adopted new tax rules for financial institutions based on the "destination source" principle, that is, where the customer or the secured property is located. The Multistate Tax Commission has proposed regulations recommending that states switch from "residence" taxation of financial institutions to destination source taxation by changing the nexus rules from physical presence in the state to an "economic presence."

Divergent state income tax rules can result in multiple taxation of income. Multiple state taxation can result if financial institutions are subject to tax under destination source rules in the state of the customer (the "market" state) and under residence rules in the state of domicile (the "headquarter" state). Multiple state taxation has significant economic implications for financial service customers, for state governments and their tax authorities, for the financial service industry, and for U.S. capital markets.

State governments' increased revenue needs plus regulatory and technological changes in the financial services industry have focused attention on the taxation of the financial services industry, particularly the taxation of out-of-state institutions. Switching from a residence-based tax to a destination source tax may increase taxes on out-of-state financial institutions with only a partial offset from lower taxes on in-state financial institutions. Such a change, however, will have potentially negative economic impacts on the state's residents and businesses.

This chapter describes the potential sources of multiple taxation of interstate financial service providers, analyzes the potential economic effects of a state switching to destination source taxation when most states tax depository institutions on a residence tax basis, and provides some empirical measures of interstate financial services to show their importance for many states.

METHODS OF STATE TAXATION OF FINANCIAL INSTITUTIONS

This section describes the different methods states use to tax financial institutions, describes the terms used in the later analysis, and identifies the circumstances creating potential multiple taxation.

Taxing Jurisdiction or "Nexus"

A state generally has taxing jurisdiction over a business entity if the entity has established a nexus to the taxing jurisdiction. For most states, nexus for depository institutions has been created where the institution is domiciled, received its charter, and is physically located.

A regulation proposed by the Multistate Tax Commission[1] would establish nexus for financial institutions to a state where there is in-state ownership of property, an office or other place of business in the state, direct loans secured by in-state property, in-state presence of employees or independent contractors, or regular solicitation of in-state loans or deposits. Regular solicitation would be presumed to exist if a minimum number of residents were a debtor or creditor, the financial institution had a minimum amount of assets or deposits from state residents, or had a minimum amount of receipts from in-state sources. For example, Indiana presumes, subject to rebuttal, that a potential taxpayer regularly solicits business within Indiana if regular solicitation or transactions are conducted with twenty or more Indiana residents or the total loans and deposits attributable to Indiana exceed $5 million. This regulation would move away from a physical presence for establishing nexus and toward a concept of an "economic presence" establishing nexus.

Attribution of Income from Interstate Activity

If nexus is established, the tax base of a multistate corporation must be allocated or apportioned among the states in which the corporation conducts its business activities. There are two general approaches to apportioning income from interstate activity of financial institutions: the residence-based (or origin source) method and the destination source method.

The residence-based method taxes the entire income of the financial institution in the state in which it is domiciled. Under the residence-based method, the state in which the financial institution is chartered or incorporated attributes 100 percent of the income to itself.

Some states apply the typical three-factor formula for general business corporations based on equally weighted property, payroll, and receipts factors to depository institutions. With origin sourcing of receipts, the domiciliary state taxes 100 percent of the income because production facilities (e.g., property and payroll) are located in the domiciliary state, and receipts are sourced to the origin of the receipts. For purposes of this chapter, origin sourcing is treated as equivalent to the residence-based method.

The destination source method attributes income of multistate firms among different states based on the destination of receipts, with more of the income attributed to the market state. For example, Minnesota's new financial institution tax rule uses a destination source apportionment formula which applies a 15 percent weighting for payroll and property and 70 percent weighting for receipts. Minnesota sources both receipts and financial assets (e.g., loans) to the destination state, so 85 percent of income from loans to Minnesota residents from out-of-state financial institutions can be subject to Minnesota tax. Indiana and Tennessee both use a single-factor receipts formula to apportion income of out-of-state financial institutions that have nexus to the state.

One state, Indiana, has adopted a combination of the two approaches called the dual system. Under the dual system, in-state financial institutions are taxed according to the residence-based method with a tax credit for income taxes paid to other states. Out-of-state financial institutions are taxed under the destination sourcing method.

Some states use a so-called throwback rule which changes the site of the receipts factor from the destination state to the origin state if the company has nexus but an insufficient connection with the destination state.

Sources of Multiple Taxation

Multiple taxation can arise from nonuniform state taxation in several circumstances. First, if states do not recognize the nexus to another state, then there is potential for multiple taxation. For example, a state enacting an "economic presence" nexus rule could create nexus with a depository institution domiciled in another state. Nexus based on physical presence of the depository institution, which has been consistent with the regulatory limitations on depository institutions, is inconsistent with an "economic presence" nexus. A domiciled financial institution in a residence method state is taxed on 100 percent of its income in that state, yet would also be subject to tax on income earned from loans or services provided to a state enacting an economic presence nexus and destination source attribution rules.

Second, multiple taxation can occur if the apportionment formulas are inconsistent across states. Nonuniform apportionment rules result from different factors included in the formulas, differences in the weighting of the factors, and differences in the definition of similar factors. For example, Indiana and Tennessee include only a single receipts factor, while Minnesota employs the typical three-factor formula. Minnesota weights receipts by 70 percent and property and payroll by only 15 percent, compared with its equal weighting of the three factors for general business corporations. Minnesota includes loans in its property factor, whereas most states do not include financial assets in the property factor.

Third, differences in the rules governing the sourcing of factors can result in multiple taxation even with uniform apportionment formulas. For example, sourcing of receipts can attribute income to the destination state or the origin state. New York generally sites receipts from loans to where the greater portion of the income-producing activity relating to the loan is performed. This occurs generally to the origin state in which the lending bank is physically located. The same receipts from the loan would be sourced to the state where the borrower lives or the property is secured under destination sourcing rules.

Lending or financial services provided from financial institutions in residence-based states to destination sourcing states where nexus has been created can result in significant multiple taxation of the income. For example, a financial institution headquartered in a residence-based state lending to a borrower in a destination source tax state with a single receipts factor formula, such as Indiana or Tennessee, would have 200 percent of the income subject to state taxation. The entire income would be subject to tax in both the residence-based state and in the destination source state. As another example, loans from a residence-based state institution to Minnesota borrowers would have 185 percent of the income subject to state tax. The entire income would be subject to tax in the residence-based state, and 85 percent of the income—70 percent from the receipts factor and 15 percent from the property (loan) factor—would be subject to tax in Minnesota.

EFFECTS OF ONE STATE SWITCHING TO DESTINATION SOURCE TAXATION

A uniform residence-based state tax system (with the same tax base and tax rate) would have the same economic effects and same total state tax revenues as a uniform destination source tax system. The allocation of revenue among the states would be different, but the overall economic effects would be the same. Thus, the adverse economic effects of destination source taxation occur principally because most states still tax depository institutions under the residence principle. States considering switching from residence to destination source taxation of financial institutions, given the current environment of nonuniform taxation, must weigh the economic effects of such a change.

Economic Effects of a Switch to a Destination Source Tax

If a state (or a small group of states) switches from a residence-based tax to a destination source tax, the tax will be newly imposed on out-of-state financial institutions lending or providing services to in-state residents. In addition, the switch will reduce the tax on in-state financial institutions to the extent that they lend or provide services out of state. For this analysis, the destination source tax will be assumed to be apportioned 100 percent by receipts, similar to the Tennessee tax.

A destination source tax will provide an incentive to *both* in-state and out-of-state financial institutions to reduce lending to residents of the state. This occurs because a destination source tax increases the opportunity cost of lending to in-state borrowers relative to lending to borrowers in residence-tax states. Lenders can receive higher after-tax rates of return from lending to borrowers in residence-based states than to borrowers in destination source states, everything else being equal.

The higher opportunity cost of lending to borrowers in a destination source tax state will result in a reduction in financial services supplied to state residents and businesses and an increase in the cost of financial services supplied. The reduction in capital availability will depend on the elasticity of demand for particular loans and financial services. The effect will be greatest on marginal borrowers who tend to be low-income individuals and higher-risk businesses.

A switch to destination source taxation might encourage financial institutions to relocate from a residence-based state to a destination source state. For example, the multiple taxation of out-of-state institutions lending in-state could be avoided if a holding company established a subsidiary within the state to lend to in-state borrowers. Further, all state corporate tax could be avoided by having that subsidiary lend only to out-of-state customers located in residence-based states. It is important to note, however, that relocation of financial institutions into the destination source state would not reduce the effect of the destination source tax on credit availability and prices because all institutions would have an increased opportunity cost of lending to in-state borrowers.

Destination Source Tax with a Throwback Rule or a Dual Tax

The economic effects described above are potentially different if the state switches to a destination source tax but has a throwback rule taxing the income to the state of domicile of the financial institution if it is not taxed elsewhere. In this case, a state switching to a destination source tax may not significantly affect the state tax liability of in-state banks and would not necessarily increase their opportunity cost of lending to in-state residents. Similarly, if the state adopts a dual tax system (with in-state institutions taxed under the residence principle and out-of-state institutions taxed under the destination source principle), then the in-state banks will remain indifferent between lending to in-state and out-of-state borrowers. In both cases, the additional tax would be imposed only on out-of-state banks lending to in-state borrowers.

If in-state financial institutions cannot meet all of the financial service demands of in-state residents (a "capital importing" state), then the additional tax on out-of-state institutions will affect financial service costs and capital availability. In a capital importing state, savings from within the state are less than the quantity demanded at the national market interest rate. If capital from other states were not available, then the interest rate in the capital importing state would have to be higher. Because out-of-state financial institutions provide funds *at the margin* to capital importing states, a destination sourcing tax will reduce capital availability to that state.

A switch to a dual tax system by a capital exporting state may not affect capital availability because in-state institutions could meet the needs of in-state residents. In-state institutions may replace out-of-state institutions in providing financial services to state residents. This substitution, however, is likely to involve additional costs that would be reflected in higher prices. Reduced competition, reduced economies of scale, and increased concentration of geographic lending risks would likely result in some upward pressure on the costs of financial services provided by in-state financial institutions.

Capital importing states might attempt to become capital exporting states by attracting additional lendable funds. However, these additional lendable funds can only be attracted through higher deposit rates which increase the financial institutions' cost of funds and thus increase lending rates.

Economic Costs of Additional Revenue

One of the attractions of destination source taxation is the additional revenue from out-of-state financial institutions. However, the additional tax revenue collected from out-of-state financial institution under a destination source tax system is likely to be less than the additional burden on state residents and businesses.

Figure 13.1 shows the market for lendable funds in a capital importing state. The supply curve, S_i, is the lendable funds available from in-state financial institutions. Funds are available from out-of-state lenders at the national market interest rate r_m. At this rate, the quantity supplied by in-state institutions, Q_1, is less than the quantity demanded by the state's residents, Q_0. The difference is lent by out-of-state financial institutions. If a destination source tax is imposed, the opportunity cost of lending to in-state borrowers increases for out-of-state financial institutions. They require a pretax yield, r_1, that exceeds r_m by the amount of destination source tax per dollar loaned. The higher rate reduces quantity demanded from Q_0 to Q_2.

At the higher pretax rate, the amount of lending by in-state institutions increases to Q_3; the amount of lending by out-of-state institutions falls to $Q_2 - Q_3$. The amount of additional tax liability from out-of-state financial institutions is shown by area CDFE—the amount of out-of-state lending multiplied by the amount of destination source tax per dollar loaned.

State residents and business borrowers will pay higher prices as a result of the destination source tax. The additional monetary cost of financial services to in-state consumers as a result of the destination source tax will be area ABFE—total borrowing multiplied by the amount of the destination source tax per dollar loaned. In addition, state

FIGURE 13.1
Economic Costs and Tax Collections
in a Capital Importing State
Enacting a Destination Source Tax

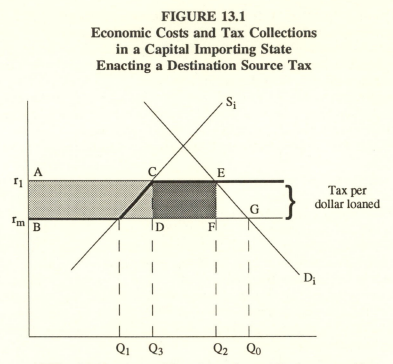

ABFE = Additional cost of financial services paid by in–state residents
CDFE = Tax collected from out–of–state financial institutions

borrowers will bear the burden of reduced capital availability—area EQ_2Q_0G.

Thus, a capital importing state, switching to a destination source tax, is likely to impose larger economic costs on its residents than it will collect in taxes from out-of-state financial institutions. Higher borrowing cost for in-state firms would be an additional cost of doing business in the state and thus make in-state firms less competitive in selling products nationally.

The effects of one state switching to destination source taxation will not necessarily occur immediately or in differential interest rates to the state's borrowers. Initially, the new destination source tax on out-of-state financial institutions would reduce the profitability of those financial institution, because they have outstanding loans and services to state residents. Interstate financial service providers and in-state institutions are likely to react initially by altering their lending away from the most risky in-state borrowers. This reduction in credit availability will take the form of tighter credit standards and higher downpayments for in-state residents and businesses. As financial institutions adopt their pricing practices to reflect the differential state taxation, less obvious higher fees and charges on the state's consumers will occur in lieu of or in addition to higher interest rates.

MEASURES OF INTERSTATE FINANCIAL SERVICES

The debate and discussion of taxation of interstate financial services has occurred without much empirical information on the extent of such services. Data on interstate capital flows and financial services have not been available, so many states do not know whether they are net capital importers or net capital exporters. As noted earlier, the potential economic effects of a state switching to destination source taxation are greater for capital importing states.

In-State Depository Institution Lending as a Percentage of Total Private Borrowing by State

We constructed a measure of states' likely capital importing status. Total lending by in-state depository institutions is compared with an estimate of the total private borrowing in the state. This ratio indicates the potential capacity of each state's financial institutions to provide credit to state borrowers at current market interest rates.

Total depository institution lending by state was obtained from regulatory information for commercial banks, savings and loan associations, and credit unions. Total lending for home mortgages, credit cards, other household borrowing, commercial and industrial loans, and all other loans were added for these institutions in each state.

Total private sector borrowing had to be estimated. Estimates of household borrowing by state were developed from regressions of historical national totals of mortgage, credit card, automobile, and other installment borrowing. Estimates of state borrowing by nonfinancial corporations were developed using information on borrowing rates of different industries from corporate financial data and the distribution of economic activity by industry for each state.

In 1989, depository institutions accounted for 45 percent of total home mortgages, 74 percent of credit card loans, 82 percent of other household installment loans, and 52 percent of nonfinancial business debt. Other lenders including insurance companies, government-sponsored agencies and mortgage pools, finance companies, pension funds, and nonfinancial businesses also hold significant amounts of total credit market claims. Because most of these other lenders would not be subject to a destination source tax, the tax would penalize depository institutions relative to other lenders.

Table 13.1 shows the ratio of in-state depository institution lending to estimated private borrowing by type of debt and by state. Depository institution lending was 52 percent of total household and nonfinancial business debt outstanding in 1989. The percent of state private borrowing that is currently lent by in-state depository institutions is less than 52 percent because some of their lending is currently to out-of-state borrowers.

The last column of Table 13.1 shows the ratio for all private borrowing by state. The ratio varied from 364 percent in Delaware to 7 percent in Alaska. Thirteen states plus the District of Columbia had above-average in-state depository institution lending as a percent of the state's total private borrowing. The remaining two-thirds of the states had below-average ratios, and thus are likely to be net capital importers.

States' ratios of in-state depository institution lending to state borrowing vary by type of loan. Several states have low total ratios yet exceed 100 percent for household borrowing other than for mortgages and credit cards. Large differences between types of loans may reflect specialization in those types of loans or imprecision in the estimates of borrowing for individual categories. The relative position of states for total lending and borrowing is the best indicator of whether a state is a net capital exporter or net capital importer.

Out-of-State Primary Banking Relationships

A second measure of the extent of cross-border lending and financial services was constructed from survey data on out-of-state primary banking relationships. Primary banking relationships generally provide businesses with an assured source of credit. Primary banking relationships are generally very profitable because the businesses maintain large deposits with the bank and purchase other banking services. Primary banking relationships are important to "middle-market businesses," variously defined to include companies ranging from $10 million to $500 million in annual sales, which are too large to rely on a community bank or thrift but not large enough to access national securities markets.

TABLE 13.1
Lending by In-State Depository Institutions as
Percentage of Estimated Borrowing, 1989

State	Home Mortgage	Credit Card	Other Installment	Nonfinancial Business	Total
AL	31	33	112	36	40
AK	9	9	48	5	7
AZ	27	57	90	42	40
AR	27	14	70	25	29
CA	85	62	53	61	69
CO	22	82	61	28	29
CT	78	33	58	60	66
DE	50	7774	160	141	364
DC	71	25	103	59	63
FL	54	35	99	44	52
GA	31	87	87	34	38
HI	59	40	88	55	58
ID	13	45	112	33	30
IL	47	22	66	59	54
IN	35	33	108	33	40
IA	30	38	84	34	36
KS	41	21	72	47	46
KY	36	27	113	30	37
LA	33	42	86	19	26
ME	32	25	94	36	38
MD	44	81	72	56	54
MA	62	28	64	79	69
MI	32	26	81	52	46
MN	27	42	90	47	43
MS	24	16	115	25	30
MO	42	20	70	47	46
MT	15	20	96	18	21
NE	35	122	79	54	51
NV	20	1001	61	22	43
NH	48	152	79	47	54
NJ	50	16	51	46	47

TABLE 13.1 (continued)

State	Home Mortgage	Credit Card	Other Installment	Nonfinancial Business	Total
NM	22	32	89	20	24
NY	43	45	118	123	90
NC	44	46	81	43	46
ND	35	36	115	39	42
OH	43	78	104	45	50
OK	25	9	81	23	27
OR	22	103	82	41	37
PA	33	20	93	69	53
RI	50	57	88	123	81
SC	35	76	85	42	44
SD	19	2616	137	41	104
HI	59	40	88	55	58
TN	31	40	101	30	36
TX	26	12	72	26	29
UT	33	77	116	36	41
VT	41	44	80	40	43
VA	53	85	109	52	59
WA	35	70	73	39	40
WV	31	23	126	20	31
WI	42	45	73	38	43
WY	16	22	81	9	14
Total U.S.	45	74	82	52	52

Source: Price Waterhouse estimates.

A sample of 6,000 corporations (of which 4,601 reported a primary banking relationship) was used to measure the percentage of out-of-state primary banking relationships in 1989. Fifteen percent of corporations reporting a primary banking relationship used an out-of-state bank.

Table 13.2 shows the percentage of out-of-state banking relationships by state. Eight states had more than 30 percent of corporations in the state reporting an out-of-state primary banking relationship. These were Delaware, Indiana, Kansas, Maryland, New Hampshire, Nevada, Vermont, and West Virginia. Medium-sized companies with annual sales ranging from $50 million to $500 million were more likely than average to have an out-of-state primary banking relationship (22 percent). Mining (28 percent), transportation and public utilities (21 percent), and manufacturing firms (16.5 percent) were most likely to use an out-of-state bank.

Potential Increases in Annual Interest Costs of an Average Mortgage and Middle-Market Business

To illustrate the potential impact on borrowers for mortgage and commercial loans, an estimate of the direct tax impact in terms of higher interest rates was calculated. The actual incidence of a state's destination source tax is uncertain and may take the form of reduced lending to higher-risk borrowers or the form of higher fees and other noninterest charges. Thus, the following calculations are illustrative of the potential magnitude of a switch to destination source taxation by one state. The potential additional interest cost necessary to provide the same after-tax rate of return to an interstate financial institution lending to a borrower in a destination source state is calculated. The calculation assumes a state corporate income tax similar to the Indiana financial institution tax: an 8.5 percent tax rate apportioned by a single receipts factor. The average mortgage loan on new homes in 1989 was $117,000. Based on data from the *Functional Cost Analysis* of the Federal Reserve Board, the net earnings rate on mortgage loans ranged from 2.25 percent for large banks to 2.65 percent for small banks in 1989. The interest cost necessary to compensate for the additional state tax ranges from 0.21 percent for large banks to 0.25 percent for small banks. This would represent an increase in annual mortgage payments of $218 to $264 on an average 30-year mortgage loan.

A medium-sized manufacturing company with total assets of $35 million and total debt of $10.85 million could face added annual interest costs of $12,700 to $20,965 if the additional state tax on financial institutions were passed through to the borrower. The average net earnings rate on commercial loans ranged from 1.26 percent for small banks to 2.08 percent for large banks in 1989.

Lending activity, of course, involves a large number of relatively small transactions, which can be very significant in the aggregate. The aggregate impact of the additional interest cost on an "average" state which accounted for 2 percent of total U.S. borrowing could be as high as $110 million annually for individuals with a comparable increase for nonfinancial businesses. These costs would be higher if the compliance

TABLE 13.2
Percentage of Firms with Out-of-State
Primary Banking Relationships, 1989

State[1]	Percentage of Firms	State[1]	Percentage of Firms
Delaware	70.0	Oklahoma	13.9
New Hampshire	46.9	Alabama	13.5
Vermont	40.0	Idaho	13.3
Nevada	37.5	Missouri	13.3
Maryland	34.3	Nebraska	13.3
Kansas	34.1	Montana	12.5
West Virginia	31.3	Pennsylvania	12.0
New Jersey	28.8	Rhode Island	11.8
Alaska	28.6	Texas	11.7
Iowa	27.7	Minnesota	11.7
Connecticut	27.2	Maine	10.3
Arkansas	26.9	Oregon	10.2
South Carolina	26.7	Washington	9.5
Tennessee	24.6	North Carolina	9.2
Indiana	20.8	Hawaii	9.2
Virginia	20.2	Utah	9.1
Arizona	19.5	New York	9.0
New Mexico	18.2	Ohio	8.9
Colorado	17.6	Illinois	8.7
Kentucky	17.5	California	8.0
Wisconsin	16.7	Dist. Columbia	7.1
Mississippi	16.1	Massachusetts	5.5
Michigan	15.9	North Dakota[2]	N.A.
Georgia	15.1	South Dakota[2]	N.A.
Louisiana	14.6	Wyoming[2]	N.A.
Florida	14.1		

Source: Standard and Poors Compumark database. Sample by Price Waterhouse.

[1]States arrayed according to percentage.
[2]Sample includes fewer than 5 companies.

and administrative costs associated with the tax change could also be passed forward to borrowers.

CONCLUSION

States considering switching from residence to destination source taxation of financial institutions must consider the potential economic effects. Such a change is not a "free lunch" with only additional tax revenues from out-of-state financial institutions. Given the nonuniformity of state tax rules, financial institutions would have an incentive to reduce lending and financial services to consumers in a state enacting a destination source tax system, unless they were compensated for the additional tax. Reduced capital availability would be most likely to occur in "market" or capital importing states.

Higher credit costs in the state would be harmful to state economic development efforts and to higher-risk individual and small business borrowers. The potential revenue increase from out-of-state financial institutions is likely to be smaller than the economic costs borne by the state's residents and businesses.

Technological and regulatory changes in the financial services sector are bringing all types of financial institutions in closer competition. Depository institutions, insurance companies, mutual funds, security firms, and even nonfinancial corporations are increasingly providing similar savings and investment vehicles and other financial services. In addition, the U.S. Treasury recently proposed a comprehensive banking reform that would authorize nationwide banking and branching, new financial activities of banks, and commercial ownership of banking organizations.

Changes to the Federal tax rules in the last decade have reflected these trends by moving toward taxing all financial institutions more similarly. Increased differential tax treatment of financial service providers at the state level could exacerbate barriers to interstate capital flows and the efficient provision of financial services.

NOTE

1. Proposed Multistate Tax Commission Regulations IV. 18(i): Attribution of Income from the Business of a Financial Institution.

14
Neutral Taxation of Financial Institutions During the 1990s

WILLIAM F. FOX and MICHAEL P. KELSAY

In recent years, there has been considerable state-level discussion of effective methods for taxing financial institutions. Arguments often have implied that the major concern is whether money center or market states will receive corporate income tax payments. However, the thesis of this chapter is that neutral taxation and reduced opportunities for tax avoidance are the important issues. The major conclusion is that a tax structure that apportions revenues according to destination or market principles is superior for both money center and market states to existing tax structures that apportion according to production.

CURRENT BANKING ENVIRONMENT

State taxation of financial institutions developed in an era when the institutions were presumed to operate inside a single state. This section describes two major changes that have dramatically expanded cross-state banking and potentially limited the effectiveness of existing tax structures. These changes are movements toward interstate banking and branchless banking.

Interstate Banking

As the 1980s began, the banking system was strongly regulated and technological innovations for delivering banking services were in their infancy. Federal legislation permitting limited interstate banking had been in place for several decades, but the effect had been small. During the 1980s, the prohibitions against interstate banking that had been embedded in our financial structure for more than fifty years began to crumble both in fact and in practical effect. Several factors led to the dramatic trend toward interstate banking, including ingenious means devised by financial institutions for delivering financial services across geographic boundaries and state-level expansion of interstate banking powers. This section describes the federal legislation, state legislation and shifts in banking practices that have been essential to the development of interstate banking.

Prior to considering the other important factors in interstate banking, it is imperative to remember that technological advances in the collection, storage, and transmission of information facilitated innovative processes in the industry. For example, advances in computer technology allowed "electronic banking" to be operationally and economically feasible. Point of sale terminals (POST) and automated clearinghouses (ACH), automated teller machines (ATM), and electronic funds transfer systems (EFTS) made it increasingly attractive to expand both the scope of financial services and the geographic span of market areas. Over the past five years, the growth of ATM terminals has increased about 10 percent per year with over 85,000 terminals in use nationwide at the end of 1990. Further, computer terminals or television linkups allow financial institutions to deliver financial services directly into the home.

Federal Legislation

Federal legislation during the past several decades has increasingly permitted interstate banking. There are currently four federal statutes that restrict branching and interstate banking. The McFadden Act, which was passed in 1927 and amended by the Banking Act of 1933, restricted the in-state branching powers of national banks to those of state-chartered banks.[1]

Three subsequent acts expanded interstate banking capabilities. The Douglas Amendment to the Bank Holding Company Act of 1956 prevented nondomiciled multibank holding companies from acquiring a bank in another state unless the state specifically authorized the purchase. However, there was a grandfather provision in the Act for transactions made by holding companies that were formed before the Bank Holding Company Act of 1956. Twelve corporations—seven domestic and five foreign firms—were included in this provision. The result of the federal legislation is that states have the final authority on branching within their borders, as well as in determining whether an interstate acquisition will be allowed.

The Garn-St. Germain Act facilitated interstate banking as well. Provisions of the Act authorized banking institutions to acquire failing banks and thrifts in states other than those in which they were presently located. In addition, the International Banking Act of 1978 and Section 25(A) of the Federal Reserve Act, commonly known as the Edge Act, allowed for limited interstate banking through international banking provisions.

Industry Practices

Banks have increased their interstate banking activities through creative manipulation of existing statutes. One way is through a chain banking agreement in which individuals, instead of corporations, own banks in multiple states. This device circumvents the restrictions of the Bank Holding Company Act of 1956 that limit corporate, but not individual, ownership of multistate banks. This option has been used extensively in the Midwest, particularly in Missouri and Kansas.

Another creative movement to increase interstate banking activity has been the acquisition by holding companies of noncontrolling ownership in an out-of-state bank with an option to purchase control of the institution when permitting legislation is in place. This practice is legal under the current regulatory structure.

State-Level Interstate Banking Provisions

State legislation has also permitted the spread of interstate banking. Maine became the first state to authorize interstate banking in 1975. Since then, forty-five other states and the District of Columbia have passed legislation permitting some form of interstate banking (Table 14.1). Nonetheless, the bank holding company structure remains the only means by which financial institutions are able to expand their interstate operations.

Although each state's banking laws are unique, Shoenhair and Spong (1990) classify interstate banking legislation based on two types of limitations placed on entry. One is the geographic range of entry (nationwide versus regional) and the other is whether or not the state has a reciprocity agreement. Thirty-one states allow nationwide entry in some form, and the other fifteen plus the District of Columbia only permit interstate banking within a region (Table 14.1). States with regional restrictions limit entry to financial institutions from particular

TABLE 14.1
State Laws Allowing Interstate Banking as of January 1, 1991

Nationwide entry without reciprocity	Nationwide entry with reciprocity	Regional or contiguous state entry w/reciprocity	Entry not allowed
Alaska	Connecticut	Alabama	Hawaii
Arizona	California	Arkansas	Kansas
Colorado	Delaware	District of	Montana
Idaho	Kentucky	Columbia	North Dakota
Maine	Illinois	Florida	
Nevada	Louisiana	Georgia	
New	Michigan	Indiana[3]	
Hampshire	Nebraska	Iowa	
New Mexico	New Jersey	Maryland	
Oklahoma[1]	New York	Massachusetts	
Oregon	Ohio	Minnesota	
Texas	Pennsylvania	Mississippi	
Utah	Rhode Island	Missouri	
Wyoming	South Dakota	North Carolina	
	Tennessee	South Carolina	
	Vermont	Virginia	
	Washington	Wisconsin	
	West		
	Virginia		

Source: *Banking Studies*, Division of Bank Supervision and Structure, Federal Reserve Bank of Kansas City, 1990 Annual.

[1]Bank holding companies from sates not granting reciprocal entry to Oklahoma banking organizations must wait four years before making additional acquisitions.

[2]Entry into Arkansas is contingent on submission, approval, and compliance with an extensive plan guaranteeing certain levels of community service and investment.

[3]This state is scheduled to convert to nationwide entry as follows: Indiana-July 1, 1992.

states, usually neighboring states. States with reciprocal legislation grant entry to out-of-state holding companies only if there is a reciprocal agreement in the state where the holding company is domiciled.

Loan Securitization

The recent rapid development of securitization of loan activity across geographic boundaries is perhaps the single most important way financial institutions are able to engage in cross-state activity. It is also an effective means of tax avoidance.

Securitization is not a new phenomenon, dating back at least to activities of the Federal National Mortgage Administration (Fannie Mae) in the 1930s. Although Fannie Mae was partially privatized in 1968, and moved into the conventional mortgage market in 1972, it took rapid information systems and deregulation to make securitization the dominant form of finance for a wide array of products. The standardization of mortgage contracts first by Fannie Mae and then by Freddie Mac set the stage for securitization and permitted the concept of securitization of the mortgage market to be firmly in place when the technology for securitization of nonmortgage loans was developed in 1985. The elevenfold increase in mortgage-backed securities during a five-year period is evidence of the dramatic growth (see Table 14.2).

The growth in both the volume and types of loans was then accelerated by computer technology. In addition to mortgage loans, there has been securitization of automobile loans, credit card receivables, small business loans, home equity loans, computer leases, affiliate notes, and a host of others. Lerner (1990) reports that the first asset-backed security transaction was completed on March 7, 1985, in the amount of $192 million. By 1989, the volume had mushroomed to $22.6 billion.

The industry was stimulated further when commercial banks became very dominant players in underwriting asset-backed securities. Government agencies, large investment banks, and large security dealers have developed a host of mortgage securities to facilitate this market, including pass-through certificates, collateralized mortgage obligations, interest rate swaps, interest-only and principal-only stripped securities, and REMICs (Real Estate Mortgage Investment Conduit Security).

STATE TAX STRUCTURES FOR FINANCIAL INSTITUTIONS

Although the regulatory structure and operating environment have changed dramatically over the past decade, few states have responded by revamping their tax structure to reflect this new environment. Only Indiana, Minnesota, New York, Tennessee, and West Virginia have altered their tax structures in recent years.[2]

TABLE 14.2
Mortgage-backed Pass Through Activity
of FHLMC, FNMA, and GNMA, 1981-1986
($millions)

	1981	1982	1983	1984	1985	1986
FHLMC	17.9	41.2	56.4	70.9	100.5	171.4
FNMA	.7	14.5	25.1	36.2	55.0	97.2
GNMA	14.3	16.0	50.5	27.9	45.9	98.2
TOTAL	32.9	71.6	132.0	135.0	201.4	366.7

Source: *Savings Institutions Sourcebook*, United States League of Savings Institutions, Chicago, Illinois, 1988, pp. 65-67.

Tax Structure

Historically, the choice of tax instruments has been influenced by constitutional restrictions that limit the taxation of national banks and that limit the taxation of income from federal securities.[3] As a result, only twenty-three states use the same tax structure for banks and other corporations. Taxation of national banks has gone through several periods of change, but congressional legislation in 1976 now allows states to tax national banks in any nondiscriminatory manner. The income from federal securities can only be taxed using a nondiscriminatory franchise or other nonproperty tax.

Bank taxes usually are structured using some combination of corporate income, franchise, or share taxes. Base definitions for the corporate income tax often are a variant of the federal definition, but the specific characteristics differ by state. The base for share taxes is the value of banking shares, deposits, or another indicator of intangible personal property. Franchise taxes employ either a corporate income tax or a share tax base. Thus, state taxes have either an income or an intangible property base, and the franchise tax is a legal distinction rather than a conceptually different tax base. Franchise taxes are popular because they allow inclusion of income from government securities in the base.

Seventeen states use corporate income taxes, thirty-four employ franchise taxes, and seven have share taxes (see Table 14.3).[4] Michigan taxes banks under the single business tax. These totals include twelve states that use some combination of income, franchise, and share taxes.

TABLE 14.3
State Tax Rate Applicable to Banks

State	Corporate Income Tax Rate	Franchise Tax Rate	Share Tax Rate
Alabama	0.0	6.0	0.0
Alaska[11]	9.4	0.0	0.0
Arizona[8,11]	9.3	0.0	0.0
Arkansas[11]	6.0	0.27	0.0
California[8,12]	0.0	10.74	0.0
Colorado[11]	5.1	0.0	0.0
Connecticut[8]	0.0	11.5	0.0
Delaware[11]	0.0	8.7	0.0
Dist. of Col.[13]	0.0	10.0	0.0
Florida[3]	0.0	5.5	0.2
Georgia[4]	6.0	0.0	0.0
Hawaii	0.0	11.7	0.0
Idaho[8]	8.0	0.0	0.0
Illinois	6.5	0.0	0.0
Indiana[4]	3.4	0.0	0.25
Iowa	0.0	5.0	0.0
Kansas	0.0	6.625	0.0
Kentucky	0.0	0.0	0.95
Louisiana	0.0	0.0	0.0
Maine[1]	0.0	1.0	0.015
Maryland	0.0	7.0	0.0
Massachusetts	0.0	12.54	0.0
Michigan[10]	0.0	0.0	0.0
Minnesota	0.0	9.8	0.0
Mississippi[6,11]	5.0	0.25	0.0
Missouri	0.0	7.0	0.0
Montana[8,14]	0.0	6.75	0.0
Nebraska[15]	0.0	0.0	0.0004
Nevada	0.0	0.0	0.0
New Hampshire	8.0	1.0	0.0
New Jersey[1]	0.0	9.0	0.2
N. Mexico[2,4,11]	7.6	0.0	0.0
New York	0.0	9.0	0.0
North Carolina	7.0	0.15	0.0

TABLE 14.3 (continued)

State	Corporate Income Tax Rate	Franchise Tax Rate	Share Tax Rate
North Dakota[8]	5.0	2.0	0.0
Ohio[8,16]	0.0	1.5	0.0
Oklahoma	6.0	0.125	0.0
Oregon	6.6	0.0	0.0
Pennsylvania	0.0	0.0	1.25
Rhode Island	8.0	0.00025	0.000695
South Carolina	0.0	4.5	0.0
South Dakota[8]	0.0	6.0	0.0
Tennessee	6.0	0.25	0.0
Texas[8]	0.0	0.525	0.0
Utah[7,8]	0.0	5.0	0.0
Vermont	0.0	0.00024	0.0
Virginia	0.0	1.0	0.0
Washington[5]	0.0	0.0	1.5
West Virginia	9.3	0.75	0.0
Wisconsin	0.0	7.9	0.0
Wyoming	0.0	0.0	0.0

Source: William F. Fox and Harold A. Black, "The Economic Impact of State Taxation and Regulation on Banking," The University of Tennessee, 1990b.

[1]The share tax is a franchise tax levied on assets.
[2]Levies a $50 franchise tax.
[3]Levies an intangible property tax.
[4]Levies a gross receipts tax.
[5]The share tax is the business and occupation tax.
[6]Levies a share tax, but it is a credit against the personal property tax.
[7]Has a supplemental income tax.
[8]Minimum tax is levied in the event no income is earned.
[9]The gross receipts tax is a credit against the income tax.
[10]Levies the Single Business Tax.
[11]This is the highest marginal tax rate levied on income.
[12]Corporate franchise tax rate (9.3 percent) plus ratio of personal property taxes and business license taxes paid by corporate taxpayers to the sum of net income, personal property taxes, and business taxes.
[13]Rate is 10 percent plus a 2.5 percent surtax (5 percent for taxable period September 30, 1989 to October 1, 1992).
[14]Rate is 7 percent of act income for taxpayers using water's edge apportionment.

TABLE 14.3 (continued)

[15]12.3 times 48.8 percent of maximum corporate tax rate (presently 7.81 percent for taxable incomes over $50,000), expressed in cents, multiplied by amount of average deposits of financial institution.

[16]Rate is 15 mills times the value of issued and outstanding shares of stock determined according to value of capital, surplus, and individual profits.

Several states have franchise taxes which use both an income and an intangibles base. Louisiana, Nevada, and Wyoming have no statewide tax on banking.

Tax rates on income (using either an income or income-based franchise tax) range from a high of 12.54 percent in Massachusetts (which uses a franchise tax) to zero percent in thirteen states. Rates on assets (using either a franchise or share tax) are harder to compare because the base definitions often differ, but they range from as high as the 1.5 percent business and occupations tax in Washington to zero percent in thirty-one states.

Several other aspects of the tax structure have the potential to reduce the effective rate (Table 14.4). One is deductibility of federal income tax obligations in calculation of the state tax liability, a feature of five states' tax structures. Another is exclusion of income from federal securities or the value of federal securities from the tax base. This exclusion is required in states using an income tax structure and is found also in some other state tax structures.

Finally, whether a state either requires or allows apportionment of bank income can influence effective tax rates. Income for multistate corporations is normally apportioned across states using either separate accounting or formulary apportionment. A common means is a three-factor formula that apportions to a state the share of its domestic income that corresponds to the arithmetic average of its percent of the firm's domestic sales, payrolls, and property.[5] Historically, state tax structures have given less consideration to apportionment of bank income than to income earned in other industries because banks were presumed to earn their income in a single state. Some states, such as Massachusetts, allow no apportionment and require all domiciled banks' income to be taxed in the state, regardless of where it is earned. Other states permit interstate banks to apportion but have not developed explicit rules for apportionment. A survey of the states found that only thirty-two permit apportionment, and of those only eighteen permit banks to use the three-factor formula. Few states, if any, treat bank holding companies as units

TABLE 14.4
Selected Characteristics of State Taxes on Banks

State	Apportion Bank Tax Liability	Franchise Tax Based on Income	Interest from Government Securities Taxable Federal	Interest from Government Securities Taxable State and Local
Alabama	Y	Y	Y	Y
Alaska	Y	N.A.	N	Y
Arizona[1]	Y	N.A.	N	Y
Arkansas	Y	N	N	N
California	Y	Y	Y	Y
Colorado	N	N.A.	N	N
Connecticut	Y	Y	Y	Y
Delaware	N	Y	Y	Y
Dist. of Col.[1]	Y	Y	N	Y
Florida	Y	Y	Y	Y
Georgia[1]	Y	N	N	Y
Hawaii	N	Y	Y	Y
Idaho[1]	Y	N.A.	N	Y
Illinois	Y	N.A.	N	Y
Indiana	Y	N.A.	N	N
Iowa	N	Y	Y	Y
Kansas	Y	Y	Y	Y
Kentucky	N	N.A.	N	Y
Louisiana	N	N.A.	N	N
Maine	Y	Y	Y	Y
Maryland	Y	Y	Y	Y
Massachusetts	N	Y	Y	Y
Michigan	Y	N.A.	N	Y
Minnesota	Y	Y	Y	Y
Mississippi	N	N	N	N
Missouri	N	Y	Y	Y
Montana	Y	Y	Y	Y
Nebraska	N	N.A.	N	N
Nevada	N	N.A.	N	N
New Hampshire	N	N	N	N

TABLE 14.4 (continued)

State	Apportion Bank Tax Liability	Franchise Tax Based on Income	Interest from Government Securities Taxable Federal	State and Local
New Jersey	Y	Y	Y	Y
New Mexico	Y	N.A.	N	N
New York	Y	Y	Y	Y
North Carolina	Y	N	Y	Y
North Dakota	Y	Y	Y	Y
Ohio	Y	N	Y	Y
Oklahoma	Y	N	Y	Y
Oregon	Y	N.A.	N	N
Pennsylvania	N	N.A.	N	Y
Rhode Island	N	N	N	N
South Carolina	N	Y	Y	Y
South Dakota	Y	Y	Y	Y
Tennessee	Y	N	Y	Y
Texas	N	N	N	N
Utah	Y	Y	Y	Y
Vermont	N	N	N	N
Virginia	N	N	Y	Y
Washington[1]	Y	N.A.	N	Y
West Virginia	Y	N	N	N
Wisconsin	Y	Y	Y	Y
Wyoming	N	N.A.	N	N

[1]Not all state and local government interest is taxable.

when apportioning income. This offers an opportunity for banks to engage in tax avoidance by shifting assets among states.

Evaluating Current Bank Tax Structures

The criteria traditionally used to evaluate tax systems apply to state taxes on financial industries. For taxes with their initial impact on business, the three most important are minimizing effects on economic activity, minimizing administrative and compliance costs, and obtaining sufficient revenues. This section evaluates the potential consequences of the existing tax structure in terms of these criteria. Equity implications are not considered because they are hard to judge without knowledge of incidence, something which is often difficult to determine.

Effects on Economic Activity. The economic consequence that state and local governments are most likely to consider is possible influence on the location of productive activity. The existing tax structure offers considerable potential for banks to engage in tax avoidance by adjusting their behavior, for example, by moving productive activity to lower-tax states. Certain retail bank functions, such as deposit taking, may need to be physically located close to the market, and there is likely to be little resiting of these activities because of tax differentials. However, production and wholesale activities, such as credit card services, commercial lending, and retail credit processing functions, need not be located near the market and can be sited to minimize production and tax costs.

Second, financial institutions have means to shift the location of their activities and thereby reduce their tax liabilities that are not available to other industries. One is choosing the situs for portfolios. For example, a member of a holding company in a high-tax state can securitize its loan portfolio and sell it to a member in a low-tax state. Even if the transfer pricing problem is properly handled, under conventional tax laws the high-tax state would only be able to tax income associated with making the loan, whereas the state where the securitized loan is held would be able to tax the interest. In many cases, the income may go untaxed because the situs rules in low-tax-rate states are likely to exclude interest from securitized loans from taxable income. Few states tax entire holding companies as unitary entities, so this type of avoidance is not discouraged. Further, share tax liabilities can be reduced if assets are held in income-taxing states, and income taxes can be reduced if income is transferred to share-taxing states. The latter can be accomplished (at least potentially) by transferring assets at values other than their market value. Thus, tax liabilities are altered as simply as selling assets within a combined company.

Third, tax liabilities can be reduced merely by changing the type of financial instruments held. For example, no tax liability is due on interest from holding federal securities in states using an income tax structure. Again, tax liabilities can be reduced by specializing in where particular assets are held. One means of achieving this is for bank holding company members located in income—as opposed to franchise—taxing states to be the situs for the federal securities.

Numerous empirical studies have examined the relationship between tax structures and manufacturing or other economic activities, but few have considered other specific industries such as the financial industries.[6] In one such study, Wasylenko and McGuire (1985) found evidence that the effective personal income tax rate was negatively related to employment in the finance, insurance, and real estate industries. However, they found no evidence that corporate taxes were important determinants of employment location.

In another study, Fox and Black (1990b) examined effects of the entire state business tax and regulatory structure on the location of banking activity. They considered the separate influences that taxes and regulations could have on the location of productive activities, such as employment and gross state product; on the location of financial aggregates, such as assets and liabilities; and on the portfolio choice of banks. They concluded that the largest effects have been on the portfolio decisions of banks and on the size distribution of banks. They found that taxes and regulations have caused discrete changes in banking activity, as evidenced by Delaware's and South Dakota's effectiveness in attracting a significant share of banking. However, there is little evidence that tax-rate differentials influence the situs of banking activity at the margin.

In sum, existing tax structures allow considerable opportunity for tax avoidance and can be expected to influence the situs of banking activity as measured in both real and financial terms. The uneven tax burden facing firms that arises from tax avoidance creates lower operational costs for some firms and results in competitive advantages created solely from differential tax liabilities. Tax structures with large potential for avoidance and behavior distortion can be expected to create excess burdens and to cause considerable compliance costs associated with tax planning. The concern is not different in principle from the expected effect of state taxes on the distribution of other economic activity. The difference is that in practice the tax avoidance potential is much greater for financial institutions. However, it must be noted that empirical results to date suggest that bankers have failed to take full advantage of the available opportunities to reduce their state tax burdens through careful planning. Current banking practices are consistent with the observation that each member of a bank holding company is being treated as a separate corporation rather than as part of a larger corporate entity. This likely arises because interstate banking is relatively new and because interstate banking is being conducted through holding companies. Tax planning to minimize tax burdens can be expected to improve as interstate banking matures and as true interstate branching becomes legal. The speed with which the industry has changed in recent years suggests that banks could move rapidly to engage in widespread avoidance.

Administration and Compliance. In addition to neutrality of tax structure, a major goal of sound tax policy is to keep the costs of administration and compliance to the minimum consistent with efficient enforcement. Existing tax structures score fairly high in this sense. Current tax structure and regulatory provisions require that, for a variety of purposes, information systems be capable of providing extensive information on the location of real and intangible properties. As a result, most financial institutions have extensive loan tracking systems, which, by and large, are necessary to respond to regulatory rather than tax requirements.

Enormous scale economies are to be found in the provision of data processing and other information systems for the banking sector. Costs of implementing system changes required by tax and regulatory changes can be spread over a large customer base. Thus, the additional administration and compliance costs associated with modification of the tax structure should not be prohibitive.

Revenues. The existing tax structure can be expected to generate an acceptable amount of tax revenues if financial institutions do not engage in tax avoidance. Potentially, all financial activity could be taxed either in the state of domicile or could be apportioned to other states, although the lack of well-developed apportionment rules would create some problems.

Tax avoidance raises at least two revenue issues. First is the distribution of tax revenues. Existing state corporate tax structures are focused on taxing *production* of banking services. Therefore, the revenue goes to the producing state or the state where assets are held rather than to market states, but a legitimate argument can be made that the income is generated in the market state. For example, a loan to finance housing in Tennessee could be made by a New York bank and the asset held in Delaware. Under this scenario, the income may be taxed in Delaware, though it is neither the producing nor the market state. Other corporations are taxed on a production basis as well, which may be consistent with New York imposing the tax. But unlike other industries, there is even considerable question about the degree to which New York versus Tennessee is the producing state. Much of the contention arises because analysts continue to debate the definition of bank production.

Second, tax avoidance raises the prospect of considerable revenue loss. Failure to tax all income in some states is one means of loss. For example, the income from the above example is likely to lie outside current rules for defining taxable income in every state—even in Delaware. Also, good tax planning can result in much income being taxed at low or zero tax rates through securitization and resiting of production activities.

The ability of financial institutions to engage in tax avoidance takes the issue from a mere disagreement over whether money center or destination states should get the revenue. Substantial revenue losses because of tax avoidance may mean neither type of state gets the revenue associated with their financial activity. Greater revenues may be generated for both market and money center states if a properly structured tax is imposed.

A DESTINATION TAX

The review of the financial institution tax structure in the previous section indicates that existing tax structures are deficient. Tax avoidance through shifting the situs of activities is easy. This section describes a destination tax, which can substantially overcome these problems without creating undue administrative burdens. Minnesota, Tennessee, Indiana, and West Virginia have each adopted a form of destination taxation.

The destination tax is not subject to the same problems. First, the tax levied in a market is independent of where production takes place. Thus, all competitors operating in a particular market will be subject to the same tax structure, so the playing field is leveled. Tax burdens could not be reduced by relocating assets, income, or production within the United States, so there are no tax effects on location. Second, revenues are generated in each state according to the market and cannot be avoided. This results in all income being taxed once. Money center states may object that this would allow some of their tax base to be shifted to market states. However, money center states would receive revenues according to their (often large) market. Without the destination tax they may receive considerably less revenues because of tax avoidance.

Corporate taxes normally are levied on an origination or production basis. Taxable income base is apportioned among states where goods or services are produced, for example, through the standard three-factor apportionment formula based on wages (a measure of where labor is located), property (a measure of where capital is located), and receipts (a measure of where revenues are received). Further, rules for determining the situs for each of these are chosen based on where production of the goods and services occurs. An exception to this approach is the gross premiums tax on insurance which is levied on a destination basis. The destination tax differs by apportioning revenues to the market state.

A good destinations tax has six characteristics. Each is important, but the key characteristics for designing a destination rather than origination tax are the determination of nexus and the apportionment formula.

Determination of Nexus

Nexus should be established on a solicitation basis. Thus, firms would become liable for taxes in any state where they regularly solicit business. A number of lawyers, including McCray (1987), have concluded that no constitutional restriction arises from defining nexus in these terms.

A *de minimus* rule is appropriate to limit administrative and compliance costs associated with inconsequential activity. Minnesota and Tennessee, two states that recently changed their bank tax laws, each adopted such rules.

A major issue in Minnesota and Tennessee was whether financial institutions can establish nexus solely by purchasing securities that use assets located in the respective state as collateral. It appears to be a political problem as well as a potential problem for financial markets to establish nexus solely on the basis of purchasing securities.[7] Both states have chosen not to establish nexus for firms whose only relationship with the state is the holding of securities but to include the interest earned in taxable income if firms otherwise have nexus in the state. This opens some possibility for tax avoidance.

Apportionment Formula

Factors in the apportionment formula and rules for determining situs would be altered for a destinations tax. A single-factor receipts formula rather than the traditional three-factor formula is most appropriate. Receipts would be measured by interest and other revenues (not repayment of loan principal). The reason for a single-factor formula is that receipts are the best measure of financial services used in a state; that is, receipts are the best measure of the market for financial services. Production factors, such as property and payrolls, which are normally included in apportionment formulas, are inconsistent with the destinations approach.

The situs rules used to determine where receipts occur also should be structured on a destinations basis. These situs rules would attribute interest to the state where the secured property for the loan is located, where the credit card is billed, or where the loan proceeds are applied.

Definition of a Financial Institution

A destination tax differs from the production structure imposed on other industries. Different treatment requires a precise definition of "financial institution." An important feature is that the definition be broad enough to include all entities that are substantially in competition in each market. California's definition of financial institutions is based on whether they are substantially in competition with national banks. Because most financial income comes from lending, a destinations tax should define financial institutions according to whether their principal activity is lending. The West Virginia legislation defines financial organizations even more broadly as ones engaged in earning income from loans, leasing, operating a credit card business, rendering estate or trust services, or handling deposits. This approach appears generally acceptable except that deposits are better regarded as a measure of the production rather than the market activities of a financial institution.

A rule must be developed for deciding when a firm, only part of whose activities involve lending, is a financial institution. A possible rule of thumb is to presume a firm is a financial institution if 50 percent or more of its income arises from making loans, though of course any specific percentage introduces an air of arbitrariness. West Virginia and California both adopted a 50 percent rule. Whatever rule is adopted, each corporation operating within a holding company should be evaluated separately using the rule. For example, a determination would be made independently for each of Sear's major activities, and the Discover Card may be regarded as a financial institution, but retailing and catalog activities may not be.

Combined Reporting

Combined reporting should be required for all those affiliated members of a holding company that individually meet the definition of a financial institution. This overcomes the need to make a determination of which transactions between affiliated companies are at arms length, and it prevents firms from engaging in tax avoidance by shifting the situs of assets or profits to a holding company member in another state. This guideline is appropriate, even if a destination tax is not adopted.

Basis for Taxation

States probably should use the same base for determining tax liability as they have adopted for other corporations. An asset or value added basis for tax could be justified, to ensure that both profitable and unprofitable firms have tax liabilities. However, movement to one of these tax structures should only be undertaken if there is an intent to tax all corporations with such a tax structure. The current choice in nearly every state is a corporate income base and thus should be maintained for financial institutions unless the overall tax base is to be changed.

The tax should be legally structured as a franchise tax to allow inclusion of interest earned on federal securities in the income definition. Interest earned on state and local securities also should be included in the base. According to the ruling in *Memphis Bank and Trust Co. v. Garner*, a state can only tax federal interest if it includes interest of its own and its subdivisions in the tax base.

Throwout Rules

Given the guidelines discussed above, financial institutions may have receipts that are not taxed under the rules of any state. For example, a financial institution may receive earnings from securitized loans where the market is in a state in which the firm has no presence other than ownership of the securities. These earnings would not be taxed in the destination state under the rules outlined above because the firm would not have nexus. Similarly, the receipts would not be taxed in the production state because, though nexus obviously exists, the situs rules would attribute earnings to the destination state. Another example is working capital or other loans made to interstate corporations for which the situs of the loan's use cannot be readily determined.[8] Interest from federal securities is a further example.

One appropriate treatment for receipts that would otherwise go untaxed is to throw them out of the denominator of the apportionment formula, thereby raising the share of tax base in every state in which the financial institution has nexus. In effect, this approach apportions income to each state according to its share of the receipts where situs can be identified. An alternative treatment of these receipts is to throw them back to the state of domicile. Receipts would go in the numerator of the domicile state in cases where the situs cannot be determined. This procedure is similar to using a production tax framework for that part of income where the market cannot be associated with specific states.

A third and less attractive option is to tax domiciled corporations on 100 percent of their income and to allow a credit for taxes paid in other states. Under this approach foreign corporations would be taxed using a destinations tax, and domiciled corporations would bear a total tax burden similar to a production approach. Indiana and West Virginia employ this method. This "dual approach" is inferior to the others because it requires domiciled firms to pay taxes at the higher of the home state or foreign state tax rates. This creates a disincentive to undertake economic activity in the home state.

Problems with a Destination Tax

Three problems with the proposed destination tax structure should be noted. First, a problem of either a production or destination tax structure is that corporations can avoid much of their potential tax burden by shifting income and assets to affiliates located outside the United States. This avoidance technique can only be overcome by moving away from a water's-edge approach to taxing multinational income.

Second, higher compliance costs will initially be imposed on financial institutions. The main difference from current practice is that financial institutions would need to measure their apportionment factors according to destination principles, and this would require a new system. We conclude that financial institutions have the ability to track their market because of existing regulatory requirements and internal business practices, so apportionment factors can be calculated. Nonetheless, additional compliance costs would arise for firms as they adjust their systems to collect tax-related information in a new way. Our examination of information processing systems in the banking and thrift sector led to the conclusion that a major portion of the processing is handled at the service bureau or batch-processing level, except for very large concerns. Therefore, the initial costs of implementation can be spread over a very large base, resulting in a small investment in administration costs at the firm level. Compliance costs should be no greater with the destinations tax after the systems have been developed.

Third, it is conceivable that income could be taxed more than once during the transition from production to destination taxes. That is, the same receipts could be in the apportionment factor for a destination-taxing state and a production-taxing state. This problem will become increasingly less important as more states move to a destinations tax and, as noted above, both money center and market states have an incentive to change. Further, the problem should not be exaggerated because much of the income already may be escaping taxation though avoidance opportunities. Thus, the sum of apportionment factors may be less than one, even if firms are subject to both tax structures.

NOTES

1. See Spong and Watkins (1985) for a summary of statutes relating to interstate banking.

2. See McCray (1990) for a summary of the new legislation in these states, except for the recently enacted West Virginia legislation.

3. See McCray (1987) for a summary of the constitutional and legislative history.

4. Characteristics of the bank tax structure were drawn from Commerce Clearinghouse and telephone interviews with the states.

5. The actual effects of apportionment also depend on the situs rules used to determine where the factors are located.

6. See Fox and Murray (forthcoming) for a review of some examples.

7. The concern is that financial institutions would avoid purchasing securities in those cases where it would create nexus in another state.

8. In every case, reasonable effort should be exerted to determine where the proceeds are used.

VI
State Taxation of
Insurance Companies

State taxation of insurance companies has not received nearly as much attention as their federal tax rules, yet in 1989 insurance companies paid more in state premiums taxes than in federal corporate income taxes. Chapters 15-18 point to the need to reassess the notion of state insurance taxes as a simple premiums tax with minimal economic effects, and provide a solid base from which future research can be undertaken.

In Chapter 15, John W. Weber, Jr. describes the legal framework within which insurance companies are taxed. State tax rules typically depend on how insurance companies are regulated in the state. Licensed insurers are subject to the premiums tax. Weber describes several important issues in defining the premiums tax base. In addition, he introduces the issue of retaliatory taxes and domestic preference taxes that are unique to state insurance taxation.

In Chapter 16, Thomas S. Neubig and Michael Vlaisavljevich suggest that economic distortions from differential state taxation of insurance companies could become more important in the future. In particular, the growth of self-insurance, the crumbling barriers to insurance services provided by banks and noninsurance companies, and the increased concern about the solvency of insurance companies and states' guaranty funds make state tax rules more important. They describe the insurance industry, its products, and the state tax rules.

Neubig and Vlaisavljevich identify six policy issues in the taxation of insurance companies. The issues include taxing insurance companies on premiums, whereas other corporations are subject to income taxes, state incentives for domestic companies, retaliatory taxation on out-of-state companies, premiums tax credits for guaranty fund assessments, and sales taxes on insurance services.

In Chapter 17, Martin F. Grace and Harold D. Skipper, Jr., ask whether state insurance taxation is neutral among competitors. Under the current tax rules, they explore five possible tax distortions due to differential taxation: (1) between domestic and out-of-state insurers; (2) based on insurer's legal form; (3) between different size insurers; (4) based on the insurer's product mix; and (5) between insurers and non-insurer competitors. Grace and Skipper also address the issue of differences in the level of state insurance tax burdens. They find substantial variation in the insurance industry's tax burden across states.

Barrese analyzes in Chapter 18 the economics of mutual policyholder dividends and the state guaranty fund interplay with state revenues. He discusses the potential economic elements of insurance policyholder dividends: price rebate to policyholders as customers, interest earnings to policyholders as creditors, or return on equity to mutual policyholders as shareholders. Depending on the characterization of policyholder dividends, the state tax treatment of insurance companies and their policyholders could differ.

Barrese also evaluates the consequences of insurance company insolvencies for state tax revenues. To protect policyholders from insolvent companies, most states have guaranty funds that are financed on an as-needed basis by assessments on solvent companies. These guaranty fund assessments are deductible against federal corporate taxable income, often are eligible for credits against state premiums or income tax liability, and may be recouped through higher prices on policyholders. Barrese suggests that states not ignore the total reimbursement available to insurance companies and the interplay between increasing guaranty fund assessments and state revenues.

15
Overview of State Insurance Taxation

JOHN W. WEBER, JR.

This chapter describes the system of taxing of insurance companies and insurance placements followed by virtually all states. The premiums tax on licensed insurers is the centerpiece of this system. Most state statutes include a series of provisions designed to tax all insurance transactions that take place within the state. These generally consist of the premiums tax, the tax on surplus lines placements, and the tax on direct placements and/or on "industrial insured" placements, if such placements are authorized by state law. These provisions are closely related to the state corporate franchise tax and the state unauthorized insurers law.

CORPORATE FRANCHISE TAX, PREMIUMS TAX, AND UNAUTHORIZED INSURERS LAW

In every state, it is unlawful to transact an insurance business without a license. Over the years various formulations of "transact[ing] insurance business" have been devised. In recent years, many states have adopted the essential elements of the Unauthorized Insurers Model Bill (the "Model Bill"). The Model Bill provides that any one of several activities will cause an insurer to be treated as transacting business in the state. These include making or proposing to make a contract of insurance, guaranty, or surety; taking or receiving any application for insurance; receiving or collecting premiums, commissions membership fees, assessments, etc.; issuing or delivering contracts to residents or to persons authorized to do business within the state; and directly or indirectly soliciting, negotiating, procuring, or effecting insurance or renewals.

Several exceptions allow "nonadmitted," that is, unlicensed, insurers to provide certain insurance within a state. States generally have provisions that place certain lines of insurance, for example, marine insurance, beyond the purview of the insurance regulations. Reinsurance is a generally recognized exception to state "transacting business" laws. Excess/surplus lines insurance is excepted from the general prohibition against writing insurance in a state unless licensed to do so. Placements by authorized "surplus-lines" brokers with unlicensed insurers ordinarily are not permitted unless the risk has been rejected by the licensed market, and may not be made solely to obtain better terms as to a rate or policy form than those offered in the admitted market. Lastly, there are "direct placement" laws and "industrial insured exemptions" from unauthorized insurers laws. Not all states have adopted such provisions, and some have adopted one but not the other.[1] In some states, direct placement statutes also require that the state in which the transaction occurs be a state in which the insurer is licensed.

The marine exemption may be thought of as justified on the ground that the state does not have jurisdiction over ocean marine risks. The excess and surplus lines exemption is justified on the basis of necessity—the state must provide a means for its insureds to purchase insurance that is unavailable in the licensed market. The reinsurance and industrial insured exemptions may be viewed as "sophisticated buyer" exemptions. The direct placement exemption arguably is based on a "constitutional right to purchase insurance" and consequently is available whether or not the statute specifically provides for it.[2]

The structure of a state's system of taxing insurance placements can be analyzed with reference to its unauthorized insurers statute. Licensed insurers, or those that should be licensed, are subject to the premiums tax. Placements made with state-authorized excess or surplus lines insurers are subject to an excess or surplus lines tax that is required to be paid by the broker. Direct placements or placements made pursuant to an industrial insured statute generally are subject to a "compensating" tax which is imposed at the same rate as the surplus lines tax. Although the industrial insured tax is applied in virtually every state that has such a statute, some states do not provide for a direct placement tax.[3] Marine insurance placements, which are not regulated for jurisdictional reasons, are not subject to tax.

The corporate franchise tax of virtually every state provides an exemption for insurance companies subject to state premiums tax.[4] Thus, insurance companies generally are subject to the premiums tax, rather than to the corporate franchise tax.

State premiums taxes are imposed on insurance companies doing business within the state. Generally, such insurers either are licensed or are required to be licensed pursuant to the state unauthorized insurers law.[5] One plausible analysis is that an insurer that was not "transacting an insurance business" for regulatory purposes would be exempt from the premiums tax, but conceivably could be subject to the corporate franchise tax. However, in at least one major jurisdiction, the question was resolved differently. In *Illinois Commercial Men's Association v. State Board of Equalization* (1983), the California Supreme Court approved an assessment of premiums tax against an insurer that solicited solely by mail but which used (to a significant extent) independent claims adjusters within the state. The court held that the fact that the insurer's contacts with the state were not significant enough to cause it to be "doing business" so as to be subject to insurance regulatory jurisdiction did not preclude the valid assertion of the premiums tax.[6] Thus, although the premiums tax can generally be associated with status as an insurer licensed to do business in a state, it is possible for an insurer to be subject to the premiums tax even though it is not required under the unauthorized insurers law to be licensed in the state.

The scope of California's "in lieu of" clause recently has spawned significant litigation. *Massachusetts Mutual Life Insurance Co. v. City and County of San Francisco* (1982) holds that the franchise tax applies to the noninsurance business of an insurance company.[7] The California Franchise Tax Board is in agreement with the *Massachusetts Mutual* case.[8] However, the *Massachusetts Mutual* result has been disapproved in *Mutual Life Insurance Company of New York v. City of Los Angeles* (1990).

There are other, as yet undecided, aspects of this problem. For example, should the "in lieu of" exemption apply to an insurance company that has made California investments but is not subject to the California premiums tax, either because it provides reinsurance or surplus lines insurance and thus is taxed indirectly, or because it has no noninvestment activities in California?[9] A second interesting question is the treatment of a "captive" insurer that is part of a unitary group doing business in California. There is a possibility that the Internal Revenue Service would characterize such a company as an investment vehicle rather than an insurer. Should the exemption still apply to such a company if it paid the premiums tax? If the exemption is not available, should the captive be treated as an investment vehicle which is not part of the unitary group, or should its income be characterized as passive and sited at the domicile of the company?

TAX BASE

Virtually every state imposes a tax on premiums paid to licensed insurers. Thus, insurance companies generally are not subject to tax on their income; rather, they are taxed on their net premiums. However, as noted above, the New York tax on insurance companies is imposed at a 9 percent rate on allocable net income plus an additional tax on net direct premiums. The additional tax is imposed at a 1.2 percent rate on property/casualty premiums, at a 1 percent rate on accident and health premiums, and at a 0.8 percent rate on life insurance premiums. All companies are subject to a maximum combined tax of 2.6 percent of allocable premiums. (New York Tax Law, Sections 1502, 1505, and 1510.)

California imposes a tax of 5 percent of allocable underwriting profits on ocean marine insurers. Also, the California Franchise Tax Board has taken the view that income from "noninsurance" business activities—that is, activities other than the investment of reserves and capital and surplus required to carry on the insurance business—is subject to the general corporate franchise tax.[10] The tax is generally imposed on "net premiums," that is, on gross direct premiums less return premiums and policyholder dividends. Generally, states define net premiums as including only direct placements. Reinsurance premiums are not included in the tax base, and reinsurance premiums ceded do not reduce the tax base.[11] This system works because it causes all premiums paid within the state to be subject to the tax when they are originally paid. As a matter of business practice, the premiums tax paid is reimbursed to the reinsured direct writer as a "ceding commission" when all or a portion of the policy is reinsured. It is notable that there are some statutes, including New York's, that both take reinsurance premiums into account and, correspondingly, provide a "deduction" for reinsurance ceded.

The problem of allocating or apportioning premiums to a state can be difficult, particularly with respect to multistate risks—for example, a worldwide property or liability cover, or coverage for a national fleet of trucks or railroad cars. New York has solved the problem with a "deemer" clause. That is, as a general matter, premiums that are not subject to tax in other states are deemed subject to the New York tax.[12]

State statutes often provide that different tax rates are applicable to life insurance premiums and to property/casualty insurance premiums. One ubiquitous provision allows foreign insurers a credit or a reduction in rate, on a formula basis, for investments made in securities issued by the taxing state or by its municipalities or other political subdivisions.[13]

RETALIATORY TAXES

Virtually every state has a retaliatory tax provision that allows it to increase the premiums tax on a foreign insurer doing business within the state. If, for example, state B imposes a higher premiums tax on state A insurers doing business in state B than state A would otherwise impose on state B insurers doing business in state A, state A may increase its tax to make up the difference.[14]

The U.S. Supreme Court approved an application of California's retaliatory tax statute in *Western & Southern Life Insurance Co. v. State Board of Equalization* (1981). Issues arising under retaliatory taxes tend to be very factual and difficult to conceptualize. For example, state B may have a higher tax rate but allow a credit for insurance examination fees, and the state A insurer being analyzed for comparative purposes may have paid a substantial examination fee to state A (its state of residence) but not to state B.[15] Difficult questions could also arise if state B subjects insurers to a franchise tax on their income.[16]

DOMESTIC PREFERENCE TAXES

States have had statutory schemes in which domestic insurers were subject to a lower premiums tax than foreign insurers doing business in the state. An Alabama scheme that taxed foreign insurers three to four times as heavily as domestic ones was struck down as discriminatory by the U.S. Supreme Court in *Metropolitan Life Insurance v. Ward* (1985). There was a vigorous dissent, and the Court was not required to thoroughly analyze all aspects of the domestic preference issue. Nevertheless, in recent years, between ten and fifteen states have amended their laws to avoid the domestic preference issue. For example, domestic preferences might be replaced by home office credit or employment credits.

This issue raises an interesting question with reference to the recent Supreme Court cases holding that a state that does not provide prepayment remedies for an unlawful tax must provide retrospective relief.[17]

NOTES

1. A direct placement statute generally allows any insured to purchase insurance from an unauthorized insurer outside the state. For example, New York's direct

placement law, N.Y. Ins. Code §1101(b)(ii)(E), permits risks to be placed directly with insurers not licensed in New York so long as the policies are "principally negotiated, issued, and delivered...in a jurisdiction in which the insurer is authorized to do an insurance business." The Colorado law provides rather typical direct placement and industrial insured exemptions: direct placement [Colo. Ins. Code §10-3-903(2)(d)] and industrial insured (Colo. Ins. Code §10-3-910).

2. See *State Board of Insurance v. Todd Shipyards Corp.* (1962); *Connecticut General Life Insurance Corp. v. Johnson* (1938); *St. Louis Cotton Compress Co. v. Arkansas* (1922); *Allgeyer v. Louisiana* (1897). These cases can be cited for the proposition that state residents may exercise a constitutional right to travel to another jurisdiction to negotiate and effect insurance coverage on their own behalf. It must be stressed that the doctrine, as a matter of common law, has been significantly eroded over time and is severely limited in scope.

3. For example, prior to 1990, neither New York nor California imposed a tax on direct placements, although both authorized direct placements in their unauthorized insurer statutes. However, recent New York legislation both provided an allocation formula for premiums subject to the excess lines tax and also imposed a direct placement tax at the same 3.6 percent rate as the excess lines tax. New York Tax Law, Sections 1551 and 1552. These tax rates generally range from 3 to 5 percent.

4. In at least one state (New York) the premiums tax on licensed insurers is a two-pronged tax (i.e., a franchise tax on allocable net income plus a premiums tax), subject to a maximum based on net premiums. See New York Tax Law, Sections 1501 and 1510. Even in New York this dual taxing system is embodied in a statute separate from the corporate franchise tax. Many state statutes provide that the premiums tax is in lieu of all other taxes. As discussed below, questions of interpretation of this clause can arise.

5. One interesting question is whether activities performed within a state by a foreign insurance company that are not sufficient to cause it to violate the state unauthorized insurers law, can be sufficient to cause it to be subject to either the premiums tax or the corporate franchise tax. For example, the activities may not be "mainstream" insurance activities but may be related to investment activities or corporate administration.

6. See also *People v. United National Life Insurance Co.,* 66 Cal. 2d 577, 427 P.2d 199, 58 Cal. Rptr. 599 (1967), *appeal dismissed,* 389 U.S. 330 (1967), which held that the premiums tax can be imposed on a mail-order insurer.

7. See California Constitution, Article XIII, Section 28(f).

8. Legal Ruling 427, 1987 WL 50207 (Cal. Fran. Tax. BD.).

9. See Legal Ruling 385, 1975 WL 3290 (Cal. Fran. Tax. Bd.).

10. Legal Ruling 427. But see, the discussion of the *Massachusetts Mutual* and *Mutual of New York* cases above.

11. For example, Texas imposes a 3.5 percent tax on "gross premium receipts," which are defined as direct premiums (not reinsurance) less policyholder dividends and return premiums. (Texas Insurance Code, Article 4.10). The California premiums tax is imposed at a rate of 2.35 percent on gross premiums less return premiums. Premiums for reinsurance are not included in gross premiums. (California Rev. and Tax Code, Section 12221.) Illinois imposes a 2 percent net receipts tax on "net taxable premiums," which are defined as gross premiums on direct business less return premiums and policyholder dividends. [Illinois Insurance Code, Section 409(1).]

However, the recently revised New York statute takes reinsurance premiums into account.

12. Cf. New York Tax Law, Sections 1504(b) and 1510(c). The New York law also contains a provision allowing the tax commissioner to allocate or apportion income or deductions for purposes of the income tax portion of the statute, in circumstances in which there has been an artificial arrangement to shift net income outside the state. (New York Tax Law, Section 1504.) Insurers operating in the New York Free Trade Zone are not subject to the deemer clause with respect to premiums received on Free Trade Zone risks.

13. For example, the Texas law provides that the 3.5 percent tax rate applicable to fire and casualty companies is reduced to 2.3 percent if Texas investments represent 85-90 percent of the state investments that represent the largest portion of the insurers portfolio. If Texas investments exceed 90 percent, the rate is reduced to 1.85 percent. Similarly, the 2.5 percent tax on life and accident and health insurers is reduced to 1.8 percent if Texas investments exceed 90 percent of the state investments that represent the largest portion of the insurers portfolio. The rate is 1.4 percent if Texas investments represent the largest portion. (Texas Insurance Code, Article 4.10, Section 10 and Article 4.11, Section 5B.)

14. The Pennsylvania retaliatory tax statute (40 P.S. §50) is typical: "If any other state imposes any burdens or prohibitions on insurance companies, or agents of this state doing business in such other state, which are in addition to, or in excess of, the burdens or prohibitions imposed by this Commonwealth on insurance companies and agents, like burdens and prohibitions shall be imposed on all insurance companies and agents of such other state doing business in this Commonwealth, so long as the burdens and prohibitions of such other state remain in force. In applying this section to an insurance company of another state, such company shall not be required to pay any taxes and fees which are greater in aggregate amount than those which would be imposed by the laws of such other state and any political subdivision thereof upon a like company of this Commonwealth transacting the same volume and kind of business in such other state."

15. A survey of some of the cases that have been decided in this area may be instructive regarding the scope of these issues. See, for example, *Providence Washington Insurance Co. v. Commonwealth* (Pa. Cmwlth. 1983) (a Rhode Island insurer doing business in Pennsylvania was required to pay additional tax of 1.5 percent on Pennsylvania workers compensation premiums to mirror a similar Rhode Island tax used to fund a rehabilitation center); *South Carolina v. Southern Farm Bureau Life Insurance Co.* (S. Ct. S.C., 1975) (additional taxes assessed against Mississippi insurance companies because the Mississippi premiums tax did not provide for investment credits); *Occidental Life v. Commonwealth* (Pa. Cmwlth. 1972) (in making the retaliatory tax comparison, a California insurer doing business in Pennsylvania was entitled to take into account the Pennsylvania use taxes it had paid); *Commonwealth v. Fireman's Fund Insurance Co.* (S. Ct. Pa., 1952) (in making the retaliatory tax comparison, a California insurer doing business in Pennsylvania was not entitled to take into account payments to the Fire Insurance Patrol of Philadelphia); and *Occidental Life v. Holmes* (S. Ct. Montana, 1938) (in making the retaliatory tax comparison, a California insurer doing business in Montana was not allowed to reduce the differential in the tax rate by hypothetical credit for Montana realty taxes; California imposed a 2.6

percent premiums tax, reduced by California realty taxes, whereas Montana imposed a 2.0 percent tax with no realty tax reduction.

16. A franchise tax on foreign insurers was proposed but defeated in Minnesota. Opponents argued that such a system would create difficult retaliatory tax problems.

17. *McKesson Corp. v. Division of Alcoholic Beverages and Tobacco* and *American Trucking Association v. Smith*, 496 U.S. 18, 110 S. Ct. 2238 (1990).

16
Economic Issues in State Taxation of Insurance Companies

THOMAS S. NEUBIG and MICHAEL VLAISAVLJEVICH

In 1989, insurance companies paid more in state premiums taxes than in federal corporate income taxes. In the same year, state insurance premiums taxes totaled $7.37 billion. Although federal income taxation has moved toward taxing all types of financial institutions more similarly, state taxation of insurance companies differs greatly from state taxation of banks and general business corporations. Differential state taxation is likely to exacerbate economic distortions as banks increasingly sell and underwrite insurance products, mutual funds continue to market annuity products, and businesses self-insure against health costs and property and casualty risks.

States are seeking additional revenues to address budget deficits, and they consider higher revenues from insurance companies as a potential source for such revenues. Increasing concerns about the solvency of insurance companies, which have been regulated at the state level, have resulted in a sharp increase in guaranty fund assessments in recent years. It is therefore important that increased attention be focused on the potential economic distortions from differential state taxation, especially as state taxation of insurance companies becomes more important in the future.

State taxation of insurance companies has generally relied on the premiums tax. Although the premiums tax has provided a large and stable revenue base, current premiums tax rates may place insurance companies at a competitive disadvantage. To the extent that effective state tax rates on insurance companies are higher than effective state tax rates on other industries, insurance companies will lose market share to their competitors and to self-insurance. To the extent that one state's premiums tax rates are higher than other states, the higher premiums tax will be an additional cost of doing business in that state and will burden domestic insurance companies selling insurance in other states because of the retaliatory tax unique to the insurance industry.

This chapter first describes the insurance industry, its products, and the major features of state taxation of insurance companies. It then discusses six policy issues involved in state insurance taxation and their economic implications.

THE U.S. INSURANCE INDUSTRY

The insurance industry plays an important role in the U.S. economy. By diversifying risks over a large number of individuals and businesses, the insurance industry can provide protection against personal and business risks. These risks include early death covered by life insurance; longevity covered by annuities; automobile and homeowner's liability and physical damage; workers' compensation; commercial multiperil and fire protection covered by property and casualty insurance; and hospital and physician care, dental, drugs, and long-term care covered by health insurance. The insurance industry enables individuals and businesses to insure against significant losses without the need for accumulating large savings. In addition to diversifying risks, the insurance industry also plays an important role in underwriting insurance risks to minimize moral hazard and adverse selection, administering claims reimbursements, and encouraging preventative measures and managed care. In all these ways, insurance companies provide value added to their policyholders at a lower price and/or significantly less risk than the policyholders could provide for themselves.

The insurance industry is regulated at the state level. State regulatory authorities monitor both the financial condition of companies licensed to do business in the state and their ability to pay claims. All states have insurance guarantee funds that collect assessments from companies to pay claims of insolvent companies. In the property and casualty insurance lines, many states require approval or review of premium rates to ensure that they are not inadequate, excessive, or discriminatory.

Types of Insurance Companies and Their Products

The insurance industry can be divided into six general types of companies: (1) property and casualty insurance; (2) life insurance; (3) health insurance; (4) reinsurance; (5) self-insurance; and (6) nontraditional insurance providers. This classification is somewhat arbitrary and does not include minor industry groups. In 1988, the property and casualty, life, and health segments approximately equally divided the almost $600 billion in total premiums (Table 16.1).

Property and Casualty Insurance Companies. The largest number of companies are in the property and casualty insurance business. In 1988, there were 3,849 individual property and casualty insurance companies, selling over $200 billion of direct written premiums (before reinsurance). The largest category of property and casualty insurance is automobile liability and physical damage insurance, accounting for $94 billion of premiums in 1989, followed by workers' compensation at $32 billion of premiums, commercial multiperil at $19 billion of premiums, and homeowner's insurance at $18 billion of premiums.

Life Insurance Companies. The next largest industry segment is life insurance companies. In 1989, there were 2,305 individual life insurance companies, selling $73 billion of life insurance premiums, $115 billion of annuity considerations, and $56 billion of health insurance premiums. Life insurance policies include individual and group term life insurance, permanent life insurance (a combination of savings and term insurance), and credit life insurance (term insurance coverage for outstanding debt). Life insurance companies sell both individual annuities ($49 billion in 1989) and group pension annuities ($66 billion). They also sell most of the purchased health insurance coverage ($56 billion).

Health Insurance Companies. Private health insurance is provided by commercial insurance companies (many are life companies), Blue Cross-Blue Shield plans, self-funded employer plans, and prepayment plans such as health maintenance organizations (HMOs). Of the total $192 billion of health insurance premiums in 1988, insurance companies received $98 billion of premiums and Blue Cross-Blue Shield plans $51.2 billion. Self-insured and HMO plans reported premiums of $74 billion for claims paid and administrative fees. These figures involve some double counting because almost $47 billion of self-insured premiums were paid to private insurance companies for administrative services only (ASO) to process claims or minimum premium plans (MPP) where employers self-fund their plans yet insure against very large claims.

Reinsurance Companies. Reinsurance companies specialize in insuring the risks of insurance companies directly underwriting the policies. Direct writers may want to reinsure all or a portion of their policies to minimize risk of loss or to increase their financial capacity to underwrite additional insurance. Many insurance companies now both cede (i.e., buy) and assume (i.e., sell) reinsurance to maximize their financial capabilities. Premiums for reinsurance assumed totaled over $26

TABLE 16.1
Insurance Premiums by Line of Business

	Premiums ($ billion)	
	1988	1989
Property and Casualty Insurance	202.0	215.5
Life Insurance	73.5	73.3
Annuity Considerations (Total)	103.3	115.0
Individual	43.8	59.5
Group	49.4	65.6
Health Insurance (Total)[1]	192.3	N.A.
Insurance Companies	98.2	N.A.
Self-insured and HMO	73.7	N.A.
Blue Cross-Blue Shield	51.2	N.A.

Source: Best's Aggregates and Averages, Property and Casualty Insurance, 1990, p. 120. American Council of Life Insurance, *1990 Life Insurance Fact Book*, p. 68 and 70. HIAA, *Source Book of Health Insurance Data*, 1990, p. 28.

[1]Does not equal sum of types due to duplication of self-insurance payments through insurance companies.

billion in the life insurance industry in 1988, and over $13 billion among the 146 organizations with predominantly reinsurance in the property and casualty industry.

Self-Insurance. Self-insurance by businesses has increased substantially in the last ten years, particularly for health and workers' compensation coverage. In 1988, over one-half of the commercial insurance companies' group coverage involved self-insurance by the employer (Health Insurance Association of America, 1990, p. 10). Fifty-nine percent of U.S. employers surveyed said they self-funded their group health plans in 1990.[1] Corporations and other employers establish self-funded health plans and pay insurance carriers or third-party administrators to process claims or to insure against only very large claims. Self-insurance also is increasing in commercial property and casualty insurance lines. Self insurance, excess/surplus lines insurance, captive insurers, and risk retention groups are methods of alternative risk financing. An estimated 30 percent of the commercial insurance market uses some form of self-insurance.[2] Self-insurance plans have several advantages in that they are generally exempt from state premiums taxes, are exempt under the Employee Retirement Income Security Act of 1974 (ERISA) from state regulation of health insurance—particularly minimum benefit requirements—and are exempt from state risk pools that sell insurance to the uninsured.

Nontraditional Insurers. In addition to self-insurance, the insurance industry faces competition from non-traditional insurers, particularly as the barriers within the financial services industry are lowered. Banks and mutual funds are allowed to sell annuities in direct competition with life insurance companies. Banks are also beginning to sell and underwrite credit life insurance in some states. Health maintenance organizations are in direct competition with private insurers. In the health and property and casualty insurance lines, third-party administrators provide administrative services to self-insurers. Finally, it is important to note that the federal government is an important provider of insurance, which often defines the scope of the private insurance market.

Statistical Measures of the Insurance Industry by State

Several different measures of the importance of the insurance industry to each state are presented: (1) the amount of insurance premiums sold in the state; (2) the number of companies headquartered in the state; and (3) the relative size of the insurance industry to total gross state product.

In 1989, property and casualty insurance premiums averaged $868 per capita, life insurance premiums were $257 per capita, and health insurance premiums sold by life insurance companies were $215 per capita (Table 16.2). The latter figure compares to $782 per capita for total health insurance premiums, including Blue Cross-Blue Shield and self-insurance and HMO plans. Annuities and health insurance sold by non-life insurance companies are not included in these data.

The location of headquarters generally offers significant employment opportunities for state residents. Arizona has the largest number of life insurance companies, 724 in 1989, followed by Texas with 267, Louisiana with 107, New York with 89, and Illinois with 82 (Table 16.3). Texas has the largest number of property and casualty insurance companies with 298, followed by Illinois with 295, Missouri with 218, Iowa with 203, New York with 201, and Pennsylvania with 200. The number of companies, however, does not indicate the size of the insurance sector in the state.

TABLE 16.2
Insurance Premiums by State, 1989

State	Premiums Per Capita ($)		
	Prop. & Cas.	Life	Health
Alabama	710	251	179
Alaska	1104	182	340
Arizona	744	231	214
Arkansas	671	174	148
California	1109	220	216
Colorado	786	258	226
Connecticut	1356	395	314
Delaware	1100	578	245
District of Columbia	1330	319	634
Florida	892	240	258
Georgia	845	295	247
Hawaii	997	271	99
Idaho	682	208	122
Illinois	872	285	290
Indiana	857	250	211
Iowa	747	312	213
Kansas	763	278	186
Kentucky	631	202	153
Louisiana	712	241	192
Maine	994	204	204
Maryland	910	273	192
Massachusetts	1210	293	214
Michigan	848	224	158
Minnesota	894	252	178
Mississippi	620	196	297
Missouri	779	280	252
Montana	697	212	192
Nebraska	765	296	265
Nevada	882	204	205
New Hampshire	1078	252	218
New Jersey	986	358	299
New Mexico	636	176	167
New York	992	322	290
North Carolina	664	263	195
North Dakota	764	256	157

TABLE 16.2 (continued)

State	Premiums Per Capita($)		
	Prop. & Cas.	Life	Health
Ohio	650	259	186
Oklahoma	587	204	195
Oregon	939	204	131
Pennsylvania	951	291	145
Rhode Island	1090	277	96
South Carolina	666	250	182
South Dakota	703	268	250
Tennessee	714	235	225
Texas	823	223	215
Utah	492	192	135
Vermont	968	255	206
Virginia	770	268	175
Washington	711	198	131
West Virginia	536	201	167
Wisconsin	771	237	220
Wyoming	565	213	171
All U.S.	868	257	215

Sources: American Council of Life Insurance, *1990 Life Insurance Fact Book*, p. 73; *Best's Aggregates and Averages, Property and Casualty Insurance, 1989*; *Statistical Abstract*.

In terms of employee compensation and capital income, the insurance industry accounted for approximately 2 percent of total gross state product (GSP) in 1986 (Table 16.4). Insurance carriers accounted for 1.3 percent, and agents, brokers, and services accounted for an additional 0.6 percent. Connecticut topped the list with insurance carriers representing 3.8 percent of GSP.

CURRENT STATE TAXATION OF INSURANCE COMPANIES

State taxation of insurance companies is unlike that of any other corporations. All states impose taxes on insurance premiums, even states without corporate income or franchise taxes. Several states also impose corporate income or franchise taxes on insurance companies. In such states, companies are generally allowed to credit one tax liability against the other.

When insurance premiums taxes were originally enacted in the nineteenth century and early 1900s, many states taxed "foreign" (out-of-state domiciled) companies at higher statutory rates than "domestic" (in-state domiciled) companies. Although a 1985 Supreme Court decision found discriminatory taxation unconstitutional, some states still have tax rules that may result in different effective tax rates for foreign and domestic companies. For example, special credits for investment or employment in the state are structured so that tax benefits are more likely to accrue to companies headquartered in the state.

Another unique feature of state insurance taxation is the retaliatory tax. Retaliatory taxes are imposed on foreign companies domiciled in states that have higher tax rates than the destination state's tax rate. For example, if state A has a 2 percent premiums tax on domestic and foreign insurers and state B has a 3 percent tax rate, then insurers from state B would pay a retaliatory tax of 1 percent on premiums received from state A residents. Retaliatory taxes are designed to discourage higher out-of-state taxes on domestic insurers.

State and local governments impose costs on insurance companies in addition to the premiums tax. Assessments from state insurance guaranty funds to cover unpaid claims of insolvent companies are levied as a percentage of premiums. Many states allow all or a part of the guaranty fund assessment as a credit against the premiums tax. States impose various fees on insurance companies, such as assessments for assigned risk pools for the uninsured and assessments for financing insurance departments and workers' compensation agency operations. Nonmonetary requirements such as minimum benefit levels impose additional costs on insurers.

Table 16.5 presents a summary of state taxation of insurance companies. The first two columns present the general premiums tax rate for life and property and casualty insurance companies for foreign and domestic insurers. The third column shows which states also levy income or franchise taxes on insurance companies and whether the premiums or income tax is creditable against the other. The fourth column shows which states permit an investment rate reduction or home office credit against the premiums tax. The final column shows which states allow a premiums tax credit for assessments paid to state guaranty funds, and whether the credit is the standard full recovery over five years.

TABLE 16.3
Number of Domiciled Insurance Companies
by State, 1989

State	Life Ins. Companies[1]		Property/Casualty Ins. Companies[2]	
	Number	Percent	Number	Percent
Alabama	30	1.3	31	0.8
Alaska	1	0.0	12	0.3
Arizona	724	31.4	40	1.0
Arkansas	33	1.4	29	0.8
California	59	2.6	158	4.1
Colorado	25	1.1	46	1.2
Connecticut	24	1.0	65	1.7
Delaware	65	2.8	108	2.8
Dist. of Col.	5	0.2	14	0.4
Florida	47	2.0	79	2.1
Georgia	32	1.4	58	1.5
Hawaii	6	0.3	20	0.5
Idaho	4	0.2	15	0.4
Illinois	82	3.6	295	7.7
Indiana	55	2.4	121	3.1
Iowa	37	1.6	203	5.3
Kansas	17	0.7	33	0.9
Kentucky	15	0.7	39	1.0
Louisiana	107	4.6	49	1.3
Maine	5	0.2	22	0.6
Maryland	17	0.7	41	1.1
Massachusetts	16	0.7	49	1.3
Michigan	28	1.2	63	1.6
Minnesota	26	1.1	179	4.7
Mississippi	30	1.3	21	0.5
Missouri	47	2.0	218	5.7
Montana	4	0.2	15	0.4
Nebraska	29	1.3	78	2.0
Nevada	3	0.1	5	0.1
N. Hampshire	4	0.2	36	0.9
New Jersey	13	0.6	65	1.7
New Mexico	6	0.3	13	0.3

TABLE 16.3 (continued)

State	Life Ins. Companies[1]		Property/Casualty Ins. Companies[2]	
	Number	Percent	Number	Percent
New York	89	3.9	201	5.2
N. Carolina	23	1.0	71	1.8
North Dakota	11	0.5	39	1.0
Ohio	45	2.0	158	4.1
Oklahoma	54	2.3	57	1.5
Oregon	6	0.3	19	0.5
Pennsylvania	60	2.6	200	5.2
Rhode Island	6	0.3	23	0.6
S. Carolina	23	1.0	32	0.8
South Dakota	8	0.3	50	1.3
Tennessee	27	1.2	52	1.4
Texas	267	11.6	298	7.7
Utah	16	0.7	11	0.3
Vermont	5	0.2	130	3.4
Virginia	16	0.7	47	1.2
Washington	21	0.9	25	0.6
W. Virginia	2	0.1	18	0.5
Wisconsin	28	1.2	191	5.0
Wyoming	2	0.1	7	0.2
All U.S.	2305	1.0	3849	1.0

Sources: American Council of Life Insurance, *1990 Life Insurance Fact Book,* p. 104, and Insurance Information Institute, *1990 Property/Casualty Insurance Facts,* p. 10.

[1]Mid-year 1989.
[2]1988.

TABLE 16.4
Insurance Industry as Percentage
of 1986 Gross State Product

State	Insurance Carriers	Agents, Brokers, & Services	Total Insurance
Connecticut	3.8	0.6	4.4
Nebraska	2.1	0.8	2.9
Massachusetts	1.8	0.7	2.5
Rhode Island	1.7	0.6	2.3
Pennsylvania	1.6	0.6	2.2
New Hampshire	1.6	0.6	2.2
Illinois	1.6	0.7	2.3
Iowa	1.6	0.7	2.3
Minnesota	1.5	0.7	2.2
New Jersey	1.5	0.7	2.2
Wisconsin	1.5	0.6	2.1
Maine	1.5	0.6	2.1
New York	1.5	0.7	2.2
Delaware	1.4	0.5	1.9
Ohio	1.3	0.5	1.8
Missouri	1.2	0.7	1.9
Maryland	1.2	0.6	1.8
Indiana	1.2	0.5	1.7
Georgia	1.2	0.6	1.8
Kansas	1.2	0.8	2.0
California	1.2	0.7	1.8
Washington	1.2	0.6	1.8
Florida	1.2	0.8	1.9
Texas	1.1	0.6	1.7
Alabama	1.1	0.5	1.6
Oregon	1.1	0.6	1.8
Tennessee	1.1	0.6	1.7
Colorado	1.1	0.6	1.6
Arizona	1.1	0.6	1.7
Vermont	1.1	0.7	1.8
Michigan	1.0	0.5	1.5
South Carolina	1.0	0.5	1.5

TABLE 16.4 (continued)

State	Insurance Carriers	Agents, Brokers, & Services	Total Insurance
Mississippi	1.0	0.6	1.6
South Dakota	0.9	0.6	1.6
North Carolina	0.9	0.5	1.4
Oklahoma	0.9	0.6	1.6
Virginia	0.9	0.4	1.3
Kentucky	0.9	0.5	1.4
Louisiana	0.9	0.6	1.5
Hawaii	0.9	0.5	1.4
D.C.	0.9	0.2	1.1
Utah	0.8	0.5	1.3
North Dakota	0.8	0.7	1.5
West Virginia	0.8	0.4	1.2
Idaho	0.7	0.9	1.6
New Mexico	0.7	0.4	1.1
Montana	0.7	0.5	1.2
Arkansas	0.7	0.6	1.2
Nevada	0.6	0.5	1.1
Alaska	0.4	0.3	0.7
Wyoming	0.3	0.3	0.6
U.S. Total	1.3	.6	1.9

*Source:*Bureau of Economic Analysis, Gross State Product Tape Compiled by Price Waterhouse.

TABLE 16.5
Summary of State Insurance Taxation, 1990

State	Premiums Tax Rate[1]		Income or Franchise Tax[2]	IRR or HOC[3]	Prem. Tax Credit[4]
	Life	P & C			
AL	3.0/1.0	4.0/1.0	Yes/credit	IRR	Yes
AK	2.7	2.7	No	No	No
AZ	2.0	2.0	No	No	Yes
AR	2.5	2.5	Dom. only	No	Yes
CA	2.35	2.35	No	No	No
CO	2.25/1.0	2.25/1.0	No	HOC	No
CT	2.0	2.0	Dom. only	No	Life only, NS
DE	2.0	2.0	No	No	Yes
DC	2.0	2.0	No	No	No
FL	1.75	1.75	Yes/credit	No	Yes/NS
GA	2.25	2.25	No	IRR	Life only
HI	3.19/191	4.28/2.96	No	No	Life only
ID	3.0	3.0	No	IRR	Life only
IL	2.0/0	2.0/0	Yes/credit	No	Life only, NS
IN	2.0/0	2.0/0	Dom. only	No	Yes
IA	2.0	2.0	No	No	Life only
KS	2.0/1.0	2.0/1.0	No	IRR	Yes
KY	2.0/0	2.0/1.0	No	No	Life only
LA	2.25	2.25	Yes/credit	IRR	P&C only, NS
ME	2.0	2.0	No	No	No
MD	2.0	2.0	No	No	No
MA	2.0	2.3	No	No	Life only, NS
MI[5]	0.74	0.74	Yes, SBT	No	Yes, NS
MN	2.0	2.0	No	No	No
MS	3.0	3.0	Yes/credit	No	Life only, NS
MO	2.0	2.0	Yes/credit	No	Yes, NS
MT	2.75	2.75	No	No	Life only
NE	1.0	1.0	Yes/credit	No	Yes

TABLE 16.5 (continued)

State	Premiums Tax Rate[1] Life	P & C	Income or Franchise Tax[2]	IRR or HOC[3]	Prem. Tax Credit[4]
NV	3.5	3.5	No	HOC	Yes
NH	2.0	2.0	Yes/credit	No	No
NJ	2.1	2.1	No	No	No
NM	3.0	3.0	No	IRR	No
NY[5]	0.8	1.2	Yes, max.	No	Life only, NS
NC	1.75	1.75	No	No	No
ND	2.0	1.8	No	No	Life only
OH[5]	2.5/0	2.5/0	No	No	Life only
OK	2.25	2.25	No	HOC	Life only
OR	2.25	0.00	Dom. only	No	Yes
PA	2.0	2.0	No	No	Life only, NS
RI	2.0	2.0	No	No	Life only, NS
SC	0.75	1.25	No	No	Life only
SD	2.5	2.5	No	HOC	Life only
TN	1.75	2.50	Yes/credit	IRR	Yes, NS
TX	2.4	3.5	No	IRR	Yes
UT	2.25	2.25	No	No	Yes
VT	2.0	2.0	Yes	No	Life only
VA	2.25	2.25	No	No	Yes, NS
WA	2.0	2.0	No	No	Yes
WV	3.0	3.0	No	IRR	No
WI	2.0	2.0/0	Dom. P&C only	No	Yes, P&C NS
WY	2.5	2.5	No	IRR	Yes, NS
PR	4.0/0	4.0/0	For. only	No	No

Source: Edward M. Burgh, *State and Local Taxation of Insurance Companies*; Commerce Clearing House, *State Tax Reporter*, various issues.

[1]General rate. Differential rates may apply to specific products. Rate applicable to foreign insurers listed first, where applicable.
[2]Credit for premiums tax against income tax or vice versa.
[3]Investment rate reduction (IRR); home office credit (HOC).

TABLE 16.5 (continued)

[4]Premiums tax offset generally creditable 20 percent over next 5 years. NS means non-standard premiums tax offset: less than 100 percent offset and/or different number of years.

[5]Michigan's Single Business Tax taxes gross receipts, including premiums. New York limits combined premiums and franchise tax to 2.6% of premiums. Ohio insurers have option of foreign premiums tax rate of capital and surplus tax.

Premiums Taxes

All fifty states plus the District of Columbia impose premiums taxes on insurance companies for insuring risks or property in the state. It is difficult to generalize about state premiums taxes because premiums tax rules differ greatly among the states. Many states levy premiums taxes "in lieu of" other taxes, such as state corporate income taxes, yet there are exceptions. In most states, insurance companies are also subject to property taxes.

The definition of taxable premiums may include finance or service charges or fees for administrative services. Taxable premiums may include noncash payments such as paid-up insurance from cash value or premiums netted from policyholder dividends. Taxable premiums generally exclude premiums for annuities that are part of qualified pension plans and often exclude nonqualified annuities. Several states impose the tax when annuity payments are made, subjecting both principal and investment income to tax.

Deductions against the premiums tax base are generally allowed for refunds, returned premiums, and policyholder dividends. Reinsurance premiums are excluded if the state taxes direct premiums (from policyholders) but would require a statutory deduction if gross premiums were taxed. Generally, reinsurance premiums are deductible only if the premiums were already subject to tax in the state by the direct writer.

Premiums tax rates differ by state and by line of business. Fire protection premiums are generally taxed at higher rates, with the extra tax often earmarked to local fire departments or state fire marshall operations. Premiums for annuities are generally excluded or subject to a lower tax rate. Tax rates range from zero to 4.28 percent of premiums, with most states in the 1.75-3.0 percent range. Nine states plus Puerto Rico have different premiums tax rates for foreign and domestic insurers. Twelve states plus the District of Columbia and Puerto Rico tax nonqualified annuities. Eight states allow special municipal taxation of insurance companies.

State insurance premiums taxes in the fifty states increased from $3.3 billion in 1981 to $7.3 billion in 1989 (Table 16.6). Premiums taxes grew at an average annual rate of 10.4 percent during this period, compared to an average 8.3 percent growth in total state revenues. Premiums taxes increased from 2.1 percent of total state revenues in 1985 to 2.58 percent in 1989. As a percentage of insurance premiums most likely to be subject to state premiums taxes (all lines of property and casualty, ordinary life, and health insurance sold by life insurance companies), premiums taxes increased from 1.84 percent in 1985 to 2.17 percent in 1989. Premiums taxes totalled $7.4 billion in 1989, representing 2.6 percent of total state revenues (Table 16.7). Insurance premiums taxes were 3.5 percent or more of total revenue in nine states: Alabama, Connecticut, Idaho, Kentucky, Louisiana, Mississippi, New Hampshire, Oklahoma, and South Dakota. Insurance premiums taxes increased in all states, except Michigan, between 1983 and 1989 (Table 16.7). Between 1988 and 1989, seventeen states experienced declines in insurance premiums taxes. Eleven states experienced increases greater than 20 percent. Large percentage changes were probably associated with tax law or administrative changes, whereas smaller changes occurred because of changes in the total and mix of insurance sales in the state.

Income or Franchise Taxes

Sixteen states impose corporate income or franchise taxes on insurance companies. In some states, the income tax applies to only domestic companies, only foreign companies, or to all companies. In most states, the income or franchise tax is creditable against the premiums tax, or the premiums tax is creditable against the income tax.

Most states subject insurance companies to the same income tax rules as other corporations with adjustments to federal taxable income. New York piggybacks on the federal tax rules, but allowed property and casualty insurance companies a five-year window before incorporating the 1986 Tax Reform Act changes.

Investment and Employment Incentives and Domestic Preferences

The 1985 Supreme Court decision in *Metropolitan Life Insurance Co. v. Ward* found discriminatory taxation to be unconstitutional. However, differential taxation of domestic and foreign companies still remains and takes many forms. These include exclusion of domestic companies from

TABLE 16.6
State Insurance Taxes as Percent of Total State
Collections and Premiums, 1981-1989[1]

Year	Prem. Taxes ($bill.)	Premiums Taxes as Percentage of	
		Total Taxes	Premiums[2]
1989	7.3	2.58	2.17
1988	6.9	2.62	2.11
1987	6.3	2.56	1.99
1986	5.5	2.40	1.91
1985	4.5	2.10	1.84
1984	4.1	2.11	1.97
1983	3.9	2.25	1.95
1982	3.5	2.13	1.82
1981	3.3	2.22	1.87

	Annual percentage change	
	1985-89	1981-89
Premiums Taxes	12.8	10.4
Total Taxes	7.10	8.3
Insurance Premiums	8.2	8.3

Sources: U.S. Department of Commerce, Bureau of Census, *State Government Tax Collections*, various issues; *Best's Aggregates and Averages*; American Council of Life Insurance, *1990 Life Insurance Fact Book.*

[1]Excludes District of Columbia.
[2]Includes property and casualty company premiums plus premiums for ordinary life insurance and health insurance sold by life insurance companies.

the premiums tax with and without an alternative tax, different inclusions or exclusions to the premiums tax base, and different tax rates. Several states provide tax incentives in the form of special credits that are likely to benefit domestic insurers. In particular, the premiums tax rate may be reduced for companies whose investment in the state exceeds a minimum level. In some cases, this minimum investment level is so high that only companies headquartered in the state are likely to qualify for a reduced rate. Ten states provide such investment-linked rate reductions. Four states provide special credits or rate reductions for companies with home or regional offices in the state. Other states provide special credits to domestic companies only, such as a credit for retaliatory taxes paid to other states.

Retaliatory Taxes

Retaliatory taxes are unique to the insurance industry and were enacted before discriminatory taxes were found unconstitutional. All states, except Hawaii, have retaliatory tax systems. Hawaii has the highest premiums tax rates.

Retaliatory taxes impose tax on foreign companies domiciled in states with higher tax rates than the destination state in which it sells premiums. Retaliatory taxes are paid by foreign companies selling premiums in lower tax rate states. To determine the retaliatory tax rate, states increasingly are including income taxes, fees, and guaranty assessments in addition to premiums taxes. Many also include other states' municipal taxes, if any. Retaliatory taxes may be so broad as to require different licensing or prepayment requirements on foreign companies.

The destination state's retaliatory tax may be based on its premiums tax rate before or after special credits. For example, beginning in 1985, Texas imposed retaliatory taxes based on its rate after the investment rate reduction, thereby reducing the Texas tax rate and thus increasing retaliatory tax collections. Texas later changed back to the premiums tax rate before the investment rate reduction.

Retaliatory taxes may be imposed on an aggregate basis or on a separate item-by-item basis. The aggregate basis compares the company's total state tax under the two systems. The item-by-item basis compares the individual tax or fee between the filing state and the state of domicile, and requires payment of any higher amount for each item.

Guaranty Assessments and Other Burdens

Most states have guaranty funds to pay claims of insolvent companies. Assessments for the guaranty fund are levied as a percentage of premiums. Generally, the assessments are limited to 1 or 2 percent of premiums each year, and are levied and billed as needed. Separate state

TABLE 16.7
Insurance Premiums Taxes by State, 1989

State	Amount ($mill.)	% of Total Tax Rev.	Annual % Change 1983-89	1988-89
AL	139.4	3.8	10.5	0.7
AK	19.4	1.4	5.8	-18.0
AZ	90.6	2.2	14.8	25.1
AR	60.1	2.8	7.8	35.3
CA	1314.8	3.2	12.2	14.1
CO	84.7	2.9	10.0	3.0
CT	175.9	3.7	14.6	16.5
DE	34.6	3.1	16.8	37.4
DC	30.2	1.3	11.2	0.0
FL	250.1	2.0	12.2	-20.9
GA	157.1	2.5	14.3	4.5
HI	35.1	1.6	4.0	-9.7
ID	35.5	3.5	7.1	50.9
IL	255.1	2.2	15.0	36.4
IN	103.4	1.8	10.1	-0.1
IA	84.9	2.7	9.4	4.7
KS	69.4	2.8	7.5	-4.0
KY	151.2	3.7	7.3	2.2
LA	177.0	4.5	6.4	-4.2
ME	36.6	2.3	15.0	9.4
MD	131.3	2.1	12.1	2.5
MA	301.6	3.3	14.3	21.6
MI	76.6	0.7	-4.7	74.6
MN	120.6	1.9	9.8	-4.8
MS	99.4	4.3	9.8	30.0
MO	145.4	3.1	5.5	-6.4
MT	29.1	4.0	2.7	-26.3
NE	42.1	2.9	8.6	22.0
NV	45.1	3.4	19.5	-3.0
NH	35.5	5.8	15.2	0.5
NJ	233.0	2.2	14.5	38.6
NM	40.6	2.1	8.3	-6.6
NY	582.2	2.2	17.4	18.9

TABLE 16.7 (continued)

| State | Premiums Taxes | | | |
| | Amount ($mill.) | % of Total Tax Rev. | Annual % Change | |
			1983-89	1988-89
NC	187.5	2.5	11.3	0.4
ND	14.4	2.2	6.0	-1.6
OH	252.3	2.3	8.7	4.7
OK	142.6	4.3	13.3	3.9
OR	55.9	2.2	8.6	-4.8
PA	335.2	2.7	11.2	-0.4
RI	32.7	2.8	14.5	7.7
SC	94.4	2.5	10.1	13.4
SD	23.8	5.1	8.2	1.4
TN	124.3	3.1	9.4	1.5
TX	441.6	3.2	12.0	-19.1
UT	42.1	3.0	10.6	66.4
VT	19.4	3.1	17.8	12.9
VA	190.3	2.9	13.9	5.4
WA	90.7	1.4	9.2	-3.1
WV	49.6	2.6	6.0	5.2
WI	76.7	1.2	9.0	-2.2
WY	9.8	1.7	4.1	0.8
ALL U.S.	7370.9	2.6	11.3	6.4

Source: U.S. Department of Commerce, Bureau of Economic Analysis, *State Government Tax Collections*, 1983, 1988, 1989.

guaranty funds have been established for property and casualty companies and life companies. Within the life company guaranty funds, separate funds for life, annuity, and health policies have been established.

Guaranty fund assessments have increased sharply in the last few years. Assessments for life and health guaranty associations totaled $164 million in 1989. Prior to 1983, annual assessments never exceeded $10 million; in 1987-1989 they averaged $112 million. Property and casualty guaranty fund net assessments were $775 million in 1989. Before 1984, property and casualty annual assessments never exceeded $70 million;

in 1987-1989 they averaged $715 million. Guaranty fund assessments were one-eighth of total insurance premiums taxes in 1989.

Thirty-nine states provide a credit against the premiums tax for at least some guaranty fund assessments. Thirty-eight states provide a credit for life guaranty fund assessments; twenty states for P&C fund assessments. The most common credit is for 100 percent of the assessments taken pro rata over the next five years. Several states have reduced or eliminated the credit for guaranty fund assessments. For example, Florida reduced the credit to one-tenth of 1 percent of total assessments each year.

In addition to guaranty fund assessments, insurance companies pay additional fees and licenses generally associated with the administrative costs of the state insurance regulatory agencies. Insurance companies also pay assessments for assigned state risk pools which sell insurance to the uninsured. Finally, insurance companies are subject to state mandated benefits requiring minimum health insurance coverage.

ECONOMIC IMPLICATIONS OF CURRENT TAXATION

The unique state tax rules governing insurance companies have not been extensively analyzed. With the growth of self-insurance, the crumbling barriers to insurance underwriting by banks and non-insurance companies, and the increasing concern about the solvency of insurance companies under state regulation, analysis of the economic effects of state taxation of insurance companies merits increased consideration. This section discusses six policy issues involved in state insurance taxation and their economic implications.

Premiums Taxes "In Lieu Of" General Business Taxes

Insurance companies are taxed differently from other financial institutions and other corporations. At the federal level, tax policy has moved in the direction of taxing insurance companies more like other corporations, yet some differences remain. At the state level, however, the differences are fundamental. Insurance companies are taxed on premiums and sometimes with an income or franchise tax, whereas general business corporations are subject to an income or franchise tax, or none at all.

Premiums taxation dates back to the nineteenth century, before the federal income tax. Premiums taxes are relatively easy to administer and provide a stable source of revenue. By contrast, the appropriate income tax rules for insurance companies at the federal level have evolved over the last seventy years and are still a subject of considerable debate. The annual income of the property and casualty and health insurance segments fluctuates greatly, depending on the stage of the underwriting cycle, and thus is a source of volatility in income tax revenue flows.

Low rates of premiums taxes were unlikely to create significant distortions when there were few close substitutes offered and no direct competitors. However, with the growth of self-insurance and the emergence of direct competitors, differences in the effective tax rate from state premiums taxes and the effective tax rate from general business taxation can cause distortions. If the effective tax rate from premiums taxes is higher than that from general business taxes, then there will be an incentive to self-insure against risks or to purchase insurance products from noninsurance companies.

For example, assume a life insurance company sells credit life insurance on a $20,000 automobile loan for a premium of $50 including a premiums tax of $1 (2 percent rate). Alternatively, the customer might purchase a similar policy from a bank or automobile finance company with no premiums tax. The bank might earn $10 after acquisition expenses and claims, pay 60 cents in state income tax (6 percent rate), and thus be able to sell the policy at $49.60. Although the difference in this example may seem trivial, for identical products small price differences can place competitors at a significant disadvantage.

Substantial tax-related price differentials can be expected to arise as barriers within the broadly defined financial services industry are reduced in the future. Differential state taxation may place insurance companies at a competitive disadvantage to self-insurance and other competitors if premiums tax rates are above general business tax rates.

Investment and Employment Incentives and Domestic Preferences

Differential tax treatment of foreign and domestic companies was common when insurance premiums taxation first developed in the nineteenth century. More recently, domestic preferences in the form of differential statutory tax rates on foreign and domestic insurance companies have been the focus of litigation and have been found unconstitutional.

State insurance taxation is striking as to its diversity with respect to use of the tax code to encourage in-state investment and employment. Some states have relatively straightforward premiums tax laws which apply uniform tax rates without use of credits or investment offsets. Other states make extensive use of investment offset provisions which vary statutory tax rates in relation to in-state investment activity. In addition, salary or regional home office tax credits are sometimes provided as employment incentives.

Because their goal is economic development, incentives should be evaluated in terms of their effectiveness. The effectiveness of state tax incentives for economic development is still debated (Carroll and Wasylenko, 1990; Papke, 1990). Wheaton (1986) found that state taxation of life insurance companies can reduce company growth rates, which is more likely than a company physically relocating its headquarters. Further research on the effectiveness of investment and employment incentives for insurance companies may yield significant findings given the numerous changes in state insurance taxation over the past fifteen years.

Tax incentives may encourage the development of domestic insurance companies, but at the expense of other businesses. If foreign insurance companies are taxed at a higher tax rate than domestic companies, insurance prices in the state may be determined by foreign insurers and thus reflect the higher foreign tax rate. Higher insurance prices are an additional cost of doing business in the state and may reduce the competitiveness of the state's noninsurance businesses in national markets.

The Role of Retaliatory Taxation

Retaliatory taxation is unique to the insurance industry. Retaliatory taxes were enacted when most states had discriminatory taxation of foreign insurers. The retaliatory tax is designed to reduce tax barriers to interstate business activity of domestic insurers. Retaliatory taxes provide an incentive for states to keep their taxes on insurance companies in line with those of other states.

If a state increases its premiums tax rate, there will be a number of economic effects on insurance companies and the state's revenue collections. The higher premiums tax rate is likely to increase state premiums tax revenues (because even with self-insurance and noninsurance industry competition, the price elasticity of most insurance products is still relatively inelastic). However, the higher domestic premiums tax rate will reduce the state's retaliatory tax revenues. The importance of this offsetting revenue depends on the relationship of the state's tax rate to other states' insurance tax rates and the extent to which the state's insurance purchases are from domestic or foreign insurers.

A higher premiums tax rate will also increase the amount of retaliatory taxes paid by domestic insurers to other states. The higher retaliatory tax may reduce the market share of the state's insurers in other states. If the state grants a tax credit for retaliatory tax paid in other states, then an additional tax offset occurs to the higher premiums tax collections.

In a state that relies heavily on out-of-state insurers, foreign insurers may determine prices at the margin. Thus, a state with a low premiums tax rate may still have a higher cost of insurance because of retaliatory taxes paid by foreign insurers. In this case, retaliatory taxes may provide higher profits or additional market share to domestic insurers in low tax rate states even without specific domestic preferences.

Premiums Tax Offsets For Guaranty Fund Assessments

One of the methods by which states have increased taxes on insurance companies is to reduce or eliminate the premiums tax credit for guaranty fund assessments. In states that allow recovery of assessments over five years as a credit against premiums taxes, the result is a small loss of the time value of money to the insurer (17-24 percent at a 10 percent discount rate, depending on whether the assessment is creditable in the year of the assessment).

The issue of premiums tax offsets for guaranty fund assessments raises the issue of the rationale for the premiums tax. If the premiums tax is designed simply to raise revenue for the state's general fund, then a premiums tax offset reduces the revenue available to the general fund. If the premiums tax rate is viewed as a maximum rate, then a premiums tax offset simply earmarks some of the premiums tax revenue to pay for the guaranty fund assessments, and the general fund gets the residual.

Increased assessments and increased concern about the solvency of insurance companies under state regulation will make premiums tax offsets a major issue in many states. Elimination or reduction of premiums tax offsets could substantially increase the effective premiums tax rate on insurance companies. Higher effective premiums tax rates, to the extent passed through to the state's residents and businesses, increase the cost of doing business in the state. Higher effective premiums tax rates on insurance companies would also exacerbate the tax differential between purchased insurance and self-insurance.

Sales Taxes on Insurance Services

At present, no state imposes a general sales tax on insurance services or financial services, although at least one has considered doing so. If applied to gross premiums, a sales tax would greatly overstate the value of insurance services. This occurs because insurance premiums generally include three elements: a savings element, a pure insurance (transfer) element, and a service (administrative, marketing, and entrepreneurial) element. For example, premiums received for permanent life insurance will be used to increase a policyholder's cash surrender value (the savings element), to pay current death claims (the transfer element), and to pay employee wages, suppliers, and the company's profit (the service element). For the life insurance industry, increases in policyholder reserves and benefit payments equalled 119 percent of premiums and 83 percent of total revenue in 1989. For the property and casualty insurance companies, incurred losses were equal to 78 percent of premiums and 69 percent of total revenue in 1988.

A more appropriate measure of insurance services might be the value added by the industry. However, a value added tax (VAT) for financial institutions involves difficult measurement issues, which have caused European countries to exclude or exempt financial institutions from a VAT. A sales tax on insurance services could further exacerbate the distortion between purchased insurance and self-insurance.

Nontax Burdens on Insurance Companies

In the universal quest for a "free lunch," states may impose nontax burdens on companies rather than raising taxes for spending programs. Insurance companies bear significant costs for requirements to participate in assigned risk pools which sell insurance to the uninsured. In addition, insurance companies must provide minimum benefit levels in their health insurance in many states. Over 700 state minimum benefit requirements have been identified.[3]

All industries face regulatory requirements, which impact the cost of doing business in a state. Most troubling is where regulatory burdens (or tax burdens) fall unequally on similar providers. Non-tax burdens on the insurance industry that do not apply to self-insurance or noninsurance providers can distort the efficient provision of insurance.

CONCLUSION

Although it is a relatively arcane area of state tax policy, insurance company taxation merits increased attention both from state tax policymakers and the industry for several reasons.

Insurance company taxation accounts for a significant share of states' tax revenue, roughly two times the industry's share of gross state product. Yet, states may increase insurance taxes in the future as a result of state budget deficits and increased concern about insurer solvency. States should be concerned about the effective tax rates on insurance companies because insurance costs are a cost of doing business in the state for noninsurance industries.

Litigation relating to differential state tax treatment of domestic and foreign insurers is likely to continue. State insurance tax rules are changing to eliminate differential foreign and domestic tax rates. Nonetheless, the diverse practices of the states relating to retaliatory taxation, premiums tax credit, and investment offsets have important tax policy and revenue implications.

State guaranty fund assessments have been increasing sharply, translating into higher insurance tax burdens or reduced general revenue.

State insurance taxation and other regulatory burdens are encouraging increased self-insurance which may place the state's residents at risk if the self-insuring businesses become insolvent.

NOTES

1. "Self-Insurance: More Small Firms Self-Fund Benefits," *Business Insurance*, January 28, 1991, p. 3.

2. "Self-Insurance: Companies Retain Comp Risk," *Business Insurance*, January 28, 1991, p. 3.

3. Jon Gabel, "Mandates Spurring Self-Insurance Growth," *National Underwriter*, Property & Casualty—Employee Benefits Edition, October 9, 1989, p. 9.

17
Neutrality in State
Insurance Taxation

MARTIN F. GRACE and HAROLD D. SKIPPER, JR.

Insurance companies in the United States have been taxed at the state level for at least the past 150 years. The preferred mode of nineteenth-century taxation was a levy on each insurer's premium writings in the state. Many states imposed such premiums taxes for the express purpose of funding programs related to some public good. For example, a tax levy on premiums paid for fire insurance—the most prevalent nineteenth-century insurance cover—might be used to help fund fire fighting services.[1] In other instances, a tax on fire insurance premiums was viewed as an extension of a property tax—at the time the predominant source of revenue for most states—because fire insurance premium levels were related to property values (Jones, 1965, p. 322).

Yet another, not mutually exclusive, argument for insurance premiums taxation related to the perceived need by some states to tax premiums revenues as they left the state for the coffers of the large, out-of-state, insurers in the East, because, as the states contended, funds would not remain in the state to become part of the state's property tax base (Jones, 1965, pp. 322-323). As a result, the "poor" southern and midwestern states erected what amounted to protective interstate tariff barriers in the form of discriminatory premiums taxation between insurers domiciled within the state and those domiciled elsewhere.

The question might arise as to whether such state interference with interstate commerce was permissible under the U.S. Constitution. Normally, states may not impose taxes or regulatory burdens that infringe unduly on interstate commerce.[2] However, the U.S. Supreme Court had held in 1868 that the business of insurance was not commerce.[3] As such, there could be no violation of commerce clause prohibitions if states erected interstate trade barriers in insurance.[4]

Although the Supreme Court reversed itself in 1944,[5] the practical effect of the 1868 decision was to cause insurance regulatory and taxation issues to evolve within the states' incubators. This situation led to important differences in insurer taxation among the states—many of which persist today.

Following the Supreme Court's 1944 decision, pressure developed for the U. S. Congress to pass a law that, in effect, would undo much of the Supreme Court's mischief, leaving the status quo ante largely in tact. The 1945 passage of the McCarran-Ferguson Act effectively accomplished the desired goal, reinstating the states' power to regulate and tax insurance, subject to certain constraints.[6]

Later Supreme Court cases held that the McCarran-Ferguson Act gave states very broad authority over the regulation and taxation of insurers.[7] The Court held that because the commerce clause was not a limitation on the power of Congress over interstate commerce, but a grant to Congress of supreme authority over commerce, Congress could delegate the authority to the states. The effect, in other words, was to bar insurance-related commerce clause challenges—the same result that had persisted since at least 1868.

Thus, we find today that all states subject most insurance companies doing business within the state to some form of taxation, and that the vast majority subject insurers to some type of premiums tax—nineteenth-century method of taxation. Some states, however, do impose an income tax on domestic and/or out-of-state insurers in addition to the premiums tax, although most of these states permit one form of tax as a credit against the other form. Ordinarily, the premiums tax is "in lieu of" other state taxation.

IS INSURER TAXATION NEUTRAL?

Given that state insurer taxation evolved in a relatively insulated environment, a central (and understandable) public policy question should be: Is state insurer taxation neutral among competitors? In examining this question, this section will (1) provide an overview of state premiums taxation and (2) set out the areas where neutrality problems seem to exist. No attempt is made to quantify the degree to which perceived problems might cause marketplace distortions.

State Premiums Taxation

Under the typical state premiums tax structure, the tax base is the simple total of each insurer's premium writings in the state. Both similarities and differences exist among the states. For example, premiums received from assumed reinsurance are usually excluded from the tax base because the original insurer that wrote the business would have already been subjected to a premiums tax for the direct premiums. All but twelve states permit a deduction from the tax base for dividends paid to policyholders.[8] Additionally, five states place limits on dividend deductions.[9] For life insurance companies, the premiums tax base may include premiums received for accident and health insurance, or such premiums may be taxed separately. Insurers' investment incomes are not included in the tax base.

Nine states apply lower premium tax rates to their domestic insurers than to out-of-state insurers.[10] Another eleven states provide for preferential tax treatment of their domestic insurers through other mechanisms,[11] and another three states provide a preference for some or all of their domestic insurers but for only a comparatively few out-of-state insurers.[12] Since 1981, twelve states have changed their laws to eliminate their discriminatory elements.[13] Another eight states have dealt legislatively with domestic preference taxes since 1981, but without clearly eliminating all aspects of domestic preference.[14]

Most states do not levy any premiums tax on annuity considerations paid to insurers, whether domestic or out-of-state. Those few states that tax annuity considerations typically exempt federally tax-qualified annuity plans (e.g., individual retirement annuities and annuities sold to fund other federally tax-qualified retirement plans) from premiums taxation. Generally, states treat annuities sold by out-of-state insurers the same as they do annuities sold by domestic insurers.

The premiums tax rates on out-of-state insurers vary from a low of 0.75 percent to a high of 4.28 percent. Tax rates on domestic insurers vary from zero percent to 3.5 percent. Each state's tax policy continues to reflect the insulation of the nineteenth-century and may actually cause harm to the state's insurance markets.[15]

Areas of Questionable Tax Neutrality

It appears that states have a substantial array of tax preferences and inconsistencies that logically could be expected to cause governmentally created marketplace disadvantages for some competitors. Five such areas are explored below.

Differential Taxation of Domestic and Out-of-State Insurers. As noted above, several states subject out-of-state insurers doing business within the state to higher effective taxation than that for insurers that are domiciled in the state.[16] Although a 1985 Supreme Court case held that such tax laws may violate the equal protection clause of the Constitution's Fourteenth Amendment, to date the decision has not proven to have dealt definitively with the issue.[17]

Although not a classic transactions tax,[18] the premiums tax system exhibits the negative traits of such a tax. Thus, a higher premiums tax on out-of-state insurers than on a state's domestic insurers could lead to out-of state insurers charging more for the same coverage, meeting domestic insurers' prices but marketing insurance on a selective basis only, or accepting a lower profit.

A price differential would put out-of-state insurers at a competitive disadvantage, and thus less insurance would be sold. The supply of insurance would then fall, and overall prices would be higher. This result is the same as applies with tariffs in international trade (Magee, 1972).

If out-of-state insurers charge the same price as domestic insurers and market insurance on a selective basis, they may underwrite risks more stringently, accepting only those risks that promise sufficient profitability to make up for the higher taxation. Or, they may not enter (or remain in) those market segments judged to be too low in overall profitability. In either case, a less competitive market would result because the out-of-state insurers effectively would be competing over a narrower range. Again, overall market supply would be lower than otherwise, and prices would be higher.

Finally, the out-of-state insurers could charge the same prices as their domestic competitors, compete fully in all of the same markets as their domestic competitors, and accept a smaller profit margin than their domestic competitors. Where profit margins were high, some out-of-state insurers might compete in this manner. For example, margins in the field of individually issued life insurance traditionally have been greater than in group life insurance or in the property and casualty or health insurance business. Thus, this alternative is not likely to be found in the more price competitive property and casualty, health, or group life areas. Also, as competition has intensified in the life insurance business over the past decade, this alternative is becoming more remote.

As a result of violating the neutrality principle, discriminatory taxation burdens and inhibits interstate commerce and is the very type of state protectionism that has been universally decried. Spencer L. Kimball, considered perhaps the foremost authority on U.S. insurance law and regulation, has observed that insurance regulation serves many purposes. Some are laudable, but others have potentially self- serving aspects. Discriminatory premiums taxation is a type of protectionism that is regrettably often a *political* objective of insurance regulation. Kimball (1969, p. 7) has observed:

Local protection [is] something that you can recognize all over in the state insurance statutes if you look at their underlying purposes. They range from countersignature laws for agents to discriminatory tax structures. All of these things are manifestations of a kind of parochialism in our economy that as farsighted and nationally oriented individuals, we want to resist and overcome if we can.

That local protectionism is an anathema to commerce and efficiency is widely acknowledged. The World Bank (1986, p. 22) recently commented on one argument often used to support protective measures:

It is often claimed that tariff and nontariff barriers to trade are justified as a way of savings jobs of domestic industries. But protection has many direct and indirect effects that need to be considered....Although the domestic industries producing these substitutes may gain, consumers and industrial users of the products lose. The net result is always a loss in real national income.

The International Insurance Advisory Council (IIAC) to the federal government has made similar arguments in the context of international insurance. The U.S. insurance industry believes that it is being discriminated against unfairly in its attempts to sell more insurance internationally. They argue that "there exists today an inventive array of protectionist devices denying U.S. and other foreign insurers a level playing field in the world insurance marketplace" (Parker, 1984, p. 4).

One of the key protectionist measures identified by the federal government and the IIAC is "discriminatory taxation of income and premiums" (Parker, 1984, p. 5). This and other discriminatory measures mean that although the local insurance industry might benefit in the short run, "the ultimate loser is the insurance buyer" (Parker, 1984, p. 6). As a result, it is argued that "there should be provision for taxation of alien [nondomestic] insurers on the same basis as for domestic insurers" (Parker, 1984, p. 9).

Although these arguments refer to protectionism in the provision of *international* insurance, they apply equally to protectionism in the provision of *interstate* insurance. Indeed, for the several discriminatory tax states to so inhibit U.S. insurance commerce in this manner results in a less efficient U. S. insurance industry, which, in turn, handicaps U. S. insurers in international competition.

The "Statement of Policy on Insurance Premium Taxation" adopted by the National Association of Insurance Commissioners (NAIC), an association of the nation's state insurance regulators in 1970, addresses the issue of preferential domestic taxation directly and succinctly:

This type of discrimination occurs where a lower premium tax rate is applied to domestic companies than to foreign companies and, more subtly, where tax credits are offered which tend to favor domestic companies.

While such discrimination may have been justified when insurance was an "infant industry" in some parts of the country, it is an anachronism today. It distorts competition by subsidizing some competitors, allocates tax burdens unfairly among policyholders, ignores the national nature of much of the contemporary insurance economy, and is likely to impel major insurers to make corporate or marketing changes which will enable them to escape the discrimination but which are not in the interest of a healthy insurance business functioning efficiently in the public interest (National Association of Insurance Commissioners, 1971, pp. 58,70).

Differential Taxation Based on Insurers' Legal Form. Another aspect of neutrality concerns the legal form of the insurance firm. In most states, whether an insurer is taxed and the extent of that taxation is determined to some degree by the insurer's legal form. The most common legal form for an insurer is a proprietary stock corporation. The second most common form, the mutual insurance corporation, differs from a stock insurer in that it is owned by and operated for the benefit of its policyholders (as opposed to a stock insurer's stockholders). Other common forms of insurers include nonprofit health care associations, such as Blue Cross and Blue Shield Associations, and fraternal benefit societies. There remains additional legal forms, such as Lloyds, reciprocal exchanges, and mutual aid associations, but they are much less common than the preceding forms.

Stock and mutual insurers are ordinarily taxed in a similar if not identical manner. However, fraternal life insurers—both domestic and out-of-state—are typically exempt from premiums taxation.[19] Also, until recently, Blue Cross-Blue Shield organizations and other nonprofit health care service plans were exempt from premiums taxation in almost all states. Today, about one-half of the states tax Blue Cross-Blue Shield organizations, consistent with the tax concept of neutrality among competitors.

In 1970, a task force of the NAIC evaluated such preferences among insuring organizations and recommended their abolition. The report, which was adopted by the NAIC as its policy position on insurance premiums taxation, read in part as follows:

Such discrimination may have been justified when some of the tax-favored organizations or arrangements were in their infancy, or where they were performing essentially a public service by meeting public needs unmet by existing insurance organizations. But, again, such discrimination is an anachronism today.

Today, the discriminations follow no consistent pattern or rationale, and their original rationale has been eroded by the development of a strong insurance industry and by a growing similarity between the operations of the tax-favored insurance organizations and those of other insurers. Moreover, these discriminations...have the effect of impeding competition, of providing less favorable treatment to the consumer purchasing a taxed policy, and of creating incentives for insurers to develop tax avoidance programs which also circumvent regulatory safeguards (National Association of Insurance Commissioners, 1971).

Differential Taxation of Different Size Insurers. The practical effect of the premiums tax as a basis for taxing insurance companies is that it has a disparate impact among insurers of different size and profitability. Because the tax totally excludes the investment income of insurance companies, the effect is to favor companies that have large investment incomes relative to their total income. Such are usually the older, larger, more established companies.

A companion neutrality problem with the premiums tax is its harmfulness both to new insurance companies and to those that make little or no profit. The tax must be paid irrespective of company profitability. Newly established insurance companies have little or no profit in the first few years of operation. Nonetheless, under the premiums tax structure, they are required to pay a tax. As a company matures and grows and becomes more profitable, its tax rate as a percentage of premiums remains constant, but as a percentage of total company profitability, the effective tax rate actually declines. Hence, the premiums tax system is not neutral among insurance company competitors of differing sizes and age.

Differential Taxation Based on Insurer Product Mix. Insurers usually specialize. Thus, a life insurer may write predominately annuities, term life insurance, whole life insurance, accident and health insurance, or other products. In situations where products are substitutes, taxation neutrality would hold that they should be taxed equivalently.

Thus, if a company sells annuities together with term policies, the combination could easily be sold as a substitute for whole life or other cash value policies. In fact, insurers have done so. Yet, in most states, premiums taxes levied on premiums for life insurance policies are considerably higher than premiums taxes levied on annuity considerations. The result is to encourage insurers to mimic cash value policies with combinations of other policies—arguably a matter over which government tax policy should be neutral.

Differential Taxation of Insurers and Noninsurer Competitors. Perhaps the area of greatest neutrality concern exists where insurers and their close, yet noninsurer, competitors are taxed differentially and not equivalently. Some research has been done in this area, but much more would seem to be needed (Skipper, 1987, p. 71, n. 17). However, certain dimensions of this neutrality concern can be highlighted if not quantified.

In general, neither the premium tax nor its equivalent is levied on several alternative, non-insurance funding media that compete with insurers. For example, in most states, self-funded group health benefits escape all taxation, whereas insurer-provided group health benefits are fully taxed. Similarly, in many states, employers may choose to self-fund workers' compensation coverages that have benefits subjected to no or a lower effective tax than where benefits are provided through an insured plan.

Other media compete with life insurance companies for consumers' saving dollars. We do not know whether insurers generally enjoy a competitive advantage or disadvantage vis-à-vis such competitors, but we do know that because the tax systems differ, no direct comparison is feasible. A not unreasonable inference is that the neutrality criterion is violated, if for no other reason than the dearth of analysis to prove the contrary.

DIFFERENTIAL TAX BURDENS AMONG THE STATES

Another dimension of neutrality in state insurer taxation relates to the differences among the states in insurance industry tax burdens. In contrast with the preceding section's orientation toward competitors, the focus here is potential distortions caused by differences in state insurance tax burdens. The issue is whether some states overtax (undertax) insurance relative to other states. If they do, we would expect marketplace distortions to result among the states. For example, if state A overtaxes insurers relative to other states, incentives would be created for insurers to market insurance in the states with lower tax burdens, thus spurring additional competition in such states. Based on the evolution of state insurer taxation, one would be surprised to find no substantial differences in state taxation burden.

To examine this issue, we employ the representative tax system (RTS) methodology used by the Advisory Commission on

Intergovernmental Relations (ACIR).[20] The RTS measures revenue-raising ability by estimating the tax yield resulting from applying a consistent definition of tax base and an average tax rate across states. The RTS has five basic constituents. According to the ACIR (1990, pp. 4-5) these are: (1) the revenue coverage; (2) the classification of revenues into separate sources; (3) the definition of a standardized tax base for each revenue source; (4) the definition of a standard tax rate for each revenue source; and (5) the estimation of RTS revenues for each state by applying the standard tax rate for each revenue source to the defined tax base for that state of that source and then summing the results for all sources.

Revenue coverage requires that the tax base take into account all state and local government tax sources. Because each state might use its tax base differently, a consistent revenue classification is important. Standardization of the tax base is necessary to permit interstate comparisons. The ACIR standardizes the tax base with two goals in mind. First, the standardized tax base should relate to the statutory tax base and, second, good data should be available in every state.

The tax rate used in the RTS is a weighted average of tax rates for each kind of tax. Finally, this average tax rate is applied to each state's standardized tax base to obtain the RTS measure of the state's tax capacity.

The RTS methodology allows a determination of the relative importance of different classes of taxes to state finances and to compare the intensity of the various tax classifications across states. If a state, for example, overtaxes a particular tax base—that is, the revenues from a particular tax are greater than the ACIR's definition of tax capacity for that particular tax—one could say that the tax base is overtaxed relative to the state's capacity.

Table 17.1 illustrates the extent to which each state over (under) taxes its entire (system) tax base.[21] The District of Columbia has the highest "over tax" percentage—its capacity minus revenues collected divided by its capacity is approximately 54 percent. New Hampshire has the largest "under tax" percentage using this definition. Table 17.2 illustrates the extent to which each state over (under) taxes its insurance tax base.

States that overuse their insurance tax capacity are those for which the insurance industry's tax burden is greater than the average state, and vice versa. State variations are substantial, suggesting that some states, for whatever reasons, tax insurers heavily, whereas other states do precisely the opposite. Recall that tax burdens here are those relative to the other states.

TABLE 17.1
Over (Under) Use of State System Tax Capacity for 1988

State	Over (Under) Use of Capacity (%)	State	Over (Under) Use of Capacity (%)
Dist. of Col.	53.7	Texas	-5.4
New York	51.8	Mississippi	-5.5
Alaska	27.4	California	-5.6
Wisconsin	19.4	Massachusetts	-5.9
Iowa	13.8	Wyoming	-6.5
Hawaii	12.2	Idaho	-6.8
Michigan	12.2	North Carolina	-6.9
Minnesota	12.2	Indiana	-7.0
Maryland	8.0	Virginia	-8.8
Utah	5.5	Connecticut	-9.1
Maine	4.9	North Dakota	-9.3
Rhode Island	4.3	Louisiana	-10.0
Kansas	3.5	Georgia	-10.6
Illinois	3.3	Colorado	-11.1
Washington	2.3	Oklahoma	-11.3
Montana	2.1	Kentucky	-11.8
New Jersey	0.9	West Virginia	-12.4
Vermont	0.0	Missouri	-13.7
New Mexico	-0.5	Alabama	-15.6
Oregon	-0.9	Arkansas	-15.7
Nebraska	-1.9	Delaware	-15.7
Ohio	-2.7	Tennessee	-16.9
Pennsylvania	-2.7	Florida	-17.5
Arizona	-4.0	Nevada	-30.7
South Carolina	-4.5	New Hampshire	-33.9
South Dakota	-5.1	Average	-3.9

Source: ACIR, *State Fiscal Capacity and Effort,* M-170 (1990).

TABLE 17.2
Over (Under) Use of State Insurance Tax Capacity for 1988

State	Over (Under) Use of Capacity (%)	State	Over (Under) Use of Capacity (%)
Nevada	92.5	New Hampshire	-5.9
Kentucky	85.6	Maryland	-6.0
Louisiana	76.8	Arkansas	-11.0
South Dakota	47.8	Pennsylvania	-12.1
Alaska	46.3	Georgia	-12.3
Mississippi	43.3	Ohio	-12.9
New Mexico	43.1	Washington	-14.0
Alabama	35.8	Rhode Island	-14.4
West Virginia	31.8	Oregon	-14.6
Texas	31.6	Utah	-16.2
North Carolina	28.4	North Dakota	-17.9
Kansas	11.2	Arizona	-19.6
Hawaii	11.1	Nebraska	-19.8
Connecticut	8.9	New York	-22.3
Missouri	8.3	Indiana	-24.5
South Carolina	8.2	Wisconsin	-33.7
Iowa	7.3	New Jersey	-36.6
Vermont	4.2	Illinois	-44.0
Idaho	3.5	Minnesota	-74.5
Massachusetts	2.8	Michigan	-85.0
Tennessee	0.7	California	-86.6
Colorado	-1.7	Virginia	-88.2
Delaware	-1.9	Dist. of Col.	-93.0
Florida	-3.3		
		Average	-6.7

Source: ACIR, *State Fiscal Capacity and Effort,* M-170 (1990).

It is beyond the scope of this chapter to seek public policy or other explanations for these variations or to try to determine whether, and the extent to which, they cause marketplace dislocations. Intuition suggests, however, that their magnitude is such as to have a reasonable chance of causing dislocations, especially given the competitive nature of most of the U.S. insurance industry.

Comparing the positions of states in Tables 17.1 and 17.2 suggests that states that tend to overtax their system capacity tend to undertax their insurance capacity, and vice versa. In the absence of countervailing public policy objectives, one might expect policy to be consistent across industries. Thus, if a state overtaxes system capacity by 20 percent, one might expect overtaxation of insurance tax capacity by 20 percent. But there seems to be little or no such relationship. There may be sound explanations of this result, but they are not self-evident. More research is called for on this issue.

CONCLUSION

State taxation of insurance companies remains based on nineteenth-century concepts. Divergent tax systems and tax treatments exist that call into question whether state insurer taxation is competitor neutral. Some states tax their domestic insurers at lower rates that otherwise similar out-of-state insurers. Such violations of tax neutrality are an anathema to competition.

States also tax insurer competitors differentially based solely on the insurer's legal form. The logic for continuing this practice seems questionable.

The premiums tax system, by its nature, results in differential taxation based on insurer size and profitability. Such a differential principle is sometimes defended as being desirable in that it can ensure smaller or less profitable insurers a lower relative tax burden. However, such insurers have a higher relative tax burden under the premiums tax system.

Arguably, suppliers of substitute products ought to be taxed equivalently, in the absence of overriding public policy reasons to do otherwise. Yet, existing state insurance tax systems can lead to differing tax burdens depending on product mix and on whether the supplier is an insurer. Again, neutrality principles argue for similar tax treatment of close competitors.

States should undertake an evaluation of existing taxation policies. One goal of this evaluation should be to treat companies in similar situations similarly. Thus, the states should remove discriminatory taxes benefitting domestic over out-of-state companies and alter taxes benefitting one product or producer at the expense of close substitutes.

Similarly, the states could examine their tax burdens to determine whether they are distorting their markets. The evidence suggests that such distortions might exist.

Finally, one might question whether the premiums tax system itself has outlived its usefulness. As has been suggested elsewhere, the system's chief redeeming quality is its simplicity (Skipper, 1987, pp. 133-142). However, simplicity gives rise to inequities and, besides, other, more complex, tax systems have been in place for decades and seem to function reasonably well.

Further research should focus on the interstate tax differentials described here as well as within state interindustry differentials. These interindustry differentials might have great marketplace import.

NOTES

1. For a brief introduction to the historical regulatory environment of insurance, see Meier (1987, Ch. 4). For current information, see *Social Report of the Life and Health Insurance Business,* published annually by the American Council of Life Insurance and Health Insurance Association of America.

2. U.S. Constitution, Art. I, §8 (interstate commerce power); and *Baldwin v. G.A.F. Seelig, Inc.,* 294 U.S. 511 (1935).

3. *Paul v. Virginia* (1868).

4. *Hooper v. California* (1895) finds that the business of insurance is not commerce.

5. *United States v. South-Eastern Underwriters Association* (1944).

6. Act of March 9, 1945 (McCarran-Ferguson Act), Ch. 20 §1, 59 Stat. 33 currently codified at 15 U.S.C. §1011 (1988).

7. See for example, *Prudential Insurance Company v. Benjamin,* 328 U.S. 408, 410 (1946).

8. Colorado, Florida, Louisiana, North Carolina, North Dakota, Ohio, Oklahoma, Tennessee, Utah, Virginia, Washington, and West Virginia.

9. Arkansas (health only), Hawaii (life only), Kentucky (health only), Texas (special rules), and Wisconsin (life only).

10. Four states (Alabama, Hawaii, Kansas, and Tennessee) tax both domestic and out-of-state insurers, but they tax domestics at a lower rate. Five other states (Illinois, Indiana, Kentucky, Ohio and Oregon) levy premiums taxes on out-of-state insurers, but they generally do not on domestic insurers.

11. Colorado, Georgia, Idaho, Louisiana, Mississippi, Nevada, New Mexico, South Dakota, West Virginia, and Wyoming. Texas might be considered a thirteenth state providing a domestic preference through an indirect mechanism; however, 1989 legislation phases out the preference by 1995.

12. Arkansas, Florida, and New Jersey.

13. Alaska, Arizona, Maine, Michigan, Montana, Nebraska, North Carolina, North Dakota, Oklahoma, South Carolina, Texas, and Washington.

14. Arkansas, Florida, Idaho, Mississippi, New Jersey, New Mexico, South Dakota, and Wyoming.

15. For a full discussion of this issue, see Grace and Skipper (1990).

16. This section draws in part from Skipper (1987).

17. *Metropolitan Life Insurance Co. v. Ward.* Litigation concerning the Alabama discriminatory tax that was the subject of the lawsuit in *Ward* is still pending.

18. Premiums taxes are not true transactions taxes. They are not identifiable levies applied to the transactions themselves, and they are not necessarily passed on fully to purchasers. This is because the insurance consumer does not pay the tax at the time of the transaction, as in the case of the sales tax. The tax is paid by the insurance company at the end of its tax year based on its total premiums.

19. Fraternal insurers are relatively small firms and do not account for a large percentage of total premiums. Evidently, there was a policy justification at some time for granting these companies a tax exemption. However, one should ask whether the exemption continues to serve its purpose, or does it grant a benefit to a particular organizational form without any policy rationale.

20. For a general discussion and history of the use of the RTS concept, see U.S. Advisory Commission on Intergovernmental Relations (1990, Ch. 1).

21. Relative capacity is calculated as (tax capacity - actual revenues)/tax capacity.

18
Insurance Taxation: Policyholder Dividends and Insolvencies

JAMES BARRESE

Insurance companies are subject to many forms of federal and state taxation. These include ad valorem taxes on real and personal property; franchise taxes; income taxes; taxes on capital and stock; taxes on credits and securities; taxes on surplus and reserve funds; taxes on premiums and other receipts; and business license taxes. Many states also impose a separate tax for the support of local fire departments.

In spite of this impressive array of taxes, insurance taxation is a subject fraught with misunderstanding. The interaction of regulatory requirements and tax rules create mach of the misunderstanding. Tax laws frequently begin with these purposely conservative rules and modify them to accord more closely with a normative business income concept, if the term has meaning at the level of the corporation. The current system of insurance taxation is the product of years of political negotiation, resulting in agreements between industry representatives and government to adopt a provision that will yield (subtract) a given dollar amount to (from) the tax rolls. It seems tautological to suggest that the resulting system does not accord with the best principles of taxation.

The first section of this chapter provides a sense of how far the system of taxing insurance has come from what might be considered simple, fair, and neutral. It provides a glimpse of the historical development of life insurance company taxation. Few state-specific issues are relevant in this section, but the history provides a basis for understanding how the second issue, the tax and expenditure policies relating to insurance insolvencies, might develop. The latter issue is important in that it has a significant impact on state tax and expenditure policies and has received almost no attention from tax specialists.

FEDERAL TAXATION

Most banks, thrift institutions, insurance companies, and investment companies use the same federal corporate tax rate schedule; industry tax differences center on differences in defining taxable income. Different approaches to defining taxable income exist within and between industry groups. One intragroup difference involves firms qualifying for tax treatment under the life insurance provisions of the Internal Revenue Code (IRC or Code) (Section 22).

The life insurance industry comprises both stock and mutual companies. Mutual companies are cooperatives with management directed by a board elected by policyholders. The financial capital of mutual companies derives from past contributions by policyholders and from retained earnings. The contracts issued by mutual companies generally are participating policies that entitle policyholders to receive a share of company earnings or company surplus that its board of directors may choose to distribute. The financial capital or surplus of stock companies represents the proceeds from past equity sales and their accumulated retained earnings. Most contracts issued by stock companies are nonparticipating policies.

Insurance corporations, like other corporations, are subject to corporate income taxes. Also like other corporations, including those in the airline and banking industries, insurance taxation has certain unique features in recognition of industry differences. Some tax differences relate to the nature of the product of the industry, some to the way the industry is regulated. The National Association of Insurance Commissioners (NAIC) determines a consistent set of accounting rules that must be followed by firms for regulatory purposes. The result is a system of statutory accounting principles (SAP). A primary goal of insurance regulation is to assure solvency. Consequently, the purpose of SAPs is to present an ultraconservative view of the firm's financial position. General accounting rules assume that the company will continue to operate. Statutory insurance accounting does not employ a consistent continuity concept. For example, using amortized cost to value bonds assumes that the securities will be held until maturity; the approach views the insurer as a going concern. On the other hand, a liquidation approach applies to the treatment of premiums revenues and the costs associated with writing new business.

The conservative NAIC accounting rules were adopted for purposes of federal taxation in 1921. That is, stock property and casualty companies are subject to the same tax rules applicable to general corporations, except that the special provisions set forth in IRC Sections

831 and 832 take precedence. The significant difference in the taxation of property and liability insurers is in the timing of the inclusion of underwriting income and deductions that follows state insurance department accounting rules. The Code sets forth that the annual statement is the guideline for determining the timing of taxable income. Property and liability insurers include premium income when earned—which understates income—but they report expenses when incurred.

The state laws under which insurance companies are chartered and regulated do not allow life insurance companies to set reserves at their discretion. From 1958 to 1982, state laws generally defined adequate reserves using an assumed rate of return of 3.5 or 4 percent. So, when the yield on insurance company assets began to rise above 4 percent, the assets backing permanent insurance reserves built too quickly.

TAXATION OF POLICYHOLDER DIVIDENDS

The Life Insurance Company Tax Act of 1959 recognized that the actual return on assets might exceed the rates of return required by state regulators. When the average yield on assets backing reserves exceeded the assumed rate used to set up those reserves, the law attempted to tax much of the resulting excess investment income as corporate profit. Mutual insurance companies tended to return excess investment income to policyholders as dividends on the anniversary date of each contract. These dividends represented a mix of a return of excess premium, a return of interest earned on that excess premium, and possibly a share of company profits or a return of equity.

The Life Insurance Company Tax Act of 1959 attempted to tax excess investment income. The Tax Reform Act of 1984 attempts to tax the profit rather than the investment income of life insurance companies. The 1984 law treats as revenue premiums receipts and investment income on assets. Against these revenues, the company may charge generally available business deductions and special life insurance deductions.

Among the general deductions allowed life insurers are net increases in reserves and payments of policyholder dividends. Although the law treats mutual and stock companies alike in most respects, mutual companies may not deduct all their policyholder dividends as a business expense.

The relationships between a policyholder and a mutual insurance company are not well defined in the insurance policy. A policyholder of a mutual insurance company is both an owner and a customer. A dollar flowing from the policyholder/owner to the company may be, in part, a payment for insurance services and, in part, an equity contribution. A dollar flowing from the company to the policyholder/owner may have a mix of sources, including a return of an overpayment for insurance services, interest earned on that overpayment during the period, and a return on equity. The lack of precision in the insurance contract provides the basis of a tax issue, an issue without a solution that is both theoretically correct and administratively simple.

A mutual insurance policy is a combination of term insurance, savings certificates, and an equity interest in the insurance company. The precise mix of insurance, savings, and ownership is not typically provided in the insurance contract. Because insurance premiums, interest earnings, dividends, and capital gains are treated differently under the individual and the corporate tax laws, this omission creates the basis for an arbitrary taxation of both the policyholder at the individual tax level and the insurance company at the corporate tax level.

On the other hand, precise statements of the ownership and price mix in the policy contract would result in extensive litigation by the IRS. In such a case the insurance company would likely be forced to show that its precise division was not arbitrary. There are obvious efficiency gains from a single arbitrary rule applied to similar types of contract. At a minimum, these efficiency gains include litigation savings for individuals, firms, and government. The question is how to determine the rules in a way that, while arbitrary, is not distortionary.

There is limited incentive for the federal government to determine the division of policyholder dividends. Both federal and state governments would benefit, in a revenue sense, if the entire policyholder dividend were characterized as a capital gain—that is, a return of equity. The dividend would not be a deductible expense at the corporate level and would be taxable at the individual level. Both federal and state governments would prefer to have a larger portion characterized as interest, not as a return of premium. For both levels of government, the interest would be deductible at the corporate level and taxable at the individual level. Finally, both would be harmed, in a revenue sense, for each dollar characterized as a return of premium. Again, at both the federal and state levels, the dividend would be deductible at the corporate level but not taxable at the individual level. At the state level, the issue is only slightly more complex. Because most states impose a tax that is the higher of a tax on income or a tax on premiums, if the firm paid a tax on premiums, the return of a premium introduces the possibility of a refund of taxes paid in a prior period.

The only obvious state specific issue in the determination of the character of policyholder dividends is one of administration. The issue is created because state governments typically impose a combination of income and dividend taxes. The interplay of those taxes introduces administrative problems that are not shared by the federal government. Moreover, the issue of policyholder dividend deductibility can be treated more sensibly by the states—there is no need for piggybacking.

Internal Revenue Code Treatment

The issue of policyholder dividends involves an interplay of three sections of the Internal Revenue Code: Sections 807, 808, and 809. Section 808 defines a "policyholder dividends deduction." For mutual life insurance companies the deduction of policyholder dividends is reduced by an amount determined under Section 809. When the amount of deduction to be reduced, determined under Section 809, exceeds the actual amount of policyholder dividends, the excess applies to the reserves carried forward under Section 807. The term policyholder dividend includes (1) any amount paid or credited where the amount is not fixed in the contract but depends on the experience of the company or the discretion of management, (2) excess interest, (3) premium adjustments, and (4) experience-rated refunds.

Excess interest is any amount paid or credited to a policyholder that is in excess of an interest rate determined at the prevailing state-assumed rate for the contract between the policyholder and the insurance company. The state-assumed rate for contracts is set by state insurance regulatory authorities. Premium adjustment means any reduction in the premium under an insurance or annuity contract that, but for the reduction, would be paid under the contract. Finally, experience-rated refund means any refund or credit based on the experience of the contract or group involved.

Section 809 requires a reduction of the deduction computed under Section 808 for mutual life insurance companies. The amount of the deduction allowed under Section 808 is reduced by a "differential earnings amount."

The differential earnings amount means an amount equal to the product of the life insurance company's average equity base for the taxable year, multiplied by the differential earnings rate for the year. The average equity base, subject to certain adjustments, is the mean of two values: the equity base at the close of the taxable year and at the close of the preceding taxable year.

The differential earnings rate is the excess of the imputed earnings rate for the taxable year over "the average mutual earnings rate for the second calendar year preceding the calendar year in which the taxable year begins." The imputed earnings rate for 1984 was 16.5 percent. For later taxable years the imputed earnings rate equal to 16.5 percent multiplied by the ratio of the "current stock earnings rate" divided by the "stock earnings rate of a base period."

The base period stock earnings rate is the average of the stock earning rates of the fifty largest stock companies in 1981, 1982, and 1983.[1] The current-year stock earnings rate is an average of the stock earnings rates of the fifty largest stock companies for the three years preceding the calendar year in which the taxable year begins. For example, for a calendar year taxpayer, the 1990 stock earning rate is the average of the 1987, 1988, and 1989 earnings rates for the fifty largest stock companies. Therefore, the performance of stock companies in general, not the actual performance of the company or of mutual companies, determines the taxable income of mutual insurers.

Mutual policyholder/owners typically receive policyholder dividends. Given the various relationships between the policyholder and a mutual insurance company, these dividends may be viewed as a return of excess premium, a return of interest earnings on the excess premium, a rate of return on the policyholder's equity share in the mutual insurance company, or a mix of all three. Returns of excess premiums are not taxable at the individual tax level and they are deductible under the corporate tax. Returns of interest earnings are taxable under the individual tax and are deductible under the corporate tax. Return of an equity share is taxable under the individual tax (possibly subject to special tax treatment) and is not deductible under the corporate tax.[2] To levy consistent income taxes at the individual and corporate levels, it is necessary to identify what portion of policyholder dividends falls into each category. Given that insurance companies do not specify the price return-interest-equity mix, tax departments or the tax law must make an arbitrary assignment.

Though a similar issue exists with respect to participating insurance issued by stock companies, the problem is less difficult because the policyholder does not purchase an equity interest in the insurance firm with the insurance policy. Policyholder dividends of stock insurance companies can only be comprised of price reductions and interest payments, both of which are deductible at the corporate level. At the individual tax level, the mutual-type problem does exist. Policyholder dividends issued by a stock company may be comprised of interest, which is taxable at the individual level, and returns of a price reduction, which is not taxable at the individual level.

On the other hand, precise statements of the ownership and price mix in the policy contract would result in extensive litigation by the IRS. In such a case the insurance company would likely be forced to show that its precise division was not arbitrary. There are obvious efficiency gains from a single arbitrary rule applied to similar types of contract. At a minimum, these efficiency gains include litigation savings for individuals, firms, and government. The question is how to determine the rules in a way that, while arbitrary, is not distortionary.

INSURANCE INSOLVENCY FUNDS

Individuals and firms purchase financial protection by remitting to an insurer a premium in return for a promise that the insured will be indemnified from a financial setback occasioned by certain specified events. In the United States, a system of insurance regulation has developed that attempts to ensure that insurers will have the means to satisfy their promises.

Typically, the regulatory process involves oversight of insurance company operations and the imposition of limits on behavior. The limits and oversight are designed to reduce activities that put at risk the ability of an insurer to meet its promises. The limits and rules for oversight include minimum capital and surplus requirements, rules of accounting practices, limitations on acceptable investments, marketing practices, growth rates, and other corporate activities. When the oversight portion of the state regulatory system does not suffice to keep an insurer whole, the remainder of the industry is called on to guaranty payment of the promises of the insolvent insurer. Currently, state insurance guaranty funds perform this function.

The current structure of insurance regulation has evolved through the uncoordinated efforts of the various states with periodic threats of federal action, causing the states to move in a coordinated fashion. Some coordination and uniformity among states are achieved through the actions of the NAIC, which has developed a series of "model acts" designed to govern insurer activities and state responsibilities. States are not compelled, however, to adopt these laws.

The NAIC model laws include two governing guaranty assessment funds (GFAs). The NAIC adopted a model property-liability insurer guaranty fund bill in 1969 and a similar life-health guaranty fund act in 1970. At that time, only a few states had guaranty systems. The remaining states rapidly adopted guaranty fund legislation based on or similar to the NAIC model.

The recent position of government has been that policyholders of insurance companies will not suffer the consequences of a failure of their insurer. Since the 1970s, the initial impact of insolvencies is paid for by surviving insurers through the use of guaranty fund assessments. Recent attention is focused on the rapidly increasing size of insolvencies as measured by the amount of guaranty fund assessments. In 1989, the aggregate amount of assessments exceeded $1 billion, a tenfold increase from 1980.

Guaranty Funds

Unlike S&L's, there is no explicit federal protection for insurance policyholders. Instead, in every state, claims against insolvent insurance companies are covered by state guaranty funds. When a company doing business in a state becomes insolvent and cannot pay outstanding claims, the state guaranty fund pays the claims. These guaranty fund monies are raised by assessing insurers doing business in the state.

Initially, the funds offered protection to policyholders of only certain lines of insurance, typically auto insurance, but they soon spread to other lines. To date state guaranty funds have not expanded to completely cover all lines and all insureds. For example, most guaranty funds exclude from coverage reinsurance and surplus lines insurance.

Guaranty fund laws in many states include a provision that allows insurers to recoup assessments in subsequent premiums. Some states permit explicit premium surcharges. Most states and the federal government allow guaranty fund deductions from taxes on or measured by income, and permit credits against taxes on premiums. This is not to say that insurance companies are protected from the financial consequences of the insolvency of a competitor. However, the actual impact of a $1 guaranty fund assessment on an insurer falls short of $1. How far short depends on which state issues the assessment and the rate-setting policies of each state. This chapter concentrates on the tax issues.

Tax Offsets: Federal

State insurance guaranty fund assessments are allowable as a deduction in deriving federal corporate taxable income. If an insurance company pays federal taxes, 34 percent of the assessment is initially offset through a reduction in federal taxes. Even if the company pays no current taxes, it may carry losses forward to future tax years, even those attributable to the GFA. Because some states grant a tax credit, the federal treasury recoups some of the tax outlay.

The deductibility of the insurance guaranty fund assessment from federal taxable income, like any other deduction, causes the federal government to place greater reliance on other revenue sources than would be the case absent the assessment. Taxpayers will bear these costs according to the income and geographic distributional impacts of the federal revenue system. Hence, to a degree, an assessment in one state will be exported to taxpayers in other states.

Tax Offsets: States

Most state corporate taxes on insurance firms involve more than one tax base. Typically, the taxes involve an income base, a capital base, a premium base, and a fixed dollar amount. Insurers generally pay the highest of the taxes computed on the alternative bases. Evidence suggests that insurance companies most frequently pay the tax computed on the premium tax base.

Because states adopt federal taxable income as the starting point in determining taxable state income, and because insurance firms may pay on the income tax base, the states also may be underwriting a part of the assessment. However, as noted above, for most insurance firms the premiums tax is the highest of the alternative tax computations.

Thirty states make a provision for a credit against their premiums tax that is equal to a fraction of the firm's guaranty fund assessment. Some states allow a full credit for both life and health and property and casualty assessments, whereas others restrict the credit to only one side of the industry. Twenty-seven of these states allow a full credit, though the credit, typically, is distributed over a period of time. Some of the states allow the credit only for life-health assessments, and some of these states limit the credit to assessments for a subset of contract types. Other states allow the credit only for property-casualty assessments, and one spreads recovery over different time periods depending on whether the assessment is on the property-casualty or life-health sides. The most common scheme allows the firm to offset against the premiums tax 20 percent per year for each of five years (Table 18.1); this is the suggested (optional) credit in the NAIC Model Act.

Table 18.2 is developed from information summarized in Table 18.1, the amount of 1989 guaranty fund assessments in each state, and an

TABLE 18.1
State GFA Tax Credits Available

| | Life- | Property- |
Credit Description	Health	Casualty
100% in the assessment year	10	7
20% per year for 5 years	16	11*
50% in the assessment year only	2*	0
40.366% in the assessment year	1	1
0.1% per year	1	1
No credit	21	31

Source: American Insurance Association, *State Taxation Manual, 1991* (laws as of December 1990). Note that one state offers a different credit (asterisk) to its property-casualty and life-health insurers.

TABLE 18.2
Analysis of 1989 Guaranty Fund Assessments

| | Life- | Property- | |
	Health	Casualty	Total
Guaranty fund assessments ($)	168	910	1208
Federal tax rate offset (%)	.2	12.0	10.4
State credit offsets (%)	99.0	29.4	39.1

initial assumption that firms pay only on the premiums tax base. This yields estimates of the assessment that may be offset by existing state tax credit laws. The estimates ignore the fact that the credits on the life-health side are frequently limited to particular contract types. They also ignore the reduction in the present value of credits spread over a period of years.

The estimates in Table 18.2 imply that 10.4 percent of the guaranty fund assessment is shifted from insurance companies to federal taxpayers. The cost would be borne in accordance with the distribution of the federal tax system—geographically and over the range of income.

Additionally, a weighted average 39.1 percent of the total life-health plus property-casualty assessments is estimated to be shifted from insurance companies to taxpayers in states offering guaranty fund assessment tax credits.

The tax payments by insurers before considering a tax offset would be available to finance a mix of government goods and services. The information provided in Table 18.2 suggests that an additional dollar of guaranty fund assessments would cause 10 cents to be reduced from federal tax revenues and 39 cents to be shifted from general fund revenues at the state level to a particular purpose: payment of a claim against an insolvent insurer. To maintain a balanced budget, governments would face the choice of raising other state taxes, increasing borrowing, or reducing services.

CONCLUSION

States are currently subject to increasing fiscal pressures. Many are desperately seeking new revenues. In the current climate a decrease in any revenue source is troubling. Yet, states seem to ignore the interplay of their funding of insurance regulatory oversight and the decline in revenues occasioned by the impact of increasing guaranty fund assessments. If regulatory improvements could make detection and action on troubled insurers occur prior to the need for assessments, all parties would gain. That is, policyholders would not have the discomfort of delayed and partial payments, and taxpayers would not have to bear an increasing tax burden.

NOTES

1. There are certain modifications to the computation, but, essentially, the base period stock earnings rate is the average of the 150 values (50 companies times 3 years).

2. There are exceptions to this rule, and there is often political pressure to integrate the individual and corporate tax systems. Under an integrated tax scheme, no problem would exist at the corporate level—the entire policyholder dividend would be deductible. The issue would continue to exist with respect to the individual income tax.

VII
Environmental Taxes and Fees

This part examines the role, both present and potential, of environmental taxes and fees as sources of state and local revenue and as instruments of environmental policy. In Chapter 19, Cordes describes the range of existing state and local environmental taxes and fees, presents data showing their importance as sources of general revenue and for environmental quality programs, and explains the financial incentives that environmental fees and taxes provide for businesses and consumers to change their behavior in ways that reduce environmental damage. He concludes that although environmental taxes presently raise modest amounts of revenue, they have room to grow. Although they could be increased to add to general revenues, they do not dominate traditional revenue sources for that purpose. As a means of reducing environmental damage, environmental taxes and fees are unlikely, in Cordes's view, to displace regulations and legislative mandate. But they can complement the regulatory approach by providing financial incentives to achieve improvements in environmental quality more cost-effectively.

In Chapter 20, Bohm and Kelsay analyze the use of taxes in dealing with a particular environmental problem—municipal solid waste. In principle, taxes on solid waste could be used both to fund disposal programs and to provide incentives for reducing waste generation. Bohm and Kelsay observe that at present solid waste taxes are viewed mainly as a source of revenue; tax rates typically are not high enough to deter significantly waste generation. When used to fund disposal, taxes on solid waste are user taxes and may be seen as fair for that reason. However, as a source of funds for general government, they are likely to be seen as unfair because of their regressivity.

19
State Environmental Taxes and Fees
JOSEPH J. CORDES

Reducing pollution of the environment has intangible, yet real, social benefits. According to some estimates, reducing acid rain from current levels could prevent premature deaths of as many as 50,000 people a year, improve water quality in acidic lakes and streams in the Northeast and Midwest, provide clearer skies in thirty-one states, and prevent damage to numerous stone buildings. Reducing smog and airborne particles is estimated to provide health benefits ranging from $500 million per year to perhaps as much as $10 billion per year. Reducing emissions of toxic chemicals is estimated to prevent 75 percent of the 1,500 to 2,700 new cases of fatal cancer attributable to exposure to such chemicals; to reduce the incidence of birth defects, chronic respiratory illness, and nonfatal cancers; and to reduce risks of major leaks of hazardous chemicals.

Reducing environmental pollution is also costly. About $90 billion is presently spent each year in the United States to comply with provisions of the Clean Air and Clean Water Acts, as well as with laws regulating solid and hazardous wastes, pesticides, herbicides, and fungicides, and other forms of pollution. A large share of these costs is paid by the private sector. But governments at all levels also must incur costs to monitor and enforce compliance with regulations, and to ameliorate the effects of pollution. In 1988, for example, budgeted outlays of the Environmental Protection Agency totaled almost $5 billion, and state budgets for control of air and water pollution, and hazardous and solid wastes were reported to be about $3 billion.[1]

To date, environmental quality has been improved largely through legislative mandate, even though economists and other policy analysts have extolled the virtues of using pollution taxes to give producers and/or consumers financial incentives to limit pollution. To be sure, a variety of taxes and fees are assessed on activities that pollute the environment. Federal environmental taxes, including the most recently enacted tax on chlorofluorocarbons (CFCs), are projected to raise some $2 billion in revenue in 1991. State and local governments are estimated to have raised about $700 million in 1988 from environmental taxes and fees. For the most part, however, these taxes and fees are intended to defray some or all of the public costs of pollution abatement, rather than to create financial incentives to pollute less.

Nevertheless, there has been some recent interest in expanding the use of environmental taxes. This interest is motivated more by a desire to find alternative ways of paying for government services than by a desire to increase the role of financial incentives in environmental regulation. At the same time, the search for alternative sources of revenue may create a political climate more receptive to the use of taxes and fees to regulate environmental quality, as well as to raise revenue.

What role do state and local environmental taxes and fees presently play, and what might their role be in the future? This chapter provides an overview of state and local environmental taxes organized around the following questions.

- What is the range of existing state and local environmental taxes and fees?
- How important are these taxes and fees as sources of revenue for state and local government generally, and for state and local environmental quality programs?
- What financial incentives do existing environmental fees and taxes provide for businesses and consumers to change their behavior in ways that reduce environmental pollution?
- Should environmental taxes figure more prominently as sources of general or dedicated revenue at the state and local levels, as compared with other more traditional revenue sources?
- Should environmental taxes and fees figure more prominently as instruments of state and local environmental policy, compared with more direct forms of regulating environmental quality?

RANGE AND SCOPE OF EXISTING TAXES AND FEES

The most comprehensive data on state environmental taxes and fees is from a detailed survey of the states undertaken by the National Governors' Association (1989). According to this survey, in 1988, forty-three states collected a little over $240 million from 272 different types of environmental fee and permit programs, and sixteen states collected almost $492 million from 37 different taxes associated with environmental programs.

Fees and Permits

A little under 20 percent of all fees collected, or about $42 million, could not be attributed to particular forms of pollution. About 40 percent of the $240 million in fees and permit revenue, or a total of $96 million, was raised from fees and permits associated with hazardous and solid waste. These fees and permits fell into four broad categories: (1) About $60 million was raised from permit and application fees for activities such as construction of underground storage tanks, and operation of solid waste management facilities; (2) about $12 million was raised from fees for solid waste disposal; (3) about $9 million was raised from fees assessed on the amount of waste generated at various facilities; and (4) about another $14 million was raised from hazardous and solid waste fees assessed on miscellaneous activities, such as radioactive waste fees and waste tire fees.

Fees and permits associated with air programs accounted for almost 25 percent of all environmental fees, or $56 million. Almost all of these fees, or $51 million, was raised from permits issued to owners of stationary or mobile sources of air pollution. About $4.5 million was raised from fees broadly related to emissions from various sources.

Fees and permits associated with water programs accounted for $46 million, or almost 20 percent of environmental fees. Almost 80 percent of revenues from water fee programs came from water permit fees, water rights applications, and training and certification fees for water management personnel.

Taxes

Of the $492 million raised in taxes, about $147 million could not be assigned to particular types of pollution or environmental programs.

Taxes associated with hazardous and solid waste programs raised $152 million, and taxes associated with air pollution programs raised $103 million (collected entirely in California).

Each type of tax that could be identified was generally levied on a base directly or indirectly linked to pollution. For example, taxes associated with hazardous and solid waste programs were levied on products whose use contributes to hazardous or solid wastes, or on owners of facilities that generate waste. Air pollution taxes in California were levied on motor vehicles and air emissions.

Taxes associated with water quality programs accounted for $87 million of all environmental taxes, though only about one-half of this amount came from taxing activities with a causal link to water pollution or to the benefits of improved water quality. The remainder came from dedicating a portion of other "sin tax" revenues from alcohol and tobacco taxes to water quality programs.

General vs. Dedicated Revenues

State environmental taxes and fees tended to be earmarked or dedicated to defray the costs of environmental quality programs. Almost $420 million was earmarked—or over 60 cents of every dollar raised in environmental fees and taxes. The share of revenues earmarked was higher for fees than it was for taxes. About 80 cents of every dollar from environmental fees whose purpose could be identified was earmarked for specific uses, as compared with about 50 cents of every dollar raised from taxes.

Among the various fees, the share of revenues that were earmarked varied with the reason for collecting the fee. Over 90 cents of every dollar raised from fees associated with hazardous and solid waste and water programs were earmarked, compared with about 50 cents of every dollar raised by air program fees. This general pattern was mirrored among environmental taxes, where over 80 cents of each dollar raised in connection with hazardous and solid waste and water programs was earmarked, compared with about 55 cents of each dollar raised from taxes associated with air programs.

Contribution to State Revenue

The total amount raised from state environmental fees is small compared with other sources of state revenue, such as so-called "sin" taxes. For example, in states that collected environmental fees and taxes, the total revenue raised from these sources was roughly a fourth as much as the total revenue raised from alcohol taxes and fees.

The amount raised from state environmental taxes and fees was also modest compared with revenue raised from federal environmental taxes. In 1988, when there was no federal tax on CFCs, federal environmental taxes raised about $1 billion. In 1991, with revenues from the new tax on CFCs, this amount is projected to be about $2 billion.

There are, however, notable differences in the relative importance of these taxes among the states. This may be seen in Table 19.1, where states are ranked by the total amount of revenue raised from environmental taxes and fees. In four of the five states that raised $50 million or more per year from environmental taxes and fees—California, New Jersey, Montana, and Illinois—these revenue source brought in about as much or more revenue than did alcohol taxes and fees.

Contribution to State Environmental Programs

Although almost $420 million in revenue from environmental taxes and fees was earmarked to support environmental programs, total spending on environmental programs in states that collected fees or taxes was a little over $3 billion. Earmarked sources of revenue thus defrayed about 10 cents of each dollar of spending for environmental programs.

There is quite a bit of variation around these averages among environmental programs and also among the states. Among different environmental programs, for example, dedicated environmental taxes and fees equaled about 18 percent of spending on hazardous and solid waste programs, almost one-third of spending on air programs, and 7 percent of spending on water programs. Among the states, earmarked taxes and fees equaled more than 50 percent of state spending on waste disposal and air and water quality programs in three states; between 25 and 50 percent of spending on these programs in another four states; between 10 and 25 percent of spending for environmental programs in seventeen states; and less than 10 percent of environmental spending in another seventeen states. (See Table 19.2).

The data just summarized show that many states have a good deal of room to raise environmental fees and taxes in the future. Would this be desirable? How this question is answered depends on whether environmental fees and taxes are seen mainly as revenue sources, or also as possible instruments of state and local environmental policy.

TABLE 19.1
State Revenue Raised by Environmental Taxes and Fees

State	Environmental Fees/Taxes	Alcohol Fees/Taxes
California	$115,805,000	$160,132,000
New Jersey	101,345,000	59,456,000
Montana	73,386,905	14,766,000
Florida	73,332,618	476,216,000
Illinois	50,480,600	69,828,000
Washington	45,400,639	109,364,000
New York	39,279,000	178,265,000
Minnesota	31,677,150	56,269,000
Pennsylvania	23,749,828	149,773,000
Missouri	23,019,600	26,283,000
Oregon	16,500,000	12,028,000
Maryland	14,267,719	28,383,000
Texas	10,629,840	337,035,000
Wisconsin	9,819,068	38,794,000
Colorado	9,755,000	24,428,000
Arizona	9,700,869	100,147,000
Massachusetts	9,560,000	79,712,000
Tennessee	5,535,496	64,565,000
Ohio	5,280,000	87,762,000
Connecticut	4,262,270	37,420,000
Maine	3,602,597	35,889,000
Delaware	2,210,400	5,651,000
New Hampshire	1,594,000	13,047,000
Virginia	1,514,750	101,421,000
Kentucky	1,126,050	51,215,000
Oklahoma	1,034,850	58,559,000
Iowa	1,018,000	20,311,000
Alabama	840,661	100,147,000
Arkansas	703,263	24,797,000
Nebraska	638,000	16,072,000
Michigan	590,400	131,626,000
West Virginia	500,000	14,403,000
Vermont	383,100	15,088,000
Louisiana	368,904	52,012,000
North Carolina	293,021	144,444,000

TABLE 19.1 (continued)

State	Environmental Fees/Taxes	Alcohol Fees/Taxes
Nevada	$290,615	$11,095,000
Indiana	218,719	45,663,000
South Dakota	121,470	9,197,000
Puerto Rico	114,186	N.A.
North Dakota	51,262	5,891,000
New Mexico	0	17,473,000
Total	690,000,850	2,984,627,000

Source: *Funding Environmental Programs: An Examination of Alternatives,* National Governors' Association, 1989.

TAXES AND FEES AS REVENUE SOURCES

Should environmental taxes become more important sources of state revenue? Should environmental taxes and fees cover more of the cost of future environmental programs? The answers to these questions depend on how environmental fees and taxes compare with other revenue sources, such as broad-based income, sales taxes, or excise taxes.

Three issues need to be addressed. First, compared with other taxes, are environmental fees and taxes more likely to raise revenue in ways that do not interfere with, and perhaps even promote, the efficient allocation of resources? Second, are such taxes more or less likely to distribute the burden of raising revenue fairly? Third, can such taxes raise added revenue at reasonable administrative cost?

Allocation of Resources

Taxing particular goods or activities changes market prices and generally causes less of the taxed good or activity to be produced. If there is no social purpose in restricting output of the taxed goods, consumers and producers suffer a loss in economic well-being that exceeds the amount revenue raised from taxes. This excess burden is a real cost of collecting taxes over and above any administrative costs of raising revenue.

TABLE 19.2

**Dedicated Environmental Fees and Taxes as a Percent of
Spending on Waste Disposal, Air, and Water Programs[1]**

50-100%	25-50%	10-25%	< 10%
Illinois	Missouri	Maryland	Arizona
Oregon	California	Arkansas	New Jersey
Colorado	Pennsylvania	Massachusetts	Kentucky
	Connecticut	Tennessee	Vermont
		Oklahoma	Montana
		Iowa	Florida
		Maine	Texas
		New York	North Carolina
		Washington	Virginia
		Delaware	North Dakota
		Ohio	Michigan
		West Virginia	South Dakota
		Nebraska	Louisiana
		Wisconsin	Minnesota
		New Hampshire	New Mexico
		Alabama	Indiana
		Nevada	

[1]Within each group, states are ranked by the ratio of dedicated environmental fees and taxes to state spending on waste disposal, air, and water programs.

The excess burden of taxation can be reduced, perhaps even eliminated, by choosing to tax activities whose consumption or production imposes social costs that are not reflected in market prices. Because there are gains from restricting such activities, taxing them may actually improve economic well-being, or at least reduce it less than if other "socially desirable" activities are taxed.

The production and consumption of goods and services that pollute the environment is widely believed to impose costs, such as those discussed in the introduction to this chapter, that are not fully reflected in the prices of those goods and services. This translates easily into the perception that one can "do well" (i.e., raise additional needed revenue) while "doing good" (i.e., reducing the costs of environmental pollution) by levying taxes or charges on activities that pollute.

In their current form, however, most state environmental fees, permits, and taxes do little to affect the behavior of polluters. One reason is that under many state environmental fee and tax programs, the amount of the fee or tax has little or no relation to the amount of pollution or waste discharged. For example, permits for waste disposal may be a fixed dollar amount, or the amount may vary with the size of the facility, but not directly with the volume of waste discharged or its social cost. Taxes that fund water quality programs are levied on goods that are complements to the use, and presumably enjoyment of, clean water (e.g., boats) or on all sales. Air emission fees often are fixed charges, or charges that become operative above some minimum level, and remain fixed thereafter. In each of these cases, polluters have little or no financial incentive to change their behavior, even if taxes and fees are assessed at higher rates.

In other cases, environmental fees and taxes are levied on bases such as emissions, or tons of waste, that would encourage abatement, but the taxes or fees are set at levels that are low enough to not encourage abatement by the polluter beyond levels mandated by direct federal and state regulations. These rates would, of course, go up if environmental taxes and fees were designed to bring in increased amounts of revenue, but current tax and fee rates would need to rise quite a bit before meeting or exceeding the financial incentives already implicit in existing environmental regulations.

Thus, unless points of collection for many environmental taxes and fees are changed, and tax and fee rates are raised considerably, state environmental taxes and fees are not likely to lead to further improvements in environmental quality beyond those achieved by direct regulation. For this reason, environmental taxes and fees should probably not be preferred to other taxes.

Even though state environmental taxes and fees in their current form provide weak financial incentives for producers to produce output with fewer environmental emissions, more reliance on these revenue sources may still reduce the excess burdens of raising state revenue. Current rates of environmental taxation are fairly low, so that increasing them may entail a smaller excess burden than would raising rates of other taxes, such as income, sales, and excise taxes. Moreover, even if environmental taxes and fees do not provide financial incentives for producers to cut back the amount of pollution emitted per unit of output, such taxes and fees would raise producers' costs. If these cost increases were passed on through higher market prices for the taxed goods, fewer goods that contribute to pollution would be bought and sold, which lowers pollution.

Fairness

In a competitive market, the burden of environmental excise taxes and fees will ultimately be passed on through higher prices on the goods and services produced in the industries subject to these taxes and fees. As with other excise and sales taxes, these burdens, with a few exceptions, decline as a percentage of household income as income goes up, and they rise with the share of household income that is spent on goods subject to environmental taxes and fees.

Whether this incidence of burdens is desirable depends on how fairness is defined. The burden of environmental taxes and fees is distributed regressively with respect to income. From the perspective of "ability to pay," environmental taxes and fees are no more attractive as sources of general revenue than sales and nonenvironmental excise taxes, which also distribute tax burdens regressively.

The benefit principle of taxation, in its conventional form, also does not provide a strong case for greater reliance on environmental fees and taxes. The reason is that benefits from improved environmental quality are distributed progressively with respect to income (Baumol and Oates, 1988, Ch. 15). Matching tax burdens with benefits received would thus require that spending for environmental quality be financed by progressive, instead of regressive, taxes. By this logic, general revenue sources, such as income taxes, may be reasonably fair ways to fund environmental quality programs.

An alternative perspective is that consumers and producers of goods and services that pollute should bear more of the cost of cleaning up the environment. According to this view, polluters should pay because their activities use environmental resources that belong to the public at large.

The equity argument for expanding the role of environmental fees and taxes thus rests on accepting the principle that the "polluter pays." Even if this is the case, however, only rough justice is achieved by levying taxes and fees on bases, such as permit applications, that have little relation to the physical volume or the economic and social harm of the discharge into the air or water, or of the hazardous waste material.

Administrative and Compliance Costs

A final issue is the comparative cost of collecting and administering environmental taxes and fees. At present many environmental tax and fee programs rely on simple points of collection, such as the permit application process, and low tax and fee rates, to hold down administrative costs, while ensuring a stable revenue base.

States that raise small amounts of revenue from permits and fees can continue to rely on simple, relatively low-rate permits and fees for a time, to raise increasing amounts of revenue. There are, however, limits to how high charges for simple permits and fees can be and still be regarded as fair and reasonable. Beyond these limits, raising more revenue may require taxing bases that depend on the volume of output or the volume of emissions or discharge. States that already collect significant revenues from fees and permits are likely to be at or near the limits of these revenue sources, and may need to move to more complex, and costlier to administer, environmental taxes and fees.

In these cases a relevant question is whether it would cost more to collect environmental taxes and emissions fees than to collect other excise and sales taxes. On the one hand, there would be initial start-up costs of administering new environmental taxes or fees that would not be present for existing taxes. On the other hand, many of the costs needed to monitor compliance with such taxes—such as measuring the volume of emissions or discharge at specific sources—may have to be borne anyway as part of the state's response to federal environmental programs. If so, the net additional costs of administering and collecting environmental taxes are likely to be comparable to the incremental cost of raising revenue from other sources, such as sales and excise taxes.

TAXES AND FEES AS INSTRUMENTS OF ENVIRONMENTAL POLICY

A different question is whether state environmental taxes and fees can realistically be expected to do more in the future than defray the public costs of pollution control. Some basic but useful insights can be gleaned from the extensive literature on the role of taxes and fees in environmental policy.[2]

Defining the Base of Pollution Taxes

The first point has already been mentioned above. To realize the presumed benefits of taxing pollution, many existing state environmental taxes and fees would need to be restructured so that the amount of the tax or fee paid varied with the amount of environmental harm caused by the activity. At minimum, this would mean directly taxing emissions into water or the air or discharge of hazardous and solid wastes, instead of levying taxes and fees on bases that are indirectly related to the emissions. Without this change, producers will have little incentive to invest in technologies to reduce air and water emissions and discharge of hazardous and solid waste, even at tax and fee rates set at considerably higher levels than at present.

Pollution Taxes as Complements to Regulation

In principle, environmental taxes and fees could be used to attain the socially optimal level of pollution—that is, the level at which the costs of reducing pollution by an extra unit are just balanced by the value of the environmental damages avoided. Alternatively, environmental taxes and fees could be used to complement but not supplant direct regulation of environmental quality. Pollution taxes would be enacted to provide financial incentives to meet legislatively mandated standards for environmental quality (which might or might not be socially optimal) at the lowest possible cost to society. The latter alternative is more realistic for several reasons.

Theoretical Issues

One reason is conceptual. Even if regulators knew enough about the social costs of pollution to set tax rates equal to the value of the environmental harm done by different pollutants, relying entirely on price incentives to achieve the desired level of environmental quality might not succeed.

Market incentives, including but not limited to pollution taxes, work best when the firm's incentive to maximize profits—given that market prices reflect all social costs—is consistent with maximizing the well-being of all members of society. When this is the case, making sure that market prices reflect the marginal social costs of pollution will achieve the best possible allocation of resources.

Pollution by its very nature, however, creates conditions under which simply having the "right" prices may not guarantee that resources will be allocated efficiently.[3] A simple case is one in which reducing pollution yields no benefit until pollution has been lowered below some minimum threshold level. If regulators knew the added social benefits of reducing pollution beyond the threshold level, they could levy taxes based on their estimate of the added benefits of lowering pollution.

Polluters would find it cheaper over some range to spend money on reducing pollution than to pay the tax. There would be a financial incentive to cut back pollution to the point where the cost of reducing pollution by an additional unit just equaled the tax per unit of pollution emitted. The result would be an amount of pollution below the threshold level at which benefits are assumed to become positive.

Whether this outcome would be socially optimal is uncertain. Society would be better off reducing pollution if the total social benefits (total social costs avoided) from reducing pollution beyond the threshold at which benefits become positive were greater than the social costs of controlling pollution up to that point. Providing firms with a financial incentive to equate abatement costs with taxes at the margin would not guarantee this outcome. Given that *some* resources are devoted to reducing pollution, taxes ensure that the right amount of resources will be spent on abatement. But, in the jargon of economics, this may be a "local" rather than a "global" optimum. It might be better to devote *no* resources to reducing pollution, depending on how costly it was to reach the threshold level of pollution abatement needed to reap positive benefits.

Practical Issues

Lack of knowledge about the effects and the causes of pollution is another, more important reason why taxes and fees are unlikely to play a primary role in limiting pollution. Though research continues to improve our understanding of the causes and the consequences of pollution, there is much uncertainty about its social costs.

This uncertainty is reflected in the wide range of estimates of the benefits of improving environmental quality. For example, a recent survey reported that reducing air pollution to levels specified in the Clean Air Act Amendments would produce estimated benefits ranging from $6 billion to $25 billion (Portney, 1990).

There is a wide range of estimates for the economic benefits from improving environmental quality for several reasons. Scientific evidence about the effects of pollution is highly uncertain. There is also uncertainty about how to translate the available scientific evidence into estimates of the monetary costs of pollution. Because of the uncertainty, there is no way of knowing at the present time what *the* optimal level of pollution is, and, therefore, little or no basis for setting pollution taxes to achieve this level.

The Role of Price Incentives

Because of these theoretical and practical limitations, it seems unrealistic to substitute pollution taxes and other price incentives for legislation that mandates specific levels of environmental quality. Price incentives, including taxes and fees, can, however, help achieve legislatively mandated level of environmental quality more cost-effectively.

Lowering the Cost of Controlling Pollution. Price incentives can help lower the costs of controlling pollution whenever multiple sources contribute to the overall level of pollution and, apart from considerations of cost, regulators are indifferent to how the required total reduction in pollution is distributed among the multiple sources. In such cases, it is desirable to distribute the total reduction in pollution so that the added cost of reducing emissions by an extra unit is the same at each source. This means that emissions from sources with relatively low costs of controlling pollution would be cut proportionately more than emissions from sources with relatively high costs of pollution control.

Current environmental regulations do not distribute reductions in emissions in this manner. Instead, regulations often require proportionate reductions at all sources. The result is that the added cost of controlling an extra unit of pollution varies among the different sources, and the total cost of meeting legislatively mandated environmental quality standards is higher than necessary. Costs could be lowered by shifting the responsibility for reducing emission from sources with relatively high costs of control to those with relatively low costs of control.

In such a case, taxes could help regulate pollution more efficiently, especially in the longer run. Instead of mandating proportional reductions of pollution at each source, a legislated target for overall pollution reduction could be set, and polluters could then be required to pay a tax on each unit of effluent discharged into the environment. Each polluter would have a financial incentive to reduce pollution up to the point where the added cost of abating an additional unit just equaled the tax. Because all polluters would face the same tax, the added cost of reducing an additional unit would be the same at all sources. Producers who could control environmental emissions relatively cheaply would cut back pollution proportionately more than businesses with relatively high costs of pollution control. As a result, the total reduction in pollution would be achieved at minimum social cost.

Using taxes to implement regulatory standards runs the risk of falling short of or exceeding the desired overall level of pollution abatement. If the tax rate is set "too low," pollution would be cut by less than the legislatively mandated amount. If the tax rate is set too high, pollution would be cut by more than the legislatively mandated amount.

Proponents of increased reliance on taxes argue that this shortcoming of pollution taxes can be overcome by adjusting the tax rate in response to observations on the level of emissions. If a particular tax rate resulted in less than the mandated reduction in pollution, then the tax rate would be raised. A tax rate resulting in more than the mandated reduction could be lowered. By adjusting the tax rate in this way, regulators would eventually arrive at a tax rate that gave different sources of pollution the financial incentives needed to reduce total pollution to the mandated level. Compared with mandating across-the-board reductions, taxing pollution would achieve the same overall result while requiring fewer resources to be devoted to controlling pollution. In the process, tax revenues would be collected on the amount of pollution remaining after abatement.

Several studies have compared the costs of limiting pollution by across-the-board percentage reductions in emissions at all sources, regardless of relative cost, with the cost of achieving the same total percentage change in emissions more efficiently. These studies show that substantial costs could be saved by moving away from the across-the-board approach.

One study used engineering data from Du Pont to estimate the costs of reducing hydrocarbon emissions by 85 percent in a variety of ways. The first alternative considered was source-by-source standards in which emissions from each source, both within a single Du Pont plant and across Du Pont plants, were reduced by 85 percent. The estimated total cost of this alternative was $105.7 million in 1975 dollars. The second alternative was plant-by-plant standards in which emissions from each Du Pont plant were reduced by 85 percent, but within each plant emissions were allowed to vary inversely by source with respect to the costs of controlling emissions. The cost of this alternative was $42.6 million, or 63 percent lower than in the case of source-by-source standards. The final alternative considered was a multiplant standard which allowed emissions to be traded off among plants subject to the overall limitation that 85 percent of emissions be reduced. The estimated cost of this alternative was $14.6 million (Maloney and Yandle, 1980).

The Du Pont study applies to a single firm, and to air pollution, but studies dealing with other forms of pollution have found comparable cost savings. A study of the cost of reducing halocarbon emissions in various ways found that compared with a realistic set of source-by-source controls, using emissions taxes to limit emissions would have saved roughly $120 million in costs of control—a savings of 50%—while at the same time collecting $1.4 billion in emissions tax revenues from polluters.[4] Still other studies that compare the cost of limiting emissions using direct controls with the least-cost solution find cost savings ranging from 50 percent to less than 10 percent (Baumol and Oates, 1988, Ch. 15).

Estimates such as these make pollution taxes look quite attractive. In practice there are several reasons why the use of pollution taxes as complements to direct regulation would need to be considered carefully on a case-by-case basis.

Administrative and Revenue Considerations. One reason is a pragmatic one. To use taxes and fees to supplement regulations in the manner just described would require changing the point of collection of many taxes and fees, in addition to large increases in tax and fee rates.

Higher tax and fee rates would raise significantly the amount of taxes paid by many industries whose activities pollute the air or water, or who contribute to hazardous and solid waste. For example, several crude estimates indicate that billions of dollars of revenue might be raised from taxing air pollution alone, if the taxes were set at levels high enough to encourage abatement by firms (Crandall, 1983; Terkla, 1984).

In other words, taxing pollution at rates high enough to create incentives for abatement would easily increase revenues from environmental taxes by several fold. These increased taxes would not be evenly distributed among industries and products. For example, in the case of taxes on stationary sources of air pollution, perhaps 75 percent of the additional tax burden would fall on seven industries (electric utilities, iron and steel, petroleum refining, nonferrous metals, cement, pulp and paper, and chemicals) (Congressional Budget Office, 1987).

One analyst has suggested that these impacts could be softened by taxing pollution only above some minimum threshold (Crandall, 1983). In principle, this approach could provide financial incentives for abatement beyond this threshold level while reducing the burden (and the revenue collected) from prospective taxes on pollution. It would, however, increase the costs of monitoring compliance with such taxes, and would also not provide the same long-run incentives for pollution abatement as would an across-the-board tax on all emissions (Spulber, 1985).

Variation in Environmental Harm at Different Sources. Another consideration is that pollution taxes (like other market incentives) are less appropriate when regulators care, for scientific and environmental reasons, about how reductions in emissions are distributed among different sources. In such cases, nothing may be gained by trading off higher levels of emission or discharge at one source against lower levels elsewhere. For example, it would not be appropriate to trade off more abatement at a cheaper source against less abatement at a more expensive source if regulators believe that emissions from the "more expensive" source are more harmful. It would also make little sense to do so when the environmental harm to be limited is confined to a particular geographic area. Reducing hazardous wastes more at one site may not substitute for reducing them less at others.

States may, however, be in a better position than the federal government to exploit the positive incentive effects of pollution taxes when there are regional differences in the harm done by pollution. In testimony before the House Committee on Ways and Means, the Treasury Department noted that when harm to the environment varies by region, pollution taxes levied at the same rate nationally would not be appropriate. Considerations of tax policy could preclude the federal government from taxing pollution at different rates in different regions of the country even if it would be desirable to do so for reasons of environmental policy. States would not, however, face this limitation.

Uncertain Control of Pollution. A final, important issue is that regulators must live with greater uncertainty about the level of pollution control when they tax polluters than when polluters are regulated directly. We have noted above that the consequences of such uncertainty would diminish over time as regulators observed how polluters respond to taxes, provided that regulators are able to adjust pollution tax rates to achieve legislatively mandated levels of pollution.

Fine-tuning environmental tax rates may, however, be easier said than done. If pollution tax rates cannot be changed over time, or can be changed only infrequently, the choice between pollution taxes and direct controls involves comparing the more certain control offered by direct regulations with the lower cost of control offered by pollution taxes. Relying on pollution taxes to achieve legislatively mandated standards, rather than on direct controls, would be an attractive option if a relatively low value was placed on certainty of control but the costs of control were thought to be high. In cases in which it was thought imperative to limit emissions to a given amount, the uncertainty associated with taxes would become a more serious limitation.

Alternative Policy Instruments

In considering the future role of environmental taxes and fees, it should also be recognized these are just one of several ways of introducing more price incentives into regulation of the environment.

Tradeable Permits. The benefits of environmental taxes can also be obtained by allowing polluters to trade pollution permits with each other. One possibility would be to set a desired level of environmental emissions, issue permits to pollute based on this level, and then allow permits to be bought and sold.

Under this arrangement, polluters with relatively high costs of controlling pollution would find it worthwhile to buy additional rights to pollute from polluters with relatively low costs of control. Polluters with relatively low costs of controlling pollution would find the costs of cutting back on pollution to be less than the income they could receive by selling rights to pollute.

Because the total amount of permits would be fixed to equal the legislatively mandated level of pollution, trading of pollution permits would not affect the total amount of pollution reduction. It would, however, redistribute abatement among pollution sources with high and low costs of control. As long as trades would be arranged at little or no transactions costs, pollution permits would be traded until each producer faced the same marginal cost of abatement. Like taxes, tradeable permits would lower the cost of achieving legislatively mandated levels of environmental quality. Unlike taxes, tradeable permits would produce a certain level of overall pollution control.

In the short run, tradeable permits have incentives comparable to those of pollution taxes, while avoiding the uncertainty about how much environmental emissions will be cut. In the long run, however, the effects of environmental taxes differ from those of tradeable permits when permits are distributed free of charge. Producers' profits would be lower if they paid taxes on all emissions than if they were assigned tradeable permits. Environmental taxes and fees, if adopted broadly among the states, would thus create stronger incentives in the long run for resources to exit industries that pollute than would tradeable permits.[5]

Tying Tax Abatement to Pollution Abatement. A different approach, available to the states but not to the federal government, might be to make tax abatement contingent on pollution abatement. Louisiana has begun experimenting with this approach by making the size of the exemption granted to a corporation for business property taxes conditional on how the corporation scores on an environmental quality scale.[6]

The Louisiana scheme will need to withstand legal challenges, but it is an interesting one. The approach has features of a subsidy for pollution control without the associated budgetary cost, because businesses would otherwise not have to pay any taxes because of the exemption. If, as several empirical studies suggest, location decisions of firms are not much influenced by tax abatement programs, tying tax abatement to pollution abatement may be a way of converting an otherwise financial windfall into an incentive for improved environmental quality.

CONCLUSION

State environmental taxes and fees presently raise small to modest amounts of revenue, much of which is earmarked to help defray the costs of state environmental spending. These taxes and fees have room to grow from current levels. Whether they should can be viewed from two different perspectives. One is the traditional public finance perspective that emphasizes raising revenue. The other is the perspective from environmental economics and policy that emphasizes strategies for controlling pollution.

Pollution taxes and fees have some features that make them attractive sources of revenue compared with other taxes, but the case in favor of environmental taxes is not clear-cut. Moreover, if they wish to raise more revenue, states that already collect significant environmental taxes and fees may need to levy taxes or fees on bases that will be somewhat harder to administer and monitor than the bases of existing taxes and fees.

Pollution taxes are unlikely to become a primary means of either federal or state policies for limiting pollution. For the foreseeable future, the level of environmental quality is likely to be determined by legislation rather than by market incentives. Pollution taxes can, however, complement existing regulations by providing financial incentives to achieve regulatory goals more cost-effectively. In some cases, especially where environmental policy considerations require regional variation in tax rates on pollution, states may be better suited than is the federal government to use taxes and fees to complement regulations.

NOTES

1. This is the sum of all budgeted amounts reported in response to a survey conducted by the National Governors Association (1989).

2. Portions of this section of the paper draw extensively from Cordes et al. (1990).

3. For a discussion of this issue see Baumol and Oates (1988) and Baumol and Bradford (1972).

4. For a general discussion of this and other studies see Baumol and Oates (1988, Ch. 15).

5. Baumol and Oates (1988, Ch. 15) and Spulber (1985). Permits issued and *sold* by state and local governments would provide the same financial incentives for pollution abatement as equivalent pollution taxes in both the short run and the long run.

6. For a detailed description of the Louisiana approach, see Farber et al. (1990).

20
State and Local Government Initiatives to Tax Solid and Hazardous Waste

ROBERT A. BOHM and MICHAEL P. KELSAY

To loosely quote the well-known country philosopher, Dolly Parton, the purpose of this chapter is to "talk trash." More specifically, and formally, our objective is to address four issues: The first concerns recent state and local government initiatives to fund solid waste programs. The second addresses the increasingly rancorous problem of the interstate shipment of both solid and hazardous waste. The third is a somewhat tongue-in-cheek observation regarding the relationship of solid waste collection and disposal costs with the nexus debate familiar to state sales tax analysts.

The final question is what might be expected in the future in the area of solid and hazardous waste environmental taxes. In all four instances, our focus will be on what is actually taking place in the field rather than on the conceptual and theoretical aspects of environmental taxation covered so admirably by Cordes in Chapter 19. Prior to turning to our principal task and by way of introduction, the following section reviews some of the major policy issues that have dominated the discussion of solid and hazardous waste in recent years and form the context within which the funding debate at the state and local level has taken place.

SOLID AND HAZARDOUS WASTE AND
AND ENVIRONMENTAL POLICY

The national, state, and local level debate on the proper environmental policy for solid and hazardous waste is dominated by images, facts, strategic behavior, and catch-22's. The images are those engendered by popular press accounts of overflowing landfills, wayward garbage barges, Love Canal, and Times Beach. The facts pertain to impending stricter environmental regulations on landfills and incinerators, dwindling disposal capacity, and rising costs from both of these factors. Strategic behavior refers to the difficulty public officials and private firms have in replacing aging landfills and incinerators. It has given rise to numerous descriptive and colorful acronyms: LULU (Locally Unacceptable Land Use), NIMBY (Not in My Backyard), and NIMTOF (Not in My Term of Office). The most common catch-22 involves the pricing of solid waste services to encourage reduction of waste generation and increased recycling. Often the prescription is an explicit user charge or tax. However, in many areas of the country, it is feared that such a pricing policy will lead to illegal dumping and have negative equity consequences.

Solid Waste

To most people, solid waste means garbage or, as it is more formally titled, municipal solid waste (MSW).[1] The collection and disposal of MSW has traditionally been a local government function or left to the private sector. The role of state government has been confined to a largely regulatory one. Although it is unlikely that many states will choose to get into the garbage business directly, as will be seen, conditions in the MSW market are pushing states into a more active role.

An Environmental Protection Agency (EPA) report on the characterization of solid waste indicated that Americans generated close to 160 million tons of solid waste in 1988 (U.S. Environmental Protection Agency, 1990). This figure was revised upward in 1990 to 180 million tons annually, an average of about 4.0 lbs/day on a per capita basis. This generation rate is far in excess of other developed countries. West Germany generates about 60 percent of the waste per capita that the United States does, whereas France generates only about 40 percent of the U.S. rate (National Governors' Association, 1989). It is projected that in the U.S. municipal solid waste will increase 20 percent by the year 2000.

The high level of MSW generation in the United States has raised the level of awareness with regard to disposal where 83 percent of municipal solid waste is placed in landfills, 6 percent is incinerated, and the remainder is recycled (National Conference of State Legislatures, 1990). In 1988, a survey by the EPA estimated that there were 5,500 landfills in operation at that time. The EPA projected 33 percent of those would be closed by 1996 due to capacity constraints or an inability to meet revised design criteria expected to result from congressional reauthorization and revision of the Resource Conservation and Recovery Act (RCRA) (U.S. Environmental Protection Agency, 1989b, p. 8). By 2013, the EPA estimates that the number of landfills in operation will decline to about 1,000.

In addition to running out of existing disposal capacity, many localities are finding it extremely difficult or impossible to site new landfills or any other type of solid waste facility. Recent surveys have shown that large percentages of the public do not want facilities sited locally.[2] Environmental groups and others have been extremely successful up to this time in blocking the siting of new disposal facilities. For example, all of the landfills over Long Island's aquifer recharge area, which previously had been used for disposal of 90 percent of the region's solid waste, have been closed for environmental reasons, and strict requirements have prevented the siting of new disposal capacity in the area (Council on Plastics and Packaging in the Environment, 1989). In New Jersey, there were 400 landfills in 1970; today, there are about 10, and over one-half of its solid waste must be shipped out of state.

High rates of generation and impending capacity constraints have resulted both in increased interest in alternatives to traditional disposal and states and localities becoming quite parochial with regard to existing capacity. The principal alternatives to landfills and incineration are recycling and source reduction, both of which should yield important resource conservation side benefits as well as relieving demand for disposal facilities. Initiating programs in these areas, however, will not be costless and will not eliminate the financial burden of maintaining the infrastructure needed to handle solid waste in the future.

Numerous studies have shown the dramatic increase in spending for environmental infrastructure and programs that is going to be required to meet the needs of our society. The EPA has estimated that the level of local spending will need to be increased $15 billion annually by the year 2000 just to maintain the present level of environmental services, and an additional $5.3 billion annually for the projected cost of new environmental regulations (Environmental Protection Agency, 1989a, p. 9). Specifically, the cost of solid waste regulations are estimated at $3 billion annually, about one-half of the $7 billion required to maintain the existing infrastructure. Overall, localities, can be expected to pay about 85 percent of the public cost of environmental protection.

Coupled with this increased financial burden for state and local governments is the shrinking role of the federal government. The EPA's operating budget for environmental protection has fallen since 1979 when it was $1.8 billion annually.[3] It fell sharply to $1.2 billion in

1983, and stood at $1.7 billion in 1989. In addition, the EPA has sharply cut grants to states to supplement operating budgets. These programs peaked at $499 billion annually in 1979, and stood at $318 billion annually in 1989, a decline of 36 percent. Other EPA grants to states such as superfund clean-up money, construction grants, and underground storage tank replacement funds have declined from $7.3 billion in 1978 to $3.5 billion in 1989. As another barometer of the increasing state role and shrinking federal role, the National Governor's Association has reported that federal grants as a percentage of state budgets declined from 49 to 46 percent in air programs, 49 to 43 percent in water programs, and 76 to 40 percent in hazardous and solid waste programs, as shown in Table 20.1.

Furthermore, existing capacity is not always where it is most needed. Some states have a net deficit and must export waste to states with surplus capacity. A similar mismatch often occurs within states. Faced with a growing need for capacity and an increased share of the cost, the lack of interest in importing a neighbor's environmental problems is understandable. The most glaring manifestation of this conflict lies in recent attempts by states to control the flow of interstate waste, a topic addressed directly in "The Problem of Interstate Waste," later in this chapter.

Rather than wait for new federal mandates, many states have moved forward with more stringent regulations on disposal facilities and comprehensive solid waste plans and programs. Although states may take an active role in the operation and management of disposal facilities (e.g., Connecticut, Rhode Island, Delaware, and the District of Columbia), the primary thrust of state government efforts has been toward planning and provision of services to support local solid waste programs while continuing their traditional regulatory function. State initiatives typically include planning and development of initial solid waste programs (statewide and locally); technical assistance; grant and loan programs for equipment to be used in a variety of resource recovery activities (e.g., scales, balers, mobile shredders); implementation grants for recycling and other expenses of resource recovery facilities; market development programs for recyclable materials; upgrading of collection services in rural areas (e.g., greenboxes, convenience centers); enforcement and regulatory activities; and information and education programs to encourage recycling and source reduction. The need for funds to finance these efforts has provided the primary impetus in most states to search for new revenue sources and to at least consider the possibility of employing environmental taxes.

TABLE 20.1
State Budgets and EPA Grants to States for Air, Water,
and Solid/Hazardous Waste Programs

Year	Total State Budgets (millions of 1988 dollars)		
	Air	Water	Hazardous/Solid Waste
1982	211	237	64
1983	214	275	76
1984	207	297	110
1985	203	327	147
1986	214	337	170

Year	EPA Grants as a Percentage of State Budgets		
	Air	Water	Hazardous/Solid Waste
1982	49	49	76
1983	45	38	66
1984	46	35	47
1985	48	34	41
1986	46	33	40

Source: National Governors Association, *Funding Environmental Programs: An Examination of Alternatives*, 1989, p. 5.

Hazardous Waste

Hazardous waste is a form of solid waste defined legislatively by Subtitle C of RCRA. As in the case of MSW, there has been concern with the future need for capacity, its cost, and the difficulty surrounding siting. One major difference is that the collection and disposal of hazardous waste is essentially a private business. Thus, the public sector has little direct ownership interest with regard to treatment and disposal facilities, and enters the market almost exclusively as a regulator. Furthermore, unlike MSW, where long distance interstate shipment issues are a relatively recent phenomena, hazardous waste has been shipped over long distances for many years.

Two pieces of federal legislation have dominated the public policy discussion on hazardous waste. The first is the so-called land ban promulgated in the 1984 Hazardous and Solid Waste Amendments to RCRA. The land ban prohibited the landfilling of hazardous waste that had not been pretreated; that is, landfilling is eliminated as a primary treatment alternative. Because landfilling is by far the cheapest treatment/disposal alternative, the land ban automatically raised the cost of treatment/disposal of hazardous waste and similarly raised the awareness of generators with regard to their hazardous waste production practices.

The second piece of legislation is the capacity assurance requirements found in Section 104(k) of the Superfund Amendments and Reauthorization Act of 1986 (SARA). States were required to assure the EPA that they had sufficient capacity to deal with the hazardous waste generated within their boundaries or that they had entered into an interstate agreement to manage any excess. Although this requirement had the beneficial effect of forcing states to come to grips with a long-neglected environmental planning function, it also placed states in the peculiar position of allocating disposal capacity that they did not own.

FINANCING SOLID WASTE PROGRAMS

State and local governments can implement solid waste taxes and fees with two objectives in mind. First, taxes and fees can be set at levels that will provide incentives to change patterns of behavior—for example, discourage generation, encourage recycling. To be effective, such taxes and fees would have to exceed the appropriate marginal cost of generation, disposal, and so on. This approach is normally based on the premise of the assumed existence of an environmental externality associated with solid waste generation or disposal. Hence, the behavior distortion or excess burden is considered a benefit to society. Whether the existing set of solid waste taxes and fees accommodate this Pigouvian view of the world is an empirical question that can not be answered at this time.

The second reason to implement solid waste taxes and fees is to generate revenues to fund the increased level of spending required by state and local program initiatives. The logic here is often loosely tied to the benefits approach. For example, a tax or a disposal fee may be levied on an item, such as tires, that is viewed as generating above-average costs of disposal. Most solid waste taxes and fees are dedicated to fund solid waste programs.[4]

TABLE 20.2
Use of Solid Waste Disposal Fees and Disposal Fee Surcharges

State	Rate ($/ton)	Comments
A. Disposal Fee		
Delaware	39.66	
Dist. of Col.[1]	41.65	
B. Disposal Fee Surcharge		
Arizona	0.25	
Arkansas	1.50	
California	0.75	Increase to 1.00 in 1992
Connecticut	1.00	Effective July 1, 1991
Illinois	1.27	
Indiana	0.50	
Iowa	3.00	Maximum of 3.50, July 1, 1992
Louisiana	0.20	
Maine	4.00	
Michigan	0.75	
Missouri	1.50	
Nevada	3.00	Differential out-of-state fee
New Jersey[2]	8.50	
Ohio[3]	0.79-1.70	
Oklahoma	1.50	Differential out-of-state fee
Oregon	1.00	
Pennsylvania	2.00	1.00 per ton is local option
Rhode Island	1.00	
South Dakota	3.00	
Tennessee	0.85	
Texas	0.50	
Utah[4]	0.50-2.50	
Vermont	6.00	
West Virginia	2.50	
Wisconsin	0.50	

TABLE 20.2 (continued)

Source: University of Tennessee Waste Management Research and Education Institute, *Managing Our Waste: Solid Waste Planning for Tennessee*, 1989 (Survey updated October, 1991).

[1]Basic fee of $22.36/ton combined with $19.29/ton recycling surcharge.

[2]Services tax of $0.50/ton and resource recovery tax of $8.00/ton. Resource recovery tax to expire January 1, 1996; services tax to increase by $1.50/ton January 1, 1992.

[3]Ohio has a 3-tier rate dependent upon location of waste.

[4]The fee varies for onsite and offsite waste disposal.

Funding State Programs

The disposal fee or surcharge is the most popular mechanism for financing state solid waste programs. A survey of the states indicates that as of October 1991, twenty-five states used this form of taxation, as shown in Table 20.2.[5] (Several of these states impose an additional charge on out-of-state waste as well.) This tax is levied on waste as it is disposed of, normally at the landfill, on a per ton basis. In states such as Delaware, it is meant to cover a significant portion of the cost of the service. In most states, however, the tax is a surcharge levied on top of whatever fee is charged by the local governments or private firm actually delivering the service, and the rate reflects all or part of the cost of the state's solid waste program. Surcharges range from a low of 20 cents per ton in Louisiana to a high of $8.50 per ton in New Jersey. The survey results indicate that several additional states have pending legislation or are working on solid waste legislation that will include disposal fees.

Another popular source of revenue is per unit excise taxes on elements of the solid waste stream viewed as especially troublesome or costly. For example, lead acid batteries can produce groundwater contamination, newsprint requires considerable landfill space, and tires must be shredded prior to disposal in a landfill. Table 20.3 contains information on special solid waste excise taxes. The most popular is the tire tax. Rates for these special excise taxes are generally quite modest. However, even at low rates, these taxes are capable of generating substantial amounts of revenue, especially vis-à-vis the cost of most state programs. In many cases, it appears that the rates are deliberately set low in order to have as little effect as possible on the taxed parties' behavior.

There are a number of other taxes and incentives used to finance solid waste programs, as shown in Table 20.4. A litter tax is imposed in many states. A business registration tax is charged in Nebraska and Florida. Four other states are currently using dedicated revenue from an automobile transfer tax. Two of the more aggressive states in terms of environmental programs, Minnesota and Washington, have chosen to broaden the sales tax base to include collection and disposal services. Note that several of these funding approaches involve no apparent linkage between the environmental issue and the funding source. They are merely a convenient or available source of revenue.

TABLE 20.3
Solid Waste Excise Taxes

State	Item(s) Taxed
Arkansas	Tires
California	Tires
District of Columbia	Tires
Florida	Tires, batteries, newsprint
Kansas	Tires
Louisiana	Tires
Maine	Tires, batteries, white and brown goods
Michigan	Refined oil products
Missouri	Tires
Nebraska	Tires
North Carolina	Tires
Oklahoma	Tires
Oregon	Tires
Rhode Island	Tires, used oil, antifreeze and solvents
South Carolina	Tires
Tennessee	Tires
Texas	Tires
Virginia	Tires
Washington	Tires
Washington, D.C.	Tires
Wisconsin	Tires

Source: University of Tennessee Waste Management Research and Education Institute, *Managing Our Waste: Solid Waste Planning for Tennessee*, 1989 (Survey updated October 1991).

In order to foster recycling and resource recovery programs, several states have employed incentives, that is, negative taxes, as shown in Table 20.4, Part B. These have included price preference programs for using recycled materials as well as the use of tax credits and exemptions. A significant number of states have chosen to appropriate money from their general fund or issue bonds to support all or part of their programs. Such approaches amount to using existing tax structures rather than introducing special environmental taxes.

Local Initiatives

At the local level, where the service must actually be delivered and disposal capacity must be available, the desire for incentives may be stronger than at the state level. For example, a community faced with limited landfill space may seriously desire to influence local waste disposal practices through taxes and fees rather than go through the arduous process of siting a new facility.

Disposal fees can be effective if transmitted through to actual generators. However, the common prescription by economists is a generation tax or fee. Implementation of such a tax on a statewide basis may prove impractical, especially in the case of households. On the other hand, at the local level this approach appears especially amendable to application to household generators of MSW.

Several communities are experimenting with these types of taxes or fees. Four examples are depicted in Table 20.5. The programs in Seattle, Washington; Jefferson City, Missouri; and Lansing, Michigan, are all examples of a marginal cost based generation fee; that is, households pay more on a per unit basis when they generate more waste. In Tulsa, Oklahoma a method has been devised to transmit the disposal fee directly to the generators attention. Seattle, at least, is willing to claim significant reduction in waste generation behavior.[6]

INTERSTATE SHIPMENT OF WASTE

A recent survey by the National Solid Wastes Management Association (NSWMA) highlights the extent of interstate movements of MSW (National Solid Waste Management Association, 1990b). The results show that 15 million tons were shipped in interstate commerce. Of this total, 53 percent was exported from New York and New Jersey. Another important result was that thirty-eight states both imported and

TABLE 20.4
Additional Taxes and Incentives Employed
in Solid Waste Programs

Mechanism	States Where Used (Proposed)
A. Taxes	
Automobile Transfer Tax	Illinois, Iowa, Michigan, Minnesota, West Virginia
Gross Receipts Tax	New Mexico, Tennessee, Wisconsin
Litter Tax	Maine, Nebraska, New Jersey, Ohio, Virginia, West Virginia
Business Registration Tax	Florida, Nebraska
General Sales Tax	Minnesota, Washington
B. Incentives	
Price Preferences	Arkansas, Florida, Iowa, Michigan, Minnesota, Mississippi, New Mexico
Investment Tax Credit	California, Maine, Michigan, Minnesota, New Jersey, Oklahoma, Oregon, Wisconsin
Sales Tax Exemption	Florida, Iowa, New Jersey,

Source: University of Tennessee Waste Management Research and Education Institute, *Managing Our Waste: Solid Waste Planning for Tennessee*, 1989 (Survey updated October 1991).

exported waste; five states only exported; four states only imported; and only one state (Montana) had no known interstate activity. States such as New York and New Jersey either do not have adequate disposal capacity within their borders, or the political and economic costs of disposing of waste locally have become prohibitive. Hence, they seek to transport their waste to other states. States with adequate or excess capacity, irrespective of whether it is publicly or privately owned, fear that they will become a dumping ground for out-of-state garbage. An increasing number of these states have passed legislation attempting to restrict or ban out-of-state shipments in one manner or another.

In the case of hazardous waste, the well-developed interstate treatment and disposal market has come under scrutiny because of the capacity assurance requirements of SARA. A hazardous waste-importing state such as Alabama is motivated by the same concerns as a state fearing a flood of northeastern MSW. In both instances, state initiatives to protect in-state capacity represent potential interference with interstate commerce and are subject to court challenge.

One approach adopted by many states has been to establish differential fees and charges for out-of-state waste. As shown in Table 20.6, Nevada, New Jersey, Oklahoma, Oregon, Utah, and West Virginia have enacted modest differential fees on the importation of solid waste. Differential fees for hazardous waste are generally much greater. The

TABLE 20.5
Solid Waste Financing Mechanisms at the Local Level

City	Mechanism
Seattle, WA	Per container generation fee. Residents pay a monthly fee ranging from $10.70 for a 19-gallon mini-can to $31.75 for three full-size 32-gallon cans.
Jefferson City, MO Lansing, MI	Per bag generation fee. Residents purchase a specified number of special bags initially, and then more as needed. Refuse not picked up unless in special bags. Cost per bag is $0.75 in Lansing.
Tulsa, OK	Per ton disposal fee charged directly to generator via utility bill. Rate is $42.00 per ton. Revenue supports waste-to-energy facility.

Source: Waste Age, selected issues: 1989-1991.

TABLE 20.6
Special Charges for Out-of-State Waste

State	Rate ($/ton)	Comments
Alabama	25.60 in-state 72.00 out-of- state	Out-of-state fee ruled unconsti- tutional 6-1-92.
Indiana	—	Rate based on cost of disposal in-state versus state of origin with minimum of $0.50/ton. Ruled unconstitutional 1990.
Louisiana	25.00	This is a transportation charge for hazardous waste.
New Mexico	—	Rate to be determined by December 31, 1992, and will apply to all out-of-district solid waste.
Oklahoma	1.50 2.00-8.00	Solid waste surcharge. Controlled industrial waste.
Utah	2.50	Applies to all offsite solid waste.
West Virginia	1.00	—
Wisconsin	—	Effective January 1, 1995 with rate up to $16.00/ton based on comparison of in-state and state of origin of disposal. Fee applies only to solid waste.

Source: University of Tennessee Waste Management Research and Education Institute, *Managing Our Waste: Solid Waste Planning for Tennessee*, 1989 (Survey updated October 1991).

most visible of these is the differential fee charged by Alabama. The base fee for the disposal of hazardous waste within the state is $25.60 per ton. A disposal surcharge of $72.00 per ton of hazardous waste is levied on out-of-state waste.[7]

Eschewing differential fees, some states have chosen outright bans, prohibitions, or moratoriums as ways to control out-of-state waste shipments. Nevada presently has an 18-month moratorium on the importation of out-of-state solid waste. Arkansas has a moratorium on the importation of waste that exceeds 20 percent of the existing capacity at any one landfill. This moratorium has been extended until January 1, 1993. Oklahoma bans sites from accepting more than 200 tons per day of solid waste if the waste is generated more than fifty miles from the disposal site.

The commerce clause of the U.S. Constitution grants Congress the authority to regulate interstate commerce, and restricts the ability of states to interfere with interstate commerce in restraint of trade. Several recent court decisions establish the parameters within which the states attempt to restrict the flow of interstate waste will be judged. These are summarized in Table 20.7. The benchmark case is *City of Philadelphia v. State of New Jersey* (1978), which establishes that a restriction must not be protectionist but must be based on a legitimate local concern, such as public health, that permits differentiation of in-state from out-of-state waste. Attempts to limit the importation of waste in South Carolina and Alabama have been struck down based on these tenets.

On the other hand, several court decisions have established a basis for restricting imports. For example, if there is a legitimate local concern that involves only incidental impact on interstate commerce, and in-state and out-of-state waste is treated in an evenhanded manner, then restriction is possible. Thus, a recent Michigan statute that banned out-of-state waste was upheld because it treated waste from outside the state no differently than waste from other counties within the state.

Indiana's differential fee has been ruled unconstitutional in a lower court. Likewise, the Alabama Court of Appeals ruled the Alabama differential fee unconstitutional. However, in July 1991, the Alabama Supreme Court overturned this decision. The U.S. Supreme Court has subsequently struck down this statute in June, 1992. Challenges to other states bans and differential fees are rumored daily. Obviously the atmosphere is volatile, and rulings by lower courts have yet to produce a consistent interpretation, suggesting an eventual appeal to the U.S. Supreme Court.

NEXUS, SALES TAXES AND SOLID WASTE

An important issue in sales tax policy for many states is whether sales from out-of-state mail-order houses are subject to the tax. The

TABLE 20.7
Interstate Waste Shipments and the Courts

Case	Decision
City of Philadelphia v. State of New Jersey, 437 U.S. 617 (1978)	New Jersey law prohibiting importation of waste declared in violation of commerce clause and unconstitutional. Court ruled law protectionist in intent, there being no legitimate local concern (e.g., public health) with which to distinguish in-state from out-of-state waste. Hence, law discriminated against out-of-state waste.
Hughes v. Alexandria Scrap Corp., 426 U.S. 794 96 S. Ct 2488, 49 L Ed2d 220 (1976); *County Commissioners Charles County v. Stevens*, 299 Md. 203, 473 A-2d 12 (1984); *Leffrancois v. State of Rhode Island*, 669 F. Supp. 1204 (D.R.I. 1987)	Establishes "market participant" restriction on flow of interstate commerce. Interstate waste can be restricted at publicly supported facilities as long as competing private facilities not prohibited or restricted.
Borough of Glassboro v. Glouster County Bd., 100 N.J. 134, 495A.2d 49 (1985); *Evergreen Waste Systems v. Metro Service Dist.*, 820F.2d 49 (1985); *Evergreen Waste Systems v. Metro Service Dist.*, 820F.2d 1482 (9th Cir. 1987)	Establishes that waste flow may be restricted in presence of legitimate public purpose and incidental impact on interstate commerce, and when in-state and out-of-state waste treated in even-handed manner.
Government Suppliers Consolidating Services Inc. v. State of Indiana, DC SIND NOIP 90-303-C (1990)	Struck down origin versus destination principle; determined tip fee as not operational, manifest system as a burden on interstate commerce, and public health certification as difficult to obtain.

TABLE 20.7 (continued)

Case	Decision
Hazardous Waste Treatment Council v. State of South Carolina, DC SC, No. 3:90-1402-0 (1991)	Struck down blacklist of states with barriers to development of new capacity, preference for in-state waste and limits on amount of imported waste as a violation of commerce clause.
National Solid Waste Management Assoc. v. Alabama Dept. of Environmental Management, No. 90-7047 (1991)	District Court upheld law that banned waste from states with restrictions on new hazardous waste treatment and disposal capacity or otherwise failed to comply with CERCLA capacity assurance provisions on grounds that impact on interstate commerce was minimal, there was a legitimate public concern, and intent was not protectionist. Law ruled unconstitutional on appeal. Court ruled that the law violated interstate commerce clause (1992).
Bill Kettleworth Excavating v. Michigan Dept. of Natural Resources, No. 90-1361 (May 1, 1991)	Michigan County may prohibit wastes from outside the state because it treats waste from outside the state no differently from that from other counties within the state. U.S. Supreme Court struck down this Michigan statute because Michigan's restriction, though based on county lines, had the effect of excluding garbage from outside the state (June 1, 1992).
Chemical Waste Management Inc. v. Hunt, Governor of Alabama, et al., No. 90-471 (1991)	U.S. Supreme Court ruled statute unconstitutional (June 1, 1992).

TABLE 20.7 (continued)

Source: Environmental Reporter, various dates; "Prohibitions/Restrictions on Importation of Solid Waste," Opinion No. 89-01, State of Tennessee, Office of the Attorney General, January 3, 1989; John L. Kraft, Esq., "Border Wars: Interstate Transportation and Disposal of Solid Waste," paper presented at First U.S. Conference on Municipal Solid Waste Management, June 1990.

celebrated National Bellas Hess decision and subsequent cases have established the principle that liability for the tax requires a physical presence within the state (McCray, 1985). If no physical presence exists, then there is no nexus and the sales are exempt. States have attempted to establish that nexus exists in many ways, for example, by the location of a sales office or the method of delivery. All these attempts have focused on the "front end" of the consumption cycle. It may well be that the proper place to establish nexus is at the "back end."

For example, if a typical household receives approximately 100 pounds per year of out-of-state catalogs from mail-order houses exempt from state sales tax, in a state such as Tennessee—where the authors of this chapter reside—the annual catalog disposal waste load would be 92,022 tons. Ignoring solid waste collection costs which may be from $60 to $120 per ton, the cost of disposing of these catalogs in existing Tennessee landfills might be $920,000 per year. Valuing landfill space at replacement cost, this figure escalates to about $2 million per year.

These disposal costs are born, jointly and severely, by the citizens of the state. It seems clear that a physical presence exists if the catalogs are disposed of within the state. If nothing else, there should be a tax on the privilege of using Tennessee landfills.

THE FUTURE OF WASTE TAXES AND FEES

It appears clear at this time that the principal impetus for enacting solid waste taxes or fees is revenue production as opposed to modification of waste generation behavior. The possible exception to this statement is found in local government experiments with variable rate generation fees. A standard textbook evaluation of these taxes would tell us to consider their effects on economic efficiency and equity, and to ponder their administrative feasibility and revenue stability.

Performing this exercise, we find that if there is an excess burden created, it is directed at elimination of an externality, and thus efficiency would improve. With regard to equity, these taxes and fees qualify for damnation as regressive; however, this is true of many attempts at benefits taxation. The disposal fee surcharge would appear to have significant start-up costs associated with it; however, these have not daunted a large number of states from moving ahead. State governments are well equipped to implement the various special excise taxes that are commonly suggested. Finally, because the objective is not incentives, rates will be low and revenue will be quite stable given the typical list of items subject to these types of taxes. Therefore, we conclude that in states where distributional issues are not politically paramount and preferences for general taxation are weak, more environmental taxes of the type discussed here will be seen.

If a desire to use taxation for environmental improvement should emerge, it would only strengthen our conclusion. The provisions of the 1991 Clean Air Act represent a breakthrough with regard to the use of economic incentives as a tool of environmental policy (Pytte, 1990). However, support for the command and control approach continues to be strong in both the environmental community and in the federal bureaucracy. In addition, environmental taxes are user taxes. It is not clear at this time how far the country is willing to retreat from its long-term reliance on broad-based taxes.

Given the inconsistency of recent court decisions, it is unclear how the interstate waste flow issue will be resolved. Sheer speculation suggests that explicit bans and restrictions will not survive but that some form of modest differential fee will. Given the cost of shipping waste, especially MSW, even modest fees may be sufficient to discourage interstate shipments of the magnitude that engender dumping ground hysteria.

It seems to us that the nexus issue with regard to catalog sales has led to unfair, albeit legal, shifting of the burden of taxation. We hope the suggestion made is this paper will help to consign the National Bellas Hess case to an appropriate resting place.

NOTES

1. Other forms of solid waste ignored by focusing on MSW are industrial nonhazardous waste, demolition waste, and agricultural waste.

2. See survey by the National Solid Waste Management Association (May 1990) for results of the public attitude toward garbage disposal.

3. See National Governors Association, *Funding Environmental Programs: An Examination of Alternatives* (1989), for a review of the shrinking EPA role.

4. For a review of the use of solid and hazardous waste fee programs at the state level, see National Governors Association, *Environmental Programs: An Examination of Alternatives* (1989), Appendix B.

5. For complete results of this survey, see *Managing Our Waste: Solid Waste Planning for Tennessee*, University of Tennessee Waste Management Research and Education Institute, Knoxville, TN, 1991, and Robert A. Bohm and Michael P. Kelsay, *Taxing to Fund Environmental Programs: The Case of Solid Waste*, University of Tennessee Waste Management Research and Education Institute, Knoxville, TN, 1992.

6. "Aided by Volunteers, Seattle Demonstrates Recycling Can Work," *The Wall Street Journal*, 19 July 1990, p. A1.

7. The hazardous waste facility at Emelle, Alabama, is owned and operated by Chemical Waste Management Corporation. The Supreme Court ruled this out-of-state fee unconstitutional on June 1, 1992.

Epilogue: Goals and Strategies for Business Tax Reform

The chapters in this book make it clear that while there is widespread agreement on the need to simplify business taxation and make it less distorting of private sector activity, there is no consensus on how best to do so. This is so even though many resources and much effort continue to go into contesting business taxes and developing proposals for "reforming" them.

What constitutes reform depends, of course, upon the purposes to be served by business taxation. One reason for taxing businesses is to charge them for services supplied by government and to confront them with the external costs of their activities. This can be termed the *social cost* rationale, because the objective is to confront producers with the full social cost of the inputs that they use in producing goods and services. Under this rationale, business taxes are a means of internalizing the costs of otherwise unpriced inputs used in production. A second reason for taxing businesses is to tax individuals indirectly.

The business taxes in use today are difficult to justify by either of these broad rationales. They are not effective tools for internalizing the costs of publicly provided inputs and environmental damage. And given the uncertainty about the incidence of most business taxes, they border on the capricious as a means of indirectly taxing individuals. Finally, by all accounts, state and local business taxes are complex and costly to administer and comply with.

Among the reasons for this unsatisfactory state of affairs, three stand out. First, tax policymakers apparently do not agree on the purposes to be served by business taxation; no rationale is widely accepted. Certainly, there is little indication that the statutes, court decisions, and administrative rules that define business taxes have been developed with the intent of internalizing the costs of unpriced inputs.

Second, states and localities often see conflicts between their self-interest and tax reform that would make business taxes less complicated and distorting. Indeed, they often try to use business taxes to alter the location of economic activity, even though any resulting changes in location are likely to make production less, rather than more, efficient.

Third, as economic enterprises and the products and services that they produce have increased in complexity, questions of nexus and apportionment— that is, how to divide a given business tax base among localities—have become increasingly difficult to resolve nonarbitrarily. It is increasingly difficult to determine where production takes place. And even a casual survey of the apportionment problems that arise in connection with states' taxation of corporate income raises serious doubt that multistate companies can be taxed fairly and without seriously distorting the efficiency of the economy.

RETHINK BUSINESS TAX ROLE

What are the prospects for improving the system of state business taxation? The chapters in this book illustrate that fundamental reform will require rethinking the role of business taxes in modern industrial economies. Reform must begin with and be grounded in a clear concept of the purpose(s) of business taxation. Otherwise, there is little to anchor policy debate, and the complexities and distortions of the present system could be aggravated rather than reduced. Oakland's critique in Chapter 2 of the various rationales for taxing business suggests that taxes should be imposed mainly to internalize external and public service costs—the social cost rationale. Business taxes could also be used to tax individuals indirectly. But there appears to be little reason for doing so, because individuals' incomes can be taxed directly, as income is either received or spent.

The prescription that reform be based mainly on the social cost rationale raises several issues. One is whether this approach would inhibit a state's economic growth, thus conflicting with the objective of economic development—an increasingly important concern of state and local policy makers. Certainly, a state may be more attractive as a location for production if its government subsidizes production by taxing resident businesses at less than the cost of the inputs that it provides to them. But residents of a state can gain, as a group, by subsidizing production in this manner only if some of the taxes required to finance publicly provided inputs can be exported to nonresidents. Similarly, levying taxes that do not internalize fully the external costs of production is potentially beneficial to a state's residents only if some of those costs are borne by nonresidents. Therefore, it is usually in the self-interest of the residents of a state to tax business as called for by the social cost rationale even if doing so diverts production from the state and slows economic growth.

Exceptions to this conclusion may arise when external costs and the cost of publicly provided inputs are borne in part by nonresidents. In these cases, however, what is optimal for individual states is not necessarily efficient from the perspective of the nation (all states). Indeed, to promote economic efficiency in the national economy, the best policy would be for all states to implement taxes called for by the social cost rationale. In terms of economic effects, if a state subsidizes business activity by taxing and/or charging businesses less than the full cost of the public services provided to them, it encourages inefficient resource allocation and distorts interstate commerce just as surely as it would if it were to impose a tariff on imports.

When assessing whether particular business taxes lead to inefficient resource allocation, the effects of services provided by government should be taken into account as well as taxes. Relatively high taxes in a state need not be a barrier to business activity if services provided to business are also relatively high in value. Despite this rather obvious fact, analyses of business taxes commonly use equal tax rates as the norm for efficient (nondistorting) taxes. Similarly, the question of whether a tax interferes with interstate commerce is typically resolved without considering whether the tax facilitates provision of services to interstate commerce.

Taxing businesses according to the social cost rationale would require that unprofitable as well as profitable businesses be taxed to offset the cost of publicly provided inputs and for external costs. Although this approach to taxation would encourage efficient resource allocation, it could also make otherwise profitable businesses unprofitable, and it could even make some businesses nonviable. Furthermore, it would require taxation of nonprofit, not-for-profit, and government enterprises. Thus, under the social cost rationale, ability to pay *applied to the business entity itself* is not a determinant of business taxes. If the underlying objective of business taxation is to promote efficient resource allocation, taxes should reflect the external costs that businesses generate and the inputs that they receive from government, regardless of their ability to pay.

When businesses are taxed according to the social cost rationale, the resulting incidence may be regressive. But this is not an argument against this approach if the taxes do indeed reflect social costs. For example, when markets operate efficiently, the retail price of bread increases when the price of flour or other ingredients increases, even though the resulting increase in bread price falls relatively heavily on the poor. A policy of providing free flour to bakers so that the poor do not have to pay for the cost of that input would lead to inefficiency. Similarly, failing to tax businesses for social costs implicit in their activities on the grounds that the incidence of the taxes would be regressive would lead to inefficiency.

Finally, one might argue that the difficulty of first measuring external costs and the costs of publicly provided inputs and then attributing them to particular businesses severely limits the usefulness and practicality of the social cost rationale as a guide for business tax reform. This is certainly a valid concern, to which the short reply is that if costs cannot be measured and attributed to particular businesses, there is little basis for taxing businesses except as an expedient means of taxing individuals. However, as Oakland, Cordes, and Bohm and Kelsay make clear in Chapters 2, 19, and 20, respectively, the difficulties of measuring and attributing costs do yield to analysis and research.

Regardless of the objective(s) sought, reform efforts could follow two distinct but not mutually exclusive strategies. One would be to continue present forms of taxation but make them less complicated and easier to comply with and to administer. The second would be to develop new taxes and fees that do a better job of internalizing social costs.

SIMPLIFY EXISTING TAXES

Much of the complexity of present taxes derives from the rules for establishing nexus and apportioning tax bases. In addition to being complicated and subject to continuing litigation, these rules vary from state to state. Definitions of tax bases likewise vary. The results are high administrative costs for state revenue departments and high compliance costs for business taxpayers.

This complexity and lack of uniformity could in principle be reduced if states would agree among themselves to use simple and uniform rules and definitions. But this approach has met with very limited success. The experience of more than three decades of negotiation under the Multistate Tax Compact and the Uniform Division of Income for Tax Purposes Act suggests that more direct federal government action will be required to reduce significantly existing complexities and nonuniformities. For state corporate income taxes in particular, administration and compliance costs could be reduced by federal collection, as Strauss suggests in Chapter 6, or by federal legislation to establish uniform rules for apportionment and for determining nexus.

Whether undertaken at the federal or state level, reform efforts should be, but usually have not been, guided by a consistent rationale for taxing business. The base and rates of a tax should follow from the rationale for it. Two examples illustrate how resolution of particular apportionment and nexus issues depends on the rationale for taxing.

If a sales or gross receipts tax is imposed as a means of charging businesses for services provided, then sales should be taxed in the state in which the business is located; the base should be apportioned according to state of origin (e.g., catalog sales would be taxed in the state in which the products were produced on the presumption that government services were provided by that state). However, if the objective is to tax individuals' incomes (as they spend), then the tax base should be apportioned according to state of destination (i.e., catalog sales would be taxed in the state of residence of the buyer, assuming that the tax is borne by the buyer).

As a second example, if the motive for taxing corporate income is to charge for public services that support production, then income should be apportioned according to the location of production—for example, by a two-factor (payroll and property) formula. However, if the objective is to tax indirectly individuals' incomes, then the tax base should be apportioned to the state of residence of the persons who bear the incidence of the tax. For example, the base should be assigned to states in which product is sold if the tax is forward-shifted, and to states in which the owners of the corporation reside if the tax is not shifted.

REPLACE EXISTING TAXES

Reform proposals have typically been developed on the assumption that governments will continue to rely primarily on present forms of business taxation. However, if internalizing social costs is accepted as the primary purpose for taxing businesses, improving existing taxes promises only limited progress. Fundamental reform will require new approaches to taxing (or otherwise charging) businesses for the costs of services provided by government and greater use of taxes to offset external costs.

Among the major business taxes in use by state governments, the state corporate income tax is least consistent with the social cost rationale. Significant reform could be achieved by replacing this tax with a system of taxes and fees that approximate in amount and distribution the unpriced inputs used by businesses. Replacing the state corporate income tax with a value added tax, as suggested by Oakland in Chapter 2, is one approach deserving careful consideration. More generally, a primary goal of business tax reform over the next decade should be to impose business taxes (and fees) that confront businesses individually and as a group with the external costs that they generate and the government services that they receive. And serious consideration should be given to reducing reliance on and even eliminating taxes that fail to serve this end.

Selected Bibliography

Advisory Opinion. New York State Tax Commission. Petition No. C840627B (Sept. 20, 1985).

"Aided by Volunteers, Seattle Demonstrates Recycling Can Work." (July 19, 1990). *Wall Street Journal.* pp. A1 and A5.

Allgeyer v. Louisiana. 165 U.S. 578 (1897).

Allied Signal, Inc. v. New Jersey Division of Taxation. U.S. Supreme Court, No. 91-615, June 15, 1992.

Amarada Hess Corp., et al. v. Director, Division of Taxation, New Jersey Department of the Treasury. U.S. Supreme Court, No. 87-453.

American Council of Life Insurance. (1990). *Life Insurance Factbook.* New York.

American Council of Life Insurance and Health Insurance Association of America. *Social Report of the Life and Health Insurance Business.* (Annual).

American Insurance Association. (1991). *State Taxation Manual.*

American Trucking Association v. Scheiner. 483 U.S. 266 (1987).

American Trucking Association v. Smith. (1990).

Armco, Inc. v. Hardesty. 467 U.S. 638 (1984).

Aten, R. (1986). "Gross State Product as a Measure of Fiscal Capacity." In J. Clyde Reeves (ed.), *Measuring Fiscal Capacity.* Boston, MA: Oelgeschlager, Gunn & Hain.

Bacchus Imports v. Dias. 468 U.S. 263 (1984).

Barclays Bank International Ltd. v. Franchise Tax Board. California Court of Appeal, Third Appellate District (Super. Ct. Nos. 325059 & 325061) (November 30, 1990).

Barlow, R., and Connell, J. S. (1983). "The Single Business Tax." In Harvey Brazer (ed.), *Michigan's Economic and Fiscal Structure.* Ann Arbor, MI: University of Michigan Press.

Bartels, A. (1990). "The Automated Clearinghouse Comes of Age." *The Bankers Magazine,* 173(2), 12-17.

Baumol, W., and Bradford, D. (May 1972). "Detrimental Externalities and Nonconvexities of the Production Set." *Economica,* 39, 160-176.

Baumol, W., and Bradford, D. (1970). "Optimal Departures from Marginal Cost Pricing." *American Economic Review,* 60, 265-283.

Baumol, W., and Oates, W. (1988). *The Theory of Environmental Policy,* 2nd ed. Cambridge, MA: Cambridge University Press.

Beaman, W. (1963). *Paying Taxes to Other States.* New York: The Ronald Press.

Blough, R., and Wagner, J.C. (April 1978). *U.S Income Tax Treaty with the United Kingdom: An Evaluation of Its Benefits to the United States Including Reasons for Approving the Constraints It Places on State Use of Unitary Apportionment.* Washington, D.C.: U.S. Department of Commerce, 28-34.

Bohm, R. and Kelsay, M. (1992). *Taxing to Fund Environmental Programs: The Case of Solid Waste.* Knoxville, TN: University of Tennessee Waste Management Research and Education Institute.

Braniff Airways, Inc. v. Nebraska State Board of Equalization. 347 U.S. 590 (1947).

Break, G. (1991). "Major Fiscal Trends in the 1980s and Implications for the 1990s." *Tax Notes,* 50, 517-526.

Brown, W.R. (August 1990). *Chronology of Federal Interstate Tax Legislation, 1959-1990.* Washington, D.C.: Council of State Chambers of Commerce.

Brown, W.R. (September 1988). *Tax Incentives vs. Business Climate.* Paper prepared for the NTA Business Tax Committee Meeting, Des Moines, Iowa.

Brown, W. R. (1979). "Congressional Action and Inaction on Interstate Tax Legislation." *National Tax Association-Tax Institute of America: Proceedings of the Seventy-Second Annual Conference, 1978,* 126-130.

Brown, W. R., and Cahoon, C. R. (1973). "The Interstate Tax Dilemma—A Proposed Solution." *National Tax Journal,* 26, 187-197.

Calem, P. (January/February 1987). "Interstate Bank Mergers and Competition in Banking." *Business Review.* Federal Reserve Bank of Philadelphia.

California Constitution, Article XIII, §28(f).

California Rev. and Tax Code, §12221.

Cargill, T. F. and Garcia, G. G. (1985). *Financial Reform in the 1980s.* Stanford, CA: Hoover Institution Press.

Carroll, R., and Wasylenko, M. (1990). "The Shifting Fate of Fiscal Variables and Their Effect on Economic Development." *National Tax Association-Tax Institution of America: Proceedings of the Eighty-Second Annual Conference, 1989,* 283-290.

Case of the State Freight Tax. 82 U.S. (15 Wall.) 232 (1873).

Case, K. (1986). "State Tax Policy and the Telecommunications Industry." In Council of State Policy and Planning Agencies. *The Challenge of Telecommunications: State Regulatory and Tax Policies for a New Industry.*

Chemical Waste Management Inc. v. Hunt. U.S. Supreme Court, No. 91-471.

Christian, E. S. (1981). *State Taxation of Foreign Source Income.* New York: Research Foundation of the Financial Executives Institute.

City of Philadelphia v. State of New Jersey. 437 U.S. 617 (1978).

Cohen, R. S. (July 30, 1990). "State Taxation of New Banking Procedures: A Reply." *Tax Notes,* 631-632.

Colgate-Palmolive Company v. Franchise Tax Board. Superior Court of the State of California for the County of Sacramento. Case No. 319715. December 1988.

Collins. (1988). "Economic Union as a Constitutional Value." *New York University Law Review,* 63, 43.

Commerce Clearing House, Inc. (1985). *Multistate Corporate Income Tax Guide.* Reference Material-Multistate Tax Compact.

Commerce Clearing House. *All States Tax Guide, Volume 1.*

Commerce Clearing House. *State Tax Reporter.* Various issues.

Commonwealth Edison Co. v. Montana. 453 U.S. 609 (1981).

Commonwealth v. Fireman's Fund Insurance Co. 87 A.2d 255 (S. Ct. Pa., 1952).

Communications Satellite Corp. v. Franchise Tax Board. 156 Cal. App. 3d 726, 203 Cal. Rptr. 770 (1984); *appeal dismissed,* 469 U.S. 1201 (1985).

Complete Auto Transit, Inc. v. Brady. 430 U.S. 274 (1977).

Congressional Budget Office. (1987). *Environmental Charges.* Washington, D.C.

Connecticut General Life Insurance Corp. v. Johnson. 303 U.S. 77 (1938).

Container Corp. of America v. Franchise Tax Board. 463 U.S. 159 (1983).

Cooney v. Mountain States Telephone & Telegraph Co. 294 U.S. 384 (1935).

Cooper, K., and Fraser, D. R. (1984). *Banking Deregulation and the New Competition in Financial Services.* New York: Harper & Row.

Cordes, J., Nicholson, E., and Sammartino, F. (1990). "Raising Revenue by Taxing Activities with Social Costs." *National Tax Journal,* 43, 343-356.

Council on Plastics and Packaging in the Environment. (April 1989). "The Nation's Solid Waste Crisis: An Overview." Washington, D.C.

Crandall, R. (1983). *Controlling Industrial Pollution.* Washington, D.C.: Brookings Institution.

Darcy, S. (March 1990). "States Fight to Ban Out-Of-State Wastes." *World Wastes,* 36-38.

Davenport, C. (1990). *The Unitary Tax Controversy: Articles and Comments.* Arlington, VA: Tax Analysts.

DiSanto v. Pennsylvania. 273 U.S. 34 (1927)

Duwe, R. (1986). "Interstate Banking in the Tenth District." *Banking Studies.* Federal Reserve Bank of Kansas City, 1986 Annual.

Economic Report of the President. (1991). Washington, D.C.: U.S. Government Printing Office.

Edelmann, C. M. (July 1958). "Industry's Appraisal of the Report of the Committee on Uniform Division of Income for Tax Purposes." *Taxes,* 36, 533.

Farber, S., Djoundourian, S., and Rambaldi, A. (June 1990). *Industrial Tax Exemptions.* Unpublished manuscript, Louisiana State University, Department of Economics, Baton Rouge.

Feldstein, M. (1974). "Tax Incidence in a Growing Economy with Variable Factor Supply." *Quarterly Journal of Economics,* 88, 563-70.

Fischel, W. A. (1976). "Fiscal Environmental Considerations in the Location of Firms in Suburban Communities." In E. S. Mills and W. Oates (eds.), *Fiscal Zoning and Land Use Control.* Lexington Books.

Fisher, R., and Martin, L. (1986). "Taxes and Telecommunications in an Era of Change." *Final Report of the Minnesota Tax Study Commission,* 2, 223-247.

Florida Department of Revenue. Technical Assistance Advisement, No. 91(B)-001. (March 8, 1991).

Florida Telecommunications Task Force. (1985). *Report of the Florida Telecommunications Task Force.*

Fox, W. F. (January, 1978). "Local Taxes and Industrial Location." *Public Finance Quarterly,* 6, 93-114.

Fox, W. F., and Black, H. A. (1990a). *The Economic Impact of State Taxation and Regulation on Banking.* Unpublished working paper, University of Tennessee.

Fox, W. F., and Black, H. A. (1990b). *Can State Taxation and Regulation Influence Bank Behavior?* Unpublished working paper, University of Tennessee.

Fox, W. F., and Murray, M. N. (in press). "Economic Development: Do State and Local Government Policies Matter?" In David L. Barkley (ed.), *Economic Adaptation: Alternatives for Rural America.*

Freeman v. Hewit. 329 U.S. 249 (1946).

Friedman, A.H. (November 12, 1990). *Outline of MTC National Nexus Program.* Paper presented at the NTA-TIA Sales and Use Tax Committee, San Francisco, CA.

General Motors Corp. v. Washington. 377 U.S. 436 (1964).

General Motors Corp. et al. v. Department of Revenue. U.S. Supreme Court, No. 89-1574.

Gillis, R. J. (1988). "The New Rules for Loan Fee Accounting." *The Bankers Magazine,* 171(1), 41-46.

Goldberg et al. v. Sweet. 488 U.S. 252 (1989).

Goode, R. (1951). *The Corporation Income Tax.* New York: John Wiley & Sons.

Grace, M. F., and Skipper, H. D., Jr. (1990). "Illinois Premium Taxation: Time for Repeal?" *Southern Illinois Law Journal,* 14, 345-399.

GTE Sprint Communications Corp. v. Department of Treasury. 179 Mich. App. 276, 445 N.W.2d 476, 480 (1989).

GTE Sprint Communication Corp. v. Wisconsin Bell, Inc.. 155 Wis. 2d 184, 454 N.W.2d 797 (1990).

Harding, B. W. (1988). "The Five-Year Outlook for Interstate Banking." *The Bankers Magazine,* 171(1), 25-30.

Health Insurance Association of America. (1990). *Source Book of Health Insurance Data 1989.*

Hellerstein, J. R. (1983). *State Taxation.* New York: Warren, Gorham & Lamont.

Hellerstein, W. (1990). "Preliminary Reflections on McKesson and American Trucking." *Tax Notes,* 48, 325-338.

Hellerstein, W. (1989). "State Taxation and the Supreme Court." *Supreme Court Review,* 223-259.

Hellerstein, W. (1988a). "Current Legal Issues in State Taxation of Telecommunications: A Preliminary Inquiry." *National Tax Association-Tax Institute of America: Proceedings of the Seventy-Ninth Annual Conference, 1987,* 69-75.

Hellerstein, W. (1988b). "Is Internal Consistency Foolish? Reflections on an Emerging Commerce Clause Restraint on State Taxation." *Michigan Law Review,* 87, 138-188.

Hellerstein, W., and Levine, H. (1988). "Utility Gross Receipts Taxes and Interexchange Telecommunications Carriers." *Tax Notes,* 40, 529-536.

Henderson, Y. K. (July/August 1988). "Financial Intermediaries Under Value-Added Taxation." *New England Economic Review,* 37-59.

Hooper v. California. 155 U.S. 648 (1895).

Hilton, C. (May 1989). "States Slap Fees on Hazwaste Transport." *Waste Age,* 69-71.

Hovey, H. A. (1986). "Interstate Tax Competition and Economic Development." In Steven D. Gold (ed.), *Reforming State Tax Systems* (pp. 89-100). Washington, D.C.: National Conference of State Legislatures.

Hunter, W. C., and Timme, S. G. (January/February 1987). "Concentration and Innovation: Striking a Balance in Deregulation." *Economic Review.* Federal Reserve Bank of Atlanta.

Illinois Central R.R. v. Minnesota. 309 U.S. 157, 161 (1940).

Illinois Commercial Men's Association v. State Board of Equalization. 34 Cal. 3d 839, 671 P.2d 863, 196 Cal. Rptr. 198 (S. Ct. Cal., 1983).

Illinois Insurance Code, §409(1).

Insurance Information Institute. (1990). *Insurance Facts.* Washington, D.C.

Insurance Information Institute. (1990). *1990 Property/Casualty Insurance Facts.* Washington, D.C.

International Harvester Company v. Evatt. 329 U.S. 416 (1947).

Interstate Busses Corp. v. Blodgett. 276 U.S. 245 (1928).

Japan Line Ltd. v. County of Los Angeles. 441 U.S. 434 (1979).

Joint Committee on Taxation, U.S. Congress. (1972). *General Explanation of the State and Local Fiscal Assistance of 1972.* Washington, D.C.: U.S. Government Printing Office.

Jones, E. M. (1965). "State Taxation of Insurance Companies: An Industry View." *National Tax Association-Tax Institute of America: Proceedings of the Fifty-Seventh Annual Conference, 1964*, 321-328.

Kimball, S. L. (1969). "The Regulation of Insurance." In S. L. Kimball and H. S. Deneberg (eds.), *Insurance, Government, and Social Policy.* Homewood, IL: Irwin.

Kimmel, L. H. (1953). "Economic Effects of Sales and Excise Taxes." *National Tax Association-Tax Institute of America: Proceedings of the Forty-Fifth Annual Conference, 1952*, 650-658.

Kraft, John L. Esq. (June 1990). "Border Wars: Interstate Transportation and Disposal of Solid Waste." Paper presented at the First Meeting of the First United States Conference on Municipal Solid Waste Management, Washington, D.C.

Lavey, W. (January, 1986). "Pitfalls in Taxing Telecommunications Services and Equipment." *Telematics, 3*, 3-7.

Ledebur, L. C., and Hamilton, W. (1986). "The Failure of Tax Concessions as Economic Development Incentives." In S. D. Gold (ed.), *Reforming State Tax Systems* (pp. 101-117). Washington, D.C.: National Conference of State Legislatures.

LePan, N. (1984). "Comments on Musgrave." In C. E. McLure, Jr. (ed.), *The State Corporation Income Tax: Issues in Worldwide Unitary Combination* (pp. 248-249). Stanford, CA: Hoover Institution Press.

Lerner, F. H. (October 1990). "Way-Out Bank Securities." *Bankers Monthly*, 64-65.

Levison, R. D. (1967). "Interstate Taxation and Apportionment of Bank Income." *National Tax Journal, 20*, 447-454.

Life Insurance Company Tax Act. (1959).

Magee, S. P. (1972). "The Welfare Effects of Restrictions on U.S. Trade." *Brookings Papers on Economic Activity.* Washington, D.C.: Brookings Institution, 645-701.

Maloney, M., and Yandle, B. (May/June 1980). "Bubbles and Efficiency." *Regulation*, 49-52.

Marshall, A. (1938). *Principles of Economics* (8th ed.). London: Macmillan.

Massachusetts Mutual Life Insurance Co. v. City of and County of San Francisco. 129 Cal. App. 3d. 876, 181 Cal. Rptr. 370 (1982).

McCray, S. B. (1990). "State Taxation of New Banking Procedures." *Tax Notes, 47*, 1229-1235.

McCray, S. B. (1987). "Constitutional Issues in State Income Taxes: Financial Institutions." *Albany Law Review, 51*, 895-933.

McCray, S. B. (1985). "Overturning *Bellas Hess*: Due Process Considerations." 1986 *BYU Law Review*, 265.

MCI Telecommunications v. Department of Treasury. 136 Mich. App. 28, 355 N.W.2d 627 (1984).

McIntyre, M. (January 16, 1991). [Editorial]. *Tax Notes International*.

McGoldrick v. Berwind–White Coal Mining Company. 309 U.S. 33 (1940).

McKesson Corp. v. Division of Alcoholic Beverages and Tobacco. 58 U.S.L.W. 4665 (June 4, 1990).

McLure, C. E., Jr. (1990). *Economic Perspectives on State Taxation of Multinational Corporations*. Arlington, VA: Tax Analysts.

McLure, C. E., Jr. (1983). "Tax Exporting and the Commerce Clause." In *Fiscal Federalism and the Taxation of Natural Resources*, 169.

McLure, C. E., Jr. (1986). *Economic Perspectives on State Taxation of Multijurisdictional Corporations*. Arlington, VA: Tax Analysts.

McLure, C. E., Jr. (1984). "Unitary Taxation: the Working Group Contribution." *Tax Notes*, 24, 879-883.

McLure, C. E., Jr. (1971). "Revenue Sharing: Alternative to Rational Fiscal Federalism." *Public Policy*, 19, 457-478.

McMahon, R. J. (1988). "Understanding Interest Rate Swaps." *The Bankers Magazine*, 171(5), 59-62.

Meier, K. J. (1987). *The Political Economy of Regulation: The Case of Insurance*. Albany, NY: SUNY Press.

Memphis Bank and Trust Co. v. Garner. 459 U.S. 392, 103 (1983).

Metropolitan Life Insurance v. Ward. 470 U.S. 869 (1985).

Minnesota Tax Study Commission. (1986). *Final Report of the Minnesota Tax Study Commission*. St. Paul: Butterworth.

Mobil Oil Corp. v. State Commissioner of Taxes of Vermont. 445 U.S. 451 (1980).

Moore, A. (October 1990). "Proposed Senate Bill Endangers Interstate Waste Disposal Patterns." *Waste Age*, 36.

Moorman Manufacturing Company v. Bair. 437 U.S. 267 (1978).

Musgrave, Richard. (1959). *Public Finance*, New York: McGraw-Hill.

Mutual Life Insurance Company of New York v. City of Los Angeles. 50 Cal. 3rd 402, 267, Cal. Rptr. 589, 787 P.2d 996 (1990).

Nagel, R. (1985). "The Formulaic Constitution." *Michigan Law Review*, 84, 165.

National Association of Insurance Commissioners. (1971). "NAIC Statement of Policy on Insurance Premium Taxation." *NAIC Proceedings*, 1.

National Conference of State Legislatures. (1990). *Developing Recycling Markets and Industries*. Washington, D.C.

National Governors' Association. (1989). *Funding Environmental Programs: An Examination of Alternatives*. Washington, D.C.

National Solid Waste Management Association. (1990a). "Public Attitudes Toward Garbage Disposal." Washington D.C.

National Solid Waste Management Association. (1990b). "Special Report: Interstate Movement of Municipal Solid Waste." Washington, D.C.

Norfolk & Western Ry. v. Missouri State Tax Commission. 390 U.S. 317, 323-35 (1968).

Oakland, W. (1988). "Business Taxation in Louisiana: An Appraisal." In J. Richardson (ed.), *Louisiana's Fiscal Alternatives* (pp. 159-187). New Orleans: Louisiana State University Press.

Oates, W. (August 1990). *Fiscal Federalism: An Overview*. Keynote Address before the 1990 Conference of the International Institute of Public Finance on Public Finance in a System with Several Levels of Government. Brussels, Belgium.

Ocampo, J. M. (1989). "The ABCs of Asset Securitization." *The Bankers Magazine*, 172(3), 5-9.

Occidental Life v. Commonwealth. 295 A.2d 853 (Pa. Cmwlth. 1972).

Occidental Life v. Holmes. 80 P.2d 383 (S. Ct. Montana, 1938).

Oster, C. V. (1957). *State Retail Taxation*. Columbus, OH: Ohio State Univesity Press.

Ott v. Mississippi Valley Barge Line Co. 336 U.S. 169 (1949).

Ozark Pipe Line Corp. v. Monier. 266 U.S. 555 (1925).

Papke, J. (1974). "Taxation of the Insurance Industry: An Industry Perspective." *National Tax Association-Tax Institute of America: Proceedings of the Sixty-Seventh Annual Conference on Taxation*, 59-69.

Papke, L. E. (1991). "Interstate Business Tax Differentials and New Firm Location: Evidence from Panel Data." *Journal of Public Economics*, 45(1), 47-68.

Papke, L. E. (1990). "Taxes and Other Determinants of Gross State Product in Manufacturing: A First Look." *National Tax Association-Tax Institute of America: Proceedings of the Eighty-Second Annual Conference, 1989*, 274-282.

Parker, H. G. (June 1984). *Insurance Across National Borders: Problems and Solutions*. Paper presented at the meeting of the National Association of Insurance Commissioners.

Paul v. Virginia. 75 U.S. (8 Wall.) 168 (1868).

Pierce, W. J. (October 1957). "The Uniform Division of Income Tax State Tax Purposes." *Taxes*, 35, 747-750.

Pittsburgh, C., C. & St. L. Ry. v. Backus. 154 U.S. 421 (1894).

Policy Economics Group, KPMG Peat Marwick. (1990). *A Report on the Connecticut Business Tax Structure*. Washington, D.C.

Pollock, S. H. (1991). "Mechanisms for Exporting the State Sales Tax Burden in the Absence of Federal Deductibility." *National Tax Journal*, 44, 297-310.

Pomp, R. (1986). "Simplicity and Complexity in the Contex of a State Tax System." In Steven D. Gold (ed.), *Reforming State Tax Systems* (pp. 119-141). Washington, D.C.: National Conference of State Legislatures.

Pomp, R. (1984). "State Tax Reform for the Eighties: The New York Tax Study Commission." *Connecticut Law Review*, 15, 925.

Pomper, M. (1989). "Recycling *Philadelphia v. New Jersey*: The Dormant Commerce Clause, Postindustrial Natural Resources, and the Solid Waste Crisis." *University of Pennsylvania Law Review*, 137, 1309.

Portney, P. (1990). "Economics and the Clean Air Act." *Journal of Economic Perspectives*, 4(4), 173-181.

Powell, T. R. (1918). "Indirect Encroachment on Federal Authority by the Taxing Powers of the States." *Harvard Law Review, 31*.

Providence Washington Insurance Co. v. Commonwealth. 463 A.2d 68 (Pa. Cmwlth. 1983).

Prudential Insurance Company v. Benjamin. 328 U.S. 408, 410 (1946).

Pytte, A. (October 27, 1990). "A Decade's Acrimony Lifted in the Glow of Clean Air." *Congressional Quarterly: Weekly Report,* 48(43), 3587-3592.

Ramsey, F. (1927). "A Contribution to the Theory of Taxation." *Economic Journal,* 37, 47-61.

Raymond Motor Transportation, Inc. v. Rice. 434 U.S. 429 (1978).

Regan, D. (1984). *Chairman's Report: Working Group on Worldwide Unitary Taxation.* Washington, D.C.: U.S. Treasury.

Reschovsky, A., et al. (1983). "State Tax Policy: Evaluating the Issues." Joint Center for Urban Studies of MIT and Harvard University.

Reynolds Metals Company v. Sizemore. U.S. Supreme Court, No. 89-1587.

Ring, R. J., Jr. (1989). "The Proportion of Consumers' and Producers' Goods in the General Sales Tax." *National Tax Journal,* 42, 167-179.

Rivlin, A. (1990). "The Challenge of Competition to Fiscal and Functional Responsibilities." *Intergovernmental Perspective,* 16(1), 15-16.

Robbins v. Shelby County Taxing District. 120 U.S. 489 (1887).

Rosner, M., and Derus, M.M. (1990). "The 4-R Act Provisions: A Necessary Unburdening of Commerce." *Proceedings of the Eighty-Second Annual Conference, National Tax Association-Tax Institute of America.* pp. 229-233.

Savage, D. T. (1989). "Interstate Banking Update." *The Bankers Magazine,* 172(4), 28-33.

Schneider Communications, Inc. v. Wisconsin Department of Revenue. Wisconsin Tax Appeals Commission. (January 3, 1991).

Schoettle, F. P. (1991). "Facts, Law, and Economics in Commerce Clause Challenges to State Taxes." *Tax Notes,* 50, 1149-1160.

Schoettle, F. P. (1990). "Use Taxes and the Out-of-State Seller." *Tax Notes,* 48, 463.

Schoettle, F. P. (1985). "A Three-Sector Model for Real Property Tax Incidence." *Journal of Public Economics,* 27, 355.

Schoettle, F. P. (1980). In *State Taxation of Interstate Commerce and Worldwide Corporate Income: Hearings on S 1688 Before the Subcommittee on Taxation and Debt Management Generally of the Senate Committee on Finance.* 96 Cong., 2d Sess., 816.

Sheffrin, S. M., and Fulcher, J. (1984). "Alternative Divisions of the Tax Base: How Much Is at Stake." In C. E. McLure, Jr. (ed.), *The State Corporation Income Tax: Issues in Worldwide Unitary Combination* (pp. 248-249). Stanford, CA: Hoover Institution Press.

Shoenhair, J. D., and Spong, K. (1990). "Interstate Bank Expansion: A Comparison Across Individual States." *Banking Studies,* Federal Reserve Bank of Kansas City, 1990 Annual.

Shoenhair, J. D., and VanWalleghem, J. (1989). "Interstate Banking: The Nation and Tenth District States." *Banking Studies,* Federal Reserve Bank of Kansas City, 1989 Annual.

Silver, D. B., and Axilrod, P. J. (1989). "Pushing Technology Its Limits: Securitizing C&I Loans." *The Bankers Magazine.* 172(3), 16-21.

Skipper, H. D., Jr. (1987). "State Taxation of Insurance Companies: Time for Changes." *Journal of Insurance Regulation,* 6, 121-37.

Smith, A. (1963). *An Inquiry into the Nature and Causes of the Wealth of Nations.* (L. Reynolds and W. Fellner, eds., 1963) (1st ed. 1776).

Smith, D. T. (1964) "The Value-Added Tax." *Excise Tax Compendium,* Committee on Ways and Means, House of Representatives, Congress of the United States, 89-98. Washington D.C.: U.S. Government Printing Office.

Smith, E. H. (1976). "Allocating to Provinces the Taxable Income of Corporations: How the Federal-Provincial Allocation Rules Evolved." *Canadian Tax Journal,* 24(5), 177-184.

South Carolina v. Southern Farm Bureau Life Insurance Co. 219 S.E.2d 80 (S. Ct. S.C., 1975).

Southern Pacific Communications Co. v. State Tax Commission. New York Division of Tax Appeals, Tax Appeals Tribunal, No. 800275. (May 15, 1991).

Spector Motor Services, Inc. v. O'Connor. 340 U.S. 602 (1951).

Spong, K., and Watkins, T. (Summer, 1985). "Interstate Banking: What Are the Competitive Effects?" *Banking Studies.* Federal Reserve Bank of Kansas City.

Spulber, D. (1985). "Effluent Regulation and Long-Run Optimality." *Journal of Environmental Economics and Management,* 12, 103-116.

St. Louis Cotton Compress Co. v. Arkansas. 260 U.S. 346 (1922).

State Board of Insurance v. Todd Shipyards Corp. 370 U.S. 451 (1962).

State Department of Revenue v. Telnet Corp. Alabama Civil Court of Appeals. (February 27, 1991).

State Taxation of Interstate Commerce. (September, 1965). Report of the Special Subcommittee on State Taxation of Interstate Commerce. Washington D.C.: Committee on Judiciary, House of Representatives.

State Tax on Railway Gross Receipts. 82 U.S. (15 Wall.) 284 (1873).

Strauss, R. P. (Winter, 1990). "The EC Challenge to State and Local Governments." *Intergovernmental Perspective.* Washington, D.C.: Advisory Commission on Intergovernmental Relations, 13-14.

Strauss, R. P. (1990). "Fiscal Federalism and the Changing Global Economy." *National Tax Journal,* 43, 315-320.

Strauss, R. P. (1987). *A Study of Alternative Tax Structures for the State of Washington.* Olympia, WA: Washington State Department of Revenue.

Studenski, P. (1940). "Toward a Theory of Business Taxation." *Journal of Political Economy,* 47, 621-654.

Tax Reform Act. (1984).

Terkla, D. (1984). "The Efficiency Value of Effluent Tax Revenues." *Journal of Environmental Economics and Management,* 11, 107-123.

Texas Insurance Code, Article 4.10, §10; Article 4.11, §5B.

Texas, State of. (1985). *Telecommunications Tax Options.* A Report to the Joint Select Committee on Fiscal Policy.

Thirsk, W. (1980). "Tax Harmonization in Canada." In George Break (ed.), *State and Local Finance: The Pressures of the 1980s* (pp. 53-73). Madison, WI: University of Wisconsin Press.

Touche Ross & Co. (1986). *Taxation of Telecommunications in Pennsylvania.* A Report Prepared for the Department of Revenue, Commonwealth of Pennsylvania.

Tyler Pipe Industries, Inc. v. Department of Revenue. 483 U.S. 232 (1987).

U.S. Advisory Commission on Intergovernmental Relations. (1987, 1989). *Changing Public Attitudes on Government and Taxes.* Washington, D.C.

U.S. Advisory Commission on Intergovernmental Relations. (1989). *State Taxation of Banks: Issues and Options.* Washington, D.C.

U.S. Advisory Commission on Intergovernmental Relations. *Significant Features of Fiscal Federalism,* various issues. Washington, D.C.

U.S. Advisory Commission on Intergovernmental Relations. (1990). *State Fiscal Capacity and Effort* (Report No. M-170). Washington, D.C.

U.S. Bureau of Economic Analysis. (May 1988). *Survey of Current Business.* Washington, D.C.

U.S. Department of the Treasury. (1985). *Federal-State-Local Fiscal Relations.* Washington, D.C.: U.S. Government Printing Office.

U.S. League of Savings Institutions. (1988). "Large Service Bureaus Dominate in DP Support." *Savings Institutions,* 8, 59-64.

U.S. League of Savings Institutions. (1988). *Savings Institutions Sourcebook.* Chicago, IL.

U.S. Department of the Treasury, Office of Tax Policy. (March 6, 1990). Testimony by Michael Graetz, Deputy Assistant Secretary for Tax Policy, before the Committee on Ways and Means, United States House of Representatives.

U.S. Environmental Protection Agency, Office of the Comptroller (prepared by Apogee Research, Inc.). (1990, March 1988). *Characterization of Municipal Solid Waste in the United States, 1960-2000* (Updates 1988, 1990), Final Report U.S. EPA, Office of Solid Waste and Emergency Response, Franklin Associates, Ltd.

U.S. Environmental Protection Agency, Office of the Comptroller (prepared by Apogee Research, Inc.). (1989a). *Draft Final Report: The Costs of Environmental Protection: EPA, the States, and Local Governments.* Washington, D.C.: U.S. Government Printing Office.

U.S. Environmental Protection Agency, Office of Policy, Planning, and Evaluation. (1989b). *Promoting Source Reduction and Respectability in the Marketplace.* Washington, D.C.: U.S. Government Printing Office.

U.S. Environmental Protection Agency, Office of the Comptroller (prepared by Apogee Research, Inc.). (September 1988). *Solid Waste Dilemma: An Agenda for Action: Appendices A-B-C.* Washington, D.C.: U.S. Government Printing Office.

United States v. South-Eastern Underwriters Association. 322 U.S. 533 (1944).

United States Transmission Systems, Inc. v. Board of Assessment Appeals. 715 P.2d 1249 (Colo. 1986).

University of Tennessee Waste Management Research and Education Institute. (1991). *Managing Our Waste: Solid Waste Planning for Tennessee.* Knoxville, TN.

Walker, M. (1937). *How Should Businesses Be Taxed?* New York: Tax Policy League.

Wallace v. Hines. 253 U.S. 66 (1920).

Wassall, G., and Sullivan, J. (1988). "State Taxation of Telecommunications Companies." *National Tax Association-Tax Institute of America: Proceedings of the Seventy-Ninth Annual Conference, 1987,* 342-347.

Wasylenko, M., and McGuire, T. (1985). "Jobs and Taxes: The Effect of Business Climate on State's Employment Growth Rates." *National Tax Journal,* 38, 497-511.

Western Live Stock v. Bureau of Revenue. 303 U.S. 250 (1938).

Western & Southern Life Insurance Co. v. State Board of Equalization. 451 U.S. 648 (1981).

Wheaton, W. C. (1986). "The Impact of State Taxation on Life Insurance Company Growth." *National Tax Journal,* 39, 85-95.

Wheaton, W. C. (1983). "Interstate Differences in the Level of Business Taxation." *National Tax Journal*, 36, 83-94.

Wilkie, R. (January 1959). "Uniform Division of Income for Tax Purposes." *Taxes*, 37, 65, 71.

Wisconsin v. J. C. Penney Co. 311 U.S. 435, 444 (1940).

World Bank. (1986). *World Development Report*. New York: Oxford University Press.

Index

About the Contributors

ROBERT H. ATEN is Vice-President and Chief Economist of the Manufacturers' Alliance for Productivity and Innovation (MAPI). Dr. Aten previously worked at the U.S. Department of the Treasury, the Joint Economic Committee, the New York City Office of Management and Budget, the U.S. Bureau of the Budget (now Office of Management and Budget), and the Office of the Secretary of Defense. He taught at Baruch College in the City University of New York. His university education includes a Ph.D. in economics (New York University).

JAMES BARRESE is Associate Professor of Economics, The College of Insurance, New York. His current research focuses on relations between government and the insurance industry: taxation, regulation, and international treaties.

ROBERT A. BOHM is Professor of Economics at the University of Tennessee and Associate Director of the University's Energy, Environment and Resources Center. He specializes in public finance, energy and environmental economics, and urban and regional economics. Since coming to the University of Tennessee, he has directed or co-directed twenty-six research projects and written widely in these areas. His most recent work has concentrated on determining the need for hazardous and solid waste facilities and the financing of these types of facilities.

WILLIAM R. BROWN retired in 1991 as President of the Council of State Chambers of Commerce and Executive Officer of the Committee on State Taxation (COST). He is now a consultant for the Council. Before becoming President of the Council of State Chambers of

Commerce, Mr. Brown served as Research Director of the Council of State Chambers, the Delaware Chamber of Commerce, and the Missouri State Chamber of Commerce. He is a former editor of the COST *State Tax Report* and the Institute of Property Taxation *Property Tax Report.*

GEORGE N. CARLSON is a participating principal in Arthur Andersen's Office of Federal Tax Services in Washington, D.C., where he is Director of the Economic Analysis Group. His areas of specialization are transfer pricing, state and local taxation, sales and consumption taxation, and international taxation. Before joining Arthur Andersen, Dr. Carlson served for fifteen years in the U.S. Treasury Department. From 1984 to 1986, he was Director of the Office of Tax Analysis. He was awarded the Treasury's Exceptional Service Award by Secretary James A. Baker III in 1986. From 1981 to 1984, Dr. Carlson was the Director of the Treasury's International Tax staff. Dr. Carlson received his Ph.D. in economics from the University of Illinois.

JOSEPH J. CORDES is Professor of Economics and Chairman of the economics department at The George Washington University. He holds a Ph.D. in economics from the University of Wisconsin, Madison. From 1989 to 1991, he was Deputy Assistant Director for Tax Analysis in the Congressional Budget Office. He has published numerous articles on taxation and public expenditure analysis. His recent research addresses the role of federal and state and local environmental taxes and fees, effects of cutting taxes on capital gains, and effects of tax policy and government spending programs on industrial research and development.

WILLIAM F. FOX is a fiscal policy consultant to Tennessee State Government and has worked with a number of states and developing countries in structuring and analyzing tax systems. He is Associate Director of the Center for Business and Economic Research at The University of Tennessee and Head of the economics department. He is the author of numerous publications on the subject of state and local taxes.

JAMES FRANCIS is the Director of Tax Research for the Florida Department of Revenue. Previously he was House Economist for the Finance and Taxation Committee of the Florida House of Representatives. He served as a member of the President's Tax Force on Worldwide Unitary Taxation, and is a past Chairman of the Research Section of the Federation of Tax Administrators. He received his Ph.D. in economics from the Florida State University and is a Vice-President of CFF Associates, Inc., an economics consulting firm in Tallahassee, Florida.

STEVEN GALGINAITIS is a Senior Manager with the Policy Economics Group of KPMG Peat Marwick. He specializes in business tax policy analysis and has developed computer models of business tax systems in several states. He has done extensive research on the economic and distributional effects of alternative business tax policies. He has worked previously for the Statistics of Income branch of the U.S. Department of Treasury.

GERALD M. GODSHAW is a manager in Arthur Andersen's Office of Federal Tax Services in Washington, D.C., where he is a member of the Economic Analysis Group. His areas of specialization are transfer pricing, corporate taxation, state and local taxation, and policy analysis. Prior to joining Arthur Andersen, Dr. Godshaw served as Senior Director of the WEFA Group (Wharton Econometric Forecasting Associates). Earlier in his career, Dr. Godshaw was a financial economist in the U.S. General Accounting Office and Senior Economist for the Washington-based International Business-Government Counsellors, Inc. He received his Ph.D. in economics from Syracuse University.

MARTIN F. GRACE is an Associate at the Center for Risk Management and Insurance Research and Assistant Professor at the College of Business Administration at Georgia State University. He holds a Ph.D. in economics and a J.D. from the University of Florida. Professor Grace's research interests are industrial organization and regulation and taxation issues in the insurance industry.

WALTER HELLERSTEIN is Professor of Law at the University of Georgia and is counsel to the law firm of Morrison & Foerster. He is a graduate of Harvard College and the University of Chicago Law School. He has written and practiced extensively in the field of state and local taxation.

JEFFREY L. HYDE is the Mid-Atlantic Director of State and Local Tax Services with Arthur Andersen, Washington, D.C. As a member of the Firm's Technical Specialty Team, he is involved in all aspects of multistate taxation review, analysis, and appeals. He received his BS/BA from Pennsylvania State University, JD from Dickinson School of Law and Masters of Law (Tax) from Temple University School of Law.

MICHAEL P. KELSAY is a doctoral candidate in economics at the University of Tennessee. Prior to going to the University of Tennessee in 1989, he was President and Chief Executive Officer of Argentine Savings and Loan Association in Kansas City, Kansas. He has over 15 years experience in the banking and financial services industry.

ROBERT N. MATTSON is Assistant Treasurer of IBM Corporation and an assistant professor of taxation at Pace University. He has published tax articles in a number of journals, including articles on research and development tax policy and the taxation of joint ventures. He has served as General Reporter for the International Fiscal Association on the topic of the taxation of computer software. Mr. Mattson is a member of the American Bar Association Section on Taxation, the Business Roundtable Tax Coordinating Committee, and tax committees of the International Fiscal Association, Tax Foundation, and Financial Executives Institute.

BRIAN H. McGAVIN is a research economist with the Office of Tax Research, Florida Department of Revenue. Previously he was assistant professor of economics at Florida State University. He holds a Ph.D. in economics from the University of California, Los Angeles. His academic research focused on the study of the macroeconomy and business cycles.

THOMAS S. NEUBIG is Director of Financial Sector Economics in Price Waterhouse's Washington National Tax Services. Previously, he was Director and Chief Economist of the U.S. Treasury Department's Office of Tax Analysis. He specializes in federal and state taxation of financial institutions (banks, insurance companies, finance companies, mutual funds, and secondary market issuers) and their products.

PATRICK J. NUGENT, C.P.A., is Director of Tax Legislative Affairs, MCI Telecommunications Corp. With a staff of three other professionals, he is responsible for all tax legislative interests of MCI at all levels of government, including federal. He has been active in the development of state and local taxation of nonmonopoly telecommunications companies since before the divestiture of the local telephone companies by AT&T. Mr. Nugent has presented papers at the NYU Institute on State and Local Taxation, the Texas Select Committee on Tax Equity, and at annual meetings of the Multistate Tax Commission, the National Conference of State Legislatures, and the National Tax Association. He is a graduate of Xavier University, Cincinnati, Ohio.

WILLIAM H. OAKLAND is Professor of Economics at Tulane University. He specializes in public finance with special emphasis on public goods and local fiscal theory. He is currently working on models of tax competition and local sales taxation.

THOMAS F. POGUE is Professor of Economics at the University of Iowa. His research on tax policy is widely published in professional journals. He has also served as a consultant to numerous state and local governments on questions of tax policy and economic development.

FERDINAND P. SCHOETTLE is Professor of Law at the University of Minnesota. He holds degrees in law and in economics from Harvard University and specializes in state and local taxation and public finance.

HAROLD D. SKIPPER, JR., is director of the Center for Risk Management and Insurance Research and a professor at Georgia State University. His research has focused on insurance-related public policy issues, and he has served as an expert witness in premium tax litigation. He holds a Ph.D. from the University of Pennsylvania. Professor Skipper's areas of interest include domestic and international regulation and taxation of the insurance industry.

BURNS STANLEY is retired from Ford Motor Company as Director, Governmental Tax Relations. He was Adjunct Professor of Law in taxation for twenty years at Wayne State University; President of the Tax Executives Institute (TEI); Chairman, Committee on State Taxation (COST); and, earlier, Assistant Attorney General of West Virginia for tax matters. A consultant on constitutional tax issues, he holds law degrees from Harvard and Wayne State University.

ROBERT P. STRAUSS is Professor of Economics and Public Policy at Carnegie-Mellon University. He holds a Ph.D. from the University of Wisconsin, Madison. Prior to joining the faculty at Carnegie-Mellon in 1979, he was a Brookings Economic Policy Fellow at the U.S. Treasury where he received the Exceptional Service Award for his design of the general revenue sharing legislation in 1972. From 1975-8, he served on the Staff of the Joint Committee on Taxation, U.S. Congress. He currently serves on the advisory board of several Federal statistical agencies, including the Internal Revenue Service, Statistic of Income Division and the Governments Division of the Census Bureau. In May, 1989, he was appointed to the Revenue Estimating Advisory Committee of the Joint Committee on Taxation, U.S. Congress.

MICHAEL VLAISAVLJEVICH is the Director of State and Local Services for the Policy Economics Group of KPMG Peat Marwick. During the past five years, Mr. Vlaisavljevich has directed tax simulation model, revenue estimating, and tax policy analysis projects for fifteen states as a private consultant. He has conducted studies of state business tax (including insurance), personal income tax, sales tax, property tax, and local government fiscal policy issues. Previously, Mr. Vlaisavljevich was Research Director for the Wisconsin Department of Revenue where he managed the tax policy department and revenue estimating functions. He taught public policy analysis and urban affairs at the university level and received a Master's degree from Indiana University.

JOHN W. WEBER, JR., is a Member of the firm of LeBoeuf, Lamb, Leiby & MacRae in New York City. He graduated from Vincentian Institute, received his A.B. degree from Holy Cross College, his J.D. degree from Catholic University and his LL.M. degree (Taxation) from New York University. Mr. Weber is a member of the New York, the New York State, and American Bar Associations, and a regular lecturer and writer on topics related to insurance and taxation.